A Selection from George Crabbe

LONGMAN ENGLISH SERIES

This series includes both period anthologies and selections from the work of individual authors. The introductions and notes have been based upon the most up-to-date criticism and scholarship and the editors have been chosen for their special knowledge of the material.

General Editor *Maurice Hussey*

A Selection from George Crabbe

Edited with Introduction and Notes
by

John Lucas

Longman

LONGMAN GROUP LIMITED
Longman House,
Burnt Mill, Harlow, Essex CM20 2JE, England.

This edition © Longman Group Ltd 1967

First published 1967
Sixth impression 1982

ISBN 0 582 34165 5

Printed in Hong Kong by
Dai Nippon Printing Co (H.K.) Ltd

for my Parents

The Editor

John Lucas is Professor of English at Loughborough University. Among his publications are *The Melancholy Man: A Study of Dicken's Novels; Arnold Bennett; Egilssaga, the Poems;* and *The Literature of Change.*

Contents

Acknowledgements

I should like to thank Dr Geoffrey Yarlott of the University of Nottingham, who read a draft of the Introduction and made valuable suggestions for alteration and improvement. And the vigilance of the General Editor, Maurice Hussey, saw to it that this book was a good deal better than it could have been without his guidance. The flaws that remain are my responsibility alone.

A Note on the Text

In general the text of these poems has been based on the first edition, but I have silently modernized spellings and emended punctuation where the sense required it, consulting on such occasions both the eight volume edition by Crabbe's sons, and Sir A. W. Ward's three volume edition of the *Collected Poems*.

John Lucas
Nottingham, 1967

Introduction

George Crabbe was born at Aldeburgh in 1754. Now a small town, at the time Crabbe lived there Aldeburgh was not much more than a fishing village set down on the flat and sombre-coloured land which is constantly being worn away by the action of the North Sea. The coastline around Aldeburgh is not dramatic; there are no abrupt meetings of cliff-edge and sea, no tangle of rocks and caves, few striking contrasts of colour. Instead mud-flats, sand-dunes, occasional salt-marshes. The sense of the place is strong in Crabbe's work, especially in *Peter Grimes*; it can also be found in some of the water-colours of the Norwich school of painters, particularly Crome, Cotman and Stannard, who were at work painting scenes of the east coast during the latter half of the eighteenth century.

Behind Aldeburgh mile after mile of level fen country stretches away into the English midlands. It was good farming country, but only for the great landlords who, as the eighteenth century wore on, used their policy of land enclosure to squeeze out the small independent tenant farmers. Tales of the hardships these farmers had to face would be carried to all the villages and towns, often by the farmers themselves, as they drifted about trying to find alternative work. And it is certain that some of Aldeburgh's own people were deprived of their living by the landlords' policy.

In front the sea, behind the land; and from both a precarious existence had to be won. For most of the people of Aldeburgh, and for numerous places like it scattered along that stretch of the east coast, life was framed by incessant toil and grinding poverty. And in addition these villages were very largely cut off from the outside world. For there were no swift means of transport to the main cities, few reasons for going there, and still fewer for townspeople to go to the villages. There was no national press, no quick and easy way, therefore, of knowing what was going on the other side of England, let alone the other side of the world. Of course there were consolations, grouped around the villagers' sense of isolation and their independence of provided entertainment. People made their own amusements; the community spirit was perhaps important. But we had better not sentimentalize this too much. All the evidence points to the fact that the customary extremity of hardships sapped energies that might otherwise have been devoted to creative enjoyment. In the constant fight to keep poverty at arm's length there was little time or inclination for leisure. Poverty, toil, isolation and the scarcely adequate compensations of the community spirit: these are the important facts to keep in mind about the small town where Crabbe spent his early years.

They were not happy ones. His father had the position of harbour-master, a rather better job than most, but still mean enough. He was a very intelligent man, a good amateur mathematician and a lover of poetry: Milton and Young (an eighteenth-century poet whose most famous poem *Night Thoughts* (1744) enjoyed great popularity at the time) were especial favourites. Yet what chance was there for intelligence to flower in the conditions I have outlined above? At Cambridge, not so very many miles away from Aldeburgh, Thomas Gray was composing his famous 'Elegy in a Country Churchyard' (1751) in which he admitted, rather too comfortably, that

> Full many a gem of purest ray serene,
> The dark unfathom'd caves of ocean bear:
> Full many a flower is born to blush unseen,
> And waste its sweetness on the desert air.

The life of Crabbe's father cruelly justifies those words. He became a drunkard, and his bitterness at the life he was forced to lead spilled over into domestic rows. When George Crabbe was nearly eight years old his younger brother died, at the age of eighteen months, and his parents were never to recover from this blow: 'To him that hath shall be given, from him that hath not shall be taken away.' I would think it quite certain that one of the main driving forces in Crabbe's later ambition to succeed was the memory of his father's drunken anger, and the misery of his own home life.

His schooling was every bit as miserable. He went first to an establishment at Bungay where whatever was irregular about the teaching and food was made up for by the regularity of the beatings. And when, in his twelfth year, he was transferred to a school at Stowmarket, the pattern he found there was much the same. Then, at fourteen he was apprenticed to an apothecary (a combination of chemist and surgeon) at Wickham Brook near Bury St Edmunds. This shows that his father still had pretensions enough not to want his son to become a labourer. Yet in the light of what followed the pretensions showed as absurd, the history of Crabbe's student years as tragi-comic. He began his apprenticeship with an apothecary so poor that Crabbe had to earn his living on a nearby farm, and learned next to nothing about his intended trade. That went on for two years and then he was transferred to an apothecary at Woodbridge, a town about the same size as Aldeburgh and not far from it. Here he got on much better, and not only at his apprenticeship. For he began to write verse, and during 1771-2 some poems of his were published in local newspapers. These modest successes may have acted as a spur, and he certainly gave a great deal of time to writing. The time he had off he used to become engaged. He was then eighteen, and his fiancée, Sarah Elmy, twenty-one.

Crabbe finished his apprenticeship in 1775, but when he got back to Aldeburgh – and remember it was essential for him to get work with reasonable pay if he was to marry – there was of course no money for him to set up in practice. So he had after all to take up a labouring job on the quayside. And then he did have a moment of luck. The parish set him up as official apothecary to the poor. The salary was a mere pittance, but it was at least a start. Crabbe threw himself into the study of anatomy, and at this time, too, began the interest in botany that was to last him all his life (it was a practical interest, since many drugs were made from herbs and weeds). But he could not teach himself all the anatomy he needed; for that he must go to London. So in 1776, with enough money to last him for only ten months, he set off for the capital city, leaving his shop in the hands of a neighbouring surgeon. When he returned to Aldeburgh it was to find that he had been cheated out of his practice.

How he spent the next years is not certain, but we do know that by 1780 he was living in very great poverty indeed. Marriage looked farther off than ever. But all this time Crabbe had been working at his verse, and since it now seemed certain he couldn't hope to succeed as an apothecary, the obvious alternative was to hope for the success of his poetry. And so Crabbe decided to do what many, including the great Dr Johnson, had done before him; he went to London to seek his fortune as a poet.

It may indeed have been that when Crabbe hit on the notion of making his second trip to London the example of Dr Johnson was uppermost in his mind. If so, he either did not know about, or conveniently forgot, the thousands who had made a similar effort to Johnson's and who had failed. But after a few months in London, Crabbe's failure was almost total. There is no point in going into the detail of these distressing months. It is enough to say that poem after poem was turned down by publishers, that the small stock of money dwindled away, that in spite of his resolve to keep up appearances he was reduced to pawning nearly all his clothes (he then spent the proceeds on an edition of Dryden's poems), that bills he could not meet piled up and creditors became more importunate, and that at what must have seemed the last moment he was rescued.

The man who rescued him was Edmund Burke, man of letters and political thinker, who at this time was famous for his defence of the American colonists' fight for independence and who was later to produce the work by which he is now best known, *Reflections on the Revolution in France*, in which he declared himself against the overthrow of the old order. Crabbe had been trying to gain himself a patron, but had no luck until, early in 1781, he managed to gain an interview with Burke and show him some of his verse. To his eternal credit Burke recognized the talent beneath the not very good lines he was shown, and took on himself the responsibility of seeing Crabbe's poem *The Library* through the press. It was paid for by subscription and with such a sponsor was certain to succeed financially. More important, perhaps, when it appeared it at once met with critical acclaim. Then Burke saw to it that Crabbe was ordained for the Church, one of the safest ways of making at least a modest living. The poet's future was assured.

It has been objected against Crabbe that he was behaving hypocritically in accepting this means of employment, since he had no vocation for the priesthood. But this is not a sound objection. Crabbe was a sincere believer, of that there can be no doubt. Whether he had a sense of vocation for the Church hardly comes into it; you do not commonly feel yourself fitted

4

for a career you have no chance of following. To be ordained, you needed money or patronage, and until his meeting with Burke, Crabbe had neither. As a matter of fact it is fairly certain that he was not a good vicar, but then there are many bad priests whom one would never accuse of lacking a strong sense of vocation. The worst that can be said is that because of the financial assurance being a priest brought him, Crabbe was enabled to write some splendid poetry. He did not do the Anglican Church very much harm, and it did him, and therefore us, a great deal of good.

From 1781 Crabbe's life altered. The full details can be followed up in Huchon's conscientious biographical study and in the life of Crabbe by his own son (details of these and other books are given on p. 263). A brief summary is given here. Crabbe's first appointment in 1782 was as chaplain to the Duke of Rutland, a position which he seems to have disliked. But his marriage in 1783 must have done much to offset his distaste and discomfort. In any case soon afterwards he left Rutland's service, becoming a vicar of two parishes, one in Lincolnshire, one in Leicestershire. He held these livings until 1814, the year after his wife's death, when he exchanged them for the one at Trowbridge in Wiltshire. Here he stayed until his death. As for his verse: two years after *The Library* he published *The Village* (1783), a poem much admired by Dr Johnson, who saw it in manuscript and suggested some alterations. Next came *The Newspaper* (1785), then a huge gap eventually broken by the publication of *The Parish Register* (1807), *The Borough* (1810), *Tales in Verse* (1812), *Tales of the Hall* (1819), and some more verse that was published two years after his death as *Posthumous Tales* (1834). Finally, in 1961 some previously unpublished work made its appearance.

There has been a good deal of speculation about the reasons for this curious twenty-two years' silence of Crabbe's, all the odder since his first three volumes had gained him, if not a large, an enviable reputation. I think myself that several factors combined to cause it. The first and most obvious was that *The Newspaper* marked the end of what we might call Crabbe's early period. That poem is indeed a pretty dull exercise, mechanically competent but little more. Crabbe was too honest a poet to go on writing this sort of verse when he had no need to, and we must assume that his dissatisfaction with the early work acted as one cause for the prolonged silence. But there are others. In particular it seems that there were great domestic difficulties. Crabbe has made sure that we shall not be able to pry too deeply into them, but there can be little doubt that shortly after the death of their two younger sons in 1796, his wife fell into a deep depression which lasted until her death. Crabbe seems to have felt some guilt for his wife's state, and we know that at her request he burned three novels he had written at this time. It may be that he connected his wife's mental illness with his writing; and of course he may well have been right. We simply do not know. But since we do know that there *was* a prolonged silence and that he did at this time destroy some of his work at his wife's request, it seems reasonable to suppose that she was closely connected with his silence.

Yet it may be that he burnt the novels because he was so unsure of their quality that he let his wife be judge (novel-writing, it ought to be explained, was not at the end of the eighteenth century much honoured). If this is the case then it connects with his destroying a botanical treatise at which he had laboured, because he was told by the then Vice-Master of Trinity College Cambridge that all such works should be written in Latin; and this, though the book was already at the printer's. The connection here is Crabbe's uncertainty about himself and his talent, for which there is plenty of evidence. For example, criticism of friends would cause him to rewrite his verse, even though there seems no reason to credit those friends with great literary acumen. And though during the days of his greatest fame he occasionally found his way into the literary life of London, contemporary recollections show him always slightly bemused by what he encountered. He did not feel himself to belong. And this feeling is the key to his uncertainty.

Brought up amid poverty and hardship, Crabbe was encouraged to hope for better things. These hopes were constantly thwarted until the lucky meeting with Burke, which immediately drew him into a life where he had great difficulty determining his position. On his own admission, when he was chaplain to the Rutlands he was never sure whether his place was with the family or the servants. And the leap from obscure poverty to comfort and some fame was very sudden. No wonder Crabbe was unsure of his bearings. Besides, he must have felt it odd, almost a breach in the order of things, that someone

6

like himself, poor and obscure, should have talent at all. How genuine could the talent be? Should not talent be a product of social position? The question may seem absurd, but the fact is that Crabbe would not be the only man of genius to suffer from the sense the upper classes give off, of the necessary dependence of personal ability on high birth, and the prefaces to some of his volumes are an undeniably queer mixture of arrogance and servility.

And again, Crabbe may have sensed that his verse had little in common with the newer movements in poetry. Blake's *Poetical Sketches* were published in 1783, and by the end of the century Wordsworth and Coleridge had produced the famous *Lyrical Ballads*. I am not going to insist that Crabbe felt himself out of tune with the times, but the possibility cannot be dismissed.

Yet though his uncertainty did not leave him, Crabbe began to publish again. The reason? Mainly I think that he had, and knew he had, a genuinely new vein to explore, though we should not ignore the fact that at the time he was writing *The Parish Register* his two sons were at Cambridge, and their expenses had put him in some financial difficulties. Fortunately these were removed by the enthusiastic reception of his poem, and from then on Crabbe was never seriously bothered about money. True, *The Borough* was not so well liked, but *Tales in Verse* brought him the fame and success it deserved, so much so that as a result he was able to sell the copyright of all his previous work to the publisher Murray for £3,000. When *Tales of the Hall* was published in 1819 it was the best received of all his works.

And yet *Tales of the Hall* exhausted its sales with only one edition. The vogue for Crabbe was over. It is true that the poems show a falling-off from the previous volumes, and this decline is even more marked in *Posthumous Tales*. But we cannot account for the slackening of interest in Crabbe in these terms. Wordsworth's popularity was at this time growing fast as his verse got steadily worse. The real truth of the matter is that between 1812 and 1819 Byron had more or less stolen the poetry reading public from most other poets.

As though recognizing this fact, Crabbe virtually retired to Trowbridge. After the success of *Tales in Verse* he had occasionally gone to London, where he had been fêted by such

7

literary figures as Moore, Campbell and Rogers; but now he abandoned the literary life for his official duties and the study of geology, which began to usurp the place his botanical studies had previously occupied. He did travel a little still. In 1822 for example he went to Abbotsford to meet Scott, who had long been an admirer of his work, and in 1828 he met Wordsworth – no admirer. And in between he had paid his last visit to Suffolk. But these trips were departures from a life of seclusion and calm. In his last years he was much affected by facial neuralgia and occasionally suffered great pain. He died on 3 February 1832 after a short illness.

I give these details in so flat a way because I want to emphasize how little caught up in the great issues of his time Crabbe was. You would never guess from reading his life that he lived through the years of the French revolution, of the Romantic movement, of passionate arguments about democracy, atheism, republicanism in which, so we like to feel, all men were involved. And at a personal level there are no stunning discoveries to make about Crabbe. If there are no great causes eagerly embraced and as eagerly rejected, there are likewise no spectacular love affairs (there was a brief engagement to a girl in Trowbridge shortly after his wife's death, but there is no reason to find it spectacular, if only because Crabbe always covered his tracks too well to make speculation profitable), no violent challenges to convention, no sudden failure of talent, nothing that remotely approaches a tragic death. It is all very level, very grey. Perhaps for these reasons Crabbe has commanded little attention. But there is also the important fact that we are accustomed to think of the years of his fame in terms of the Romantic achievement, and with the Romantics Crabbe does not belong. Indeed these poets have so little in common with him that if ever they do refer to him it is in scathing terms, sharpened by the spiteful awareness that he enjoyed a fame and popularity that were denied them. Wordsworth, for example, told Rogers that 'nineteen out of twenty of Crabbe's Pictures are mere matters of fact; with which the muses have as much to do as they have with a collection of medical reports, or of Law cases'. Hazlitt, in his lectures on the English poets, gave him what Keats called 'an unmerciful licking', and Keats himself wrote that he liked half of Wordsworth, and 'Crabbe not at all'. As for Coleridge, he confided in his notebook that

'In Crabbe there is an absolute defect of high imagination; he gives me little or no pleasure'. Shelley never wrote about Crabbe, but he can hardly have approved of someone who stood for interests so completely opposed to his own. Byron, indeed, is the one exception to the general chorus. In his early *English Bards and Scotch Reviewers* (1809) he made the famous remark that Crabbe was 'Nature's sternest painter and her best', and several years later told his publisher that of all worthwhile modern poets, 'Crabbe's the man'. Yet Byron, of course, is a notoriously uncertain judge; he not only thought Rogers (a mere dilettante) Crabbe's equal, but considered Moore and Campbell better poets than Wordsworth and Coleridge.

Should we then write Crabbe off, as the great Romantic poets did? Of course not. It is essential that we remember not only their inevitable jealousy of his success, but the fact that their own concerns could hardly make them sympathetic to a poet so remote from these as Crabbe was. It is interesting to know the reasons for their disapproval, but these are likely to tell us more about the poets themselves than the object of their criticism. And no matter how little he has been spoken of approvingly, the truth is that Crabbe is a major poet. Not perhaps a great one; anyway, not so great as Wordsworth. But he is a better poet than Shelley, better than Coleridge even, and if this has not been generally recognized the fault is not his but that of successive generations of readers and critics who have set aside his excellence, or not known how to come at it, or been confused by the accounts of the Romantics in whose favour he has been neglected. In the rest of this introduction I shall try to explain what Crabbe's peculiar excellence is, and why we must regard him as a major poet.

AUGUSTANISM

Before turning to Crabbe's work we should note one or two essential aspects of eighteenth-century or *Augustan* ideas that recur throughout its whole range. These stem from the single premise: that as a consequence of the Fall man is inevitably flawed and corrupt. Because of this, he should not expect too much of his own judgment and ability: caution and restraint are what he needs at all times. Reason is therefore to be preferred to the passions, since these trap a man into acting without forethought. In its own way, however, reason is to be

9

approached with caution too, because no less than any other element in human make-up it is flawed.

In this predicament no man should implicitly trust his own reason without first consulting the views of others alive and dead. Man, over the ages, has built up a society and a set of values which have proved their use and worth. A man who is wise finds out what is the traditional, approved course of action and then if he seeks to act in a contrary manner he should strive to curb himself. The Church of England, the Throne and the Civil Laws are all institutions with long valued traditions that demand complete allegiance from English people. In an attempt to further the social institutions that have grown up over a long period of time men must be content to accept the positions into which they have been born. For anybody to challenge his position would lead inevitably to a radical disturbance of all social institutions. Indeed, this fact the previous century had witnessed with the Civil War, the execution of Charles I and the overthrow of James II. We should not be surprised that Augustans were obsessed with social stability.

From what has been said so far, it follows that Augustans were also contemptuous of nonconformist religions such as Methodism which not only differed with the Established Church but also preferred to put complete trust in feelings rather than a rational belief supported by a wealth of theological study. Republicanism or any other social movement that threatened the monarchy or civil law must inevitably be outlawed. In short, an Augustan (such as George Crabbe) accepted that man should pay all his allegiance to the society he found ready-made. To depart from this would be uncivilized and in Augustan poetry the accent always falls upon the civilized, the polite and the social acceptable ways of behaving.

As a focus of such good behaviour and social excellence many writers found the City of London of unparalleled importance. The City is where men are identified with a common purpose – to serve society – and are obliged to minimize their own individuality. Such an acceptance of tradition dominates Augustan attitudes to art. For this reason originality is despised as is any work that does not show a proper respect for civilized values. To call a work of art original or barbaric is the worst insult that an Augustan can bestow.

If we look at Crabbe's poetry as a whole we find that he

sought to trace acceptable paths for individual behaviour with socially established patterns in the back of his mind. It means that for the reader all the words that describe human behaviour and psychology have to be read with especial care and that abstract nouns and their derivatives have an added weight. If we turn, for the moment, to his early poetry then we find that Crabbe knows how to apply these Augustan values but he is not yet at ease because he has not lived long enough in the City or wherever they have been responsibly discussed and tested out.

THE EARLY VERSE

The Village is undoubtedly the best of Crabbe's early works and very clearly its allegiances are with the great Augustan writers, Alexander Pope and Samuel Johnson, and the general ideas that have been sketched in already. But he could not yet do more than accept the topics these writers introduce into their work and he has nothing original or penetrating to add.

To glance at *The Village* is to see the justice of my remarks. The poem has altogether too theoretical an air about it, and unavoidably you come to feel that Crabbe overstrains the vices of village life. Of course, if he is to refer that way of life to his rigidly interpreted Augustan values there can be very little good about it. The villagers live well beyond the influence of what 'civilizes', and so,

> Here joyless roam a wild amphibious race,
> With sullen woe display'd in every face;
> Who far from civil arts and social fly,
> And scowl at strangers with suspicious eye.

It seems to me that the chief effect of those lines – and they are entirely representative – is to remind us of Crabbe's desperate uncertainty about where he himself belonged. *The Village* often reads as a renunciation of his own village past; Crabbe is pathetically keen to stand up and be counted with what he assumes is the best society has to offer. And so the motions of judgment are scrupulously and dully gone through. It is altogether too censorious, and for that very reason shows how little Crabbe is at ease with his acquired values. 'Joyless' for example is a word difficult to justify in itself – is the life that bad? – and it makes 'sullen woe' unnecessary. You might argue that Crabbe is grimly underlining the villagers' lot, and that 'joyless' by itself cannot do that; but my point is that the underlining helps us to feel the wild improbability of what's being said. And as for 'roam': it is easy to see how the word breeds, or was brought out by, 'wild'; but the consistency of the image while very well to describe a pack of wild dogs (or sea-monsters) is ludicrous when applied to the villagers, who are tied to their life in a way that is quite the opposite of nomadic.

Yet *The Village* does gain one advantage from its Augustan allegiances. Dr Johnson, who read the poem in manuscript and professed considerable admiration for it, would be certain to applaud Crabbe's scepticism about the delights of rural life. Johnson himself had spoken in *Rasselas* of some shepherds who 'were so ignorant, so little able to compare the good with the evil of the occupation, and so indistinct in their narratives and descriptions, that very little could be learned from them (ch. xix)'. Crabbe's poem may suffer from its readiness to turn villagers into ogrish beasts, but we have at least to see that his personal experience lends strength to his refusal to consider them as demigods of beauty and wisdom, dwelling in rural paradises. For this is how they were represented in a growing body of verse written during the latter half of the eighteenth century. Langhorne's *The Country Justice* (1774) is perhaps the most extended example of this type of poem. The following lines from Book 2 of the poem offer a direct challenge to Augustan values; the pleasures of the country are contrasted with the viciousness of city life.

> Has the fair Vale, where REST, conceal'd in Flowers,
> Lies in Sweet Ambush for thy careless[1] Hours,
> The Breeze, that, balmy Fragrance to infuse,
> Bathes its soft Wing in Aromatic Dews,
> The Stream, to soothe thine Ear, to cool thy Breast,
> That mildly murmers from its crystal Rest; –
> Have these less Charms to win, less Power to please,
> Than Haunts of Rapine, Harbours of Disease?

Self-consciously enough, the verse carries an air of challenge, and yet its diction and finally its attitudes are inescapably Augustan.

---

[1] 'Careless' means free from care.

A few lines (71–6) from Pope's 'Summer Pastoral' will be enough to show the extent of Langhorne's debt to what he hopes to disown.

Oh deign to visit our forsaken Seats,
The mossie Fountains, and the Green Retreats!
Where-e'er you walk, cool Gales shall fan the Glade,
Trees, where you sit, shall crowd into a Shade,
Where-e'er you tread, the blushing Flow'rs shall rise,
And all things flourish where you turn your Eyes.

As these lines make clear, Langhorne's diction is every bit as 'literary' as Pope's. In both there is the decision in favour of the generalizing epithet that resists too specific a descriptive function – compare 'fair Vale' with 'Green Retreats,' or 'sweet Ambush' with 'cool Gales' – and both aim for the typical rather than the particular, securing this by the definite article: *the* Breeze, *the* Stream and so on. In addition, the 'nature' depicted is ideal, not only in the sense that it is the best language can create, but also because it exists to serve man; its *raison d'être* is subservience to the human. Pope's 'Where-e'er *you* walk, cool Gales shall fan the Glade', is matched by Langhorne's 'The stream, to soothe *thine* Ear, to cool *thy* Breast'. But there is, of course, an important distinction to make between Pope and Langhorne, for Pope's is not intended to be a descriptive art; he does not set out to tell the literal truth about the English countryside. Langhorne does. But the literary, generalizing quality of his diction, and his underlying assumptions about nature's use, work against his purpose. All too obviously, Pope's ideal has become for Langhorne an escapist dream world that he thinks of as actual. Or if that is to put the matter unfairly, we can at least say that though Langhorne may be dissatisfied with Augustan values, he has no way of presenting his dissatisfaction; we must simply take it on trust. In short he has no actual positive to set up against what he dislikes; only a literary convention which is deliberately a far remove from the actual.

Not surprisingly Crabbe saw how absurd was the tactic that *The Country Justice* exemplifies. He would agree with Dr Johnson that 'Life must be seen before it can be known', rural life not excepted. Accordingly, *The Village* directly addresses poets like Langhorne who indulge a sort of weekend pastoralism.

> Ye gentle souls, who dream of Rural ease,
> Whom the smooth stream and smoother sonnet[1] please;
> Go! if the peaceful Cot your praises share,
> Go look within, and ask if Peace be there;
> If Peace be his – that drooping weary Sire,
> Or theirs, that Offspring round their feeble fire;
> Or hers, that Matron pale, whose trembling hand
> Turns on the wretched hearth th'expiring brand!

Even here, though, Crabbe's air of tough facing up to the brutal realities of rural life is overdone. The taut contempt of 'Whom the smooth stream and smoother sonnet please', is very nearly undermined by what follows. Epithets pile up with a glum relish that comes dangerously near to being farcical: we do not really need 'drooping' and 'weary', nor 'pale' and 'trembling'; and after drawing our attention to the 'feeble fire' it is surely gratuitous of Crabbe to provide an exclamation mark for 'th'expiring brand'. And to point out these excesses is to suggest that *The Village* is best seen, not as a realistic account of rural life, but as a corrective to the sentimentalities of poems like *The Country Justice*.

Yet the Augustan good sense that vetoed Langhorne's Romantic inclinations carried with it a weighty problem. For if rural life was as Crabbe had painted it in *The Village*, and if life was to be seen before it could be known (and thus written about), the uncomfortable conclusion followed that he should give up verse. The only life he knew anything about being rural, he ought at best to write verse saying rural life was not worth writing about, since it is far from civil arts and social; and that could not be done too often. Put thus baldly the idea may seem silly; yet I have already spoken of Crabbe's protracted silence, and to suppose it was at least partly occasioned by some crisis of purpose is not unreasonable, especially when this is seen in the context of Crabbe's acute uncertainty about his position. What we can legitimately suppose is that Crabbe did not find it easy to reconcile his real interests with his acquired principles. To glance at 'Sir Eustace Grey' is to see this more clearly.

'Sir Eustace Grey' was published in the volume of 1807, with which Crabbe broke his silence. The poem shows a consider-

---

[1] 'Sonnet' here means song – i.e. poem.

able interest in, and knowledge of mental extremity, an interest we are quick to associate with Romantic poetry. Yet Crabbe finds a cause of the madness to be in Sir Eustace Grey's enthusiastic embracing of Nonconformist religion, which we have seen the Augustans distrusted, as emotional and insufficiently rational. Moreover, the poem ends with some lines that are an unmistakable echo of Dr Johnson. Compare Crabbe's

> But ah! though time can bring relief,
>   And soften woes it cannot cure;
> Would we not suffer pain and grief,
>   To have our reason sound and sure?

with Johnson's '[the madman] has always discontent in his look, and malignity in his bosom. And, if we had the power of choice, he would soon repent who should resign his reason to secure his peace'.[1] All the same, Crabbe is undoubtedly more interested in the state of Sir Eustace Grey's mind than in making sententious reflections about the comparative joys of sanity. 'Sir Eustace Grey' has a framework of Augustan attitudes, but the real core of interest is not only Augustan. As he is in 'Peter Grimes', so here Crabbe is clearly fascinated by an extreme of mental distress, and it is an interest from which Dickens, as an admirer of Crabbe, certainly profited when he came to write of the murderers, Bill Sykes and Jonas Chuzzlewit. This is not to say that Crabbe's interests can be identified with Dickens', because his moral attitude is at once simpler and more certain. But I do want to suggest that Crabbe's interests occasionally move in the direction of Romanticism, and though his interest in mental extremity is not central to his work, the fact that he entertains it at all and is so clearly concerned with the workings of the mind brings us to this crucial point: that our estimate of Crabbe's worth is likely to be harmed if we are content to see him as late Augustan, the 'Pope in worsted stockings' for which most accounts settle.[2]

Though *The Village* is the best of his early verse, Crabbe in that poem wears his stockings with scarcely a wrinkle, and if it were all of his work that survived there would be little point in

[1] From *Review of a Free Enquiry into the Nature and Origin of Evil.*
[2] This famous phrase was coined by H. and J. Smith in 1812, in a volume of parodies of poets of the day, called *Rejected Addresses.*

trying to regard him as a major poet. He became one only when he saw where his true interests lay, and had the courage to write about them. And Crabbe's greatest triumphs are owing to his realization that he could legitimately write about those small societies which from a strict Augustan standpoint lie outside the concerns of serious literature. For his art is rooted in small societies, and he knows what Johnson did not, that more than a little can be learned from them. Even so, Crabbe did not have to overthrow completely his Augustanism in order to discover the true strengths of his art; rather these became revealed as he learned to *adapt* Augustan habits of mind and modes of thought to the subject matter of his verse. So to call him a late Augustan is to miss the force of his originality, for it makes him too simply derivative, and inevitably focuses attention on the least remarkable qualities of his art. These are generally to be found in his earlier verse. In what remains of this introduction, the focus is very emphatically on the later Crabbe.

The Parish Register was the work that broke Crabbe's twenty-two-year silence. Everywhere in it there is evidence of how far he had travelled from his early verse; an assured and flexible wit declares how fully the poet has managed to assimilate Augustan values to his subject matter. In the following lines, for example, we have a description of a lord's footman, who has returned to his native village for the day, and who, dressed in imitation of the town dandy, is out to make a glittering impression on his former acquaintances.

> Rings on his fingers shone; his milk-white hand
> Could pick-tooth case and box for snuff command:
> And thus, with clouded cane, a fop complete,
> He stalk'd, the jest and glory of the street.

Crabbe's art is to undercut Daniel's pride by a series of wittily established contrasts. Notice, for instance, how the word 'command', which hints at the social position of a lord, neatly demolishes the footman's pretensions. All he can command are a pick-tooth case and a snuff-box; for the rest he is commanded. But Crabbe leads up to the word by a bland matter-of-fact detailing of Daniel's possessions, so that the stress taken by 'command' jolts us into a sudden recognition of the word's being absurdly too big. And since Daniel cannot command anything worth while, his pride is seen to be a matter of self-deceit; and the rhyme word takes us back to the milk-white hand, a detail we now recognize as equally absurd in view of Daniel's function: he is after all a footman. Now it is true that Crabbe's judgment of Daniel depends on an Augustan sense of values; it implies the need for self-knowledge as part of social consciousness and affirms the necessity of a recognized acceptance of order and degree. But very clearly, these values are accommodated to the small society about which Crabbe is writing. Indeed this is made even more apparent in the second couplet. So much depends on the juxtaposition of *complete/ street*: the grandeur of the one is undercut by the meanness of the other. 'Complete' is a mocking celebration of Daniel's utter dedication to his foppishness, and it also manages to imply that he is so caught up in that that he has no time to be anything else. The next line exposes how pathetic Daniel's pretensions in fact are: he can only hope to succeed as a fop in the village, for in the town where fops belong he is merely a footman. But he is so ridiculously out of place in the village that he cannot impress even the villagers; he is their jest. And this double failure is the more exactly defined since the second line is a deliberate echo of a very famous one from Pope's *Essay on Man*, where man is spoken of as 'The Glory, Jest, and Riddle of the World'. Here *world* has contracted to *street*; it is the only world Daniel can hope to conquer, and he fails. We may note that Crabbe's allusion to Pope's poem is sure proof of his confidence that he can naturalize Augustan values to his own concerns.

As with any good poet, Crabbe is constantly alive to the full meaning of words. His attentiveness to language is essentially part of his vision (note for example how, in the lines just looked at, *command* and *complete* owe their richness of meaning to Crabbe's regard for the social context). Elements of this attentiveness are pointed out in A. E. Rodway's *The Romantic Conflict*,[1] and there is no point in my repeating what has been well said there. But it is worth offering an example Dr Rodway does not select, because it suggests how very subtly Crabbe can use language to register states of mind. In the section of *The Parish Register* called 'Burials', Crabbe mentions the death of a young mother and the anguish her family suffered. To suggest

[1] See esp. pp. 45–8.

the keenness of their distress, Crabbe mentions 'The fire-side chair still set, but vacant still'. If we are alert to the fact that *still* means both *as yet* and *always*, we can see how fine is Crabbe's perception. The obvious reading of the line is: 'The fire-side chair as yet set (with the implication that at some time in the future it will not be), but always vacant.' The mother's death, that is, cannot be undone. But sympathetically read, the line also allows us to take in the family's struggle to acknowledge the terrible finality of death. We do, in other words, sense a hopeless hope in the meaning, 'the fire-side chair always set but as yet vacant' (with the implication that at some time in the future it will not be). There is nothing sentimental about this psychological insight; the bleaker meaning of the words predominates, but all the same the other one legitimately tugs for its share of our attention.

I do not single out Crabbe's achievement here at random, but because it hints at something I have already mentioned in talking of 'Sir Eustace Grey' and 'Peter Grimes', and which I shall have cause to touch on again later. The fact is that much of Crabbe's important work is remarkable for its psychological subtlety, its keen enquiry into the states and processes of the human mind. But Crabbe sees neither the mind nor the individual in complete isolation. There are no solitaries of the Wordsworthian kind in his work, his outcasts (even Grimes) retain a strong sense of the society from which they have been removed, and indeed their behaviour is understandable to Crabbe on the assumption that they are social beings. To say this brings us to the true centre of his art and its essential strength. Like the Romantics Crabbe is concerned with individual lives, but unlike them he does not consider them apart from their social setting. Indeed, Crabbe retains the Augustan belief that a person is fully human only in a social context which most insistently taxes him.

Choosing to write about a small rural community Crabbe is, however, different from the Augustans. What London had been to Pope a Suffolk village is to Crabbe. This is not because he had – as some writers have maintained – an interest in poverty, but because it was a society that he knew well. For him, as for Pope, judgment of individuals necessitated a balance between their public and private claims and how they reconcile the two. For Pope London could be imagined as a paradisal city. His poem, *Windsor Forest* (1711) shows this very clearly. But at the end of the same century poets would see the capital in very different terms. Shelley spoke for all when he declared in 'Peter Bell the Third' that 'Hell is a city much like London'. The reason is soon stated: as far as the Romantic poet is concerned London was an impersonal chaos that threatened to destroy all human potential. William Cobbett, the farmer and politician who was the author of *Rural Rides*, agreed with this estimate and called London 'the Great Wen'. He was a man who would have had a good deal in common with Crabbe. To all these dissident writers, London deserved no allegiance whatever.

For the Romantic, the ideal community was not a present inescapable fact but a remote future possibility. It might be a paradise which was temporal (as in Coleridge's dream of establishing a society on the banks of the Susquehanna) or spiritual (as in the case of William Blake's heavenly city, Golgonooza). Compared with such dauntless visions it may seem fatally unimaginative of Crabbe to see in the village a community to which allegiance properly is owed, and indeed the Romantics protested that it was. Yet such a decision has the advantage of being shrewdly realistic, and also validly keeps alive Augustan habits of thought. Thus Crabbe's scrutiny of individuals bears on the manner of their commitment to society. And to put the matter this way goes far towards explaining Jane Austen's great admiration for his work, which the best of his art fully deserves, since it possesses strengths we are accustomed to think of as hers alone. The justice of my claim can be tested by a relatively minor example from *The Parish Register*.

In the third section of this poem, Crabbe includes a portrait of a Lady who, he says, 'showed her virtue by her scorn of vice'. It is easy to see how a lesser artist might coarsen the perception by making the Lady a hypocrite, insisting that her virtue is merely show. If we attempted such a reading of Crabbe's line, however, its sure-footed poise would be quite lost. As far as he is concerned the Lady's virtue is real and honourable, because it is socially proper to show scorn of vice; the community demands responsible acceptance of its standards. Yet at the same time we are not meant to feel that the Lady's attitude has been entirely vindicated, since the line lets us feel – though without losing the poise that would plunge it into denunciation – that the Lady is not holding in proper balance her private and public responsibilities. There is the unavoidable suggestion that she is content with showing scorn rather than feeling it. No doubt this puts the matter clumsily, but that is because of the irreducible poise and subtlety of a line which must surely have delighted the author of these words: 'Emma denied none of it aloud, and she agreed to none of it in private.'

It is a measure of Jane Austen's and Crabbe's unromantic art that they should be so firmly committed to the attempt to reconcile and balance the private and public claims on individuals in the small society. Unromantic, too, is their awareness of the small society as a complex web of relations which, in its respect for the subtleties of social gradations, becomes in little the harmonious world governed by order and degree that Pope had postulated on a universal scale, when he spoke of

> bearings, and the ties,
> The strong connections, nice dependencies,
> Gradations just (*Essay on Man*: Epistle I, ll. 29–31).

For both Crabbe and Jane Austen, strong connections and nice dependencies form the necessary framework of the good society, and social harmony thus depends on each person acknowledging the just gradation whereby he is assigned his place in the hierarchy. But where for the Augustans resisting place was of political consequence (for if you challenged your position you would threaten social stability and might eventually provoke civil war), in the work of Crabbe and Jane Austen the consequence is more directly moral, since in the small community everybody knows everybody else, and therefore social relationships are also personal ones. So to fail in social responsibility is to fail in the matter of personal relationships, a truth Jane Austen has Mr Knightley reveal to Emma after she has insulted Miss Bates:

Were she a woman of fortune, I would leave every harmless absurdity to take its chance; I would not quarrel with you for any liberties of manner. Were she your equal in situation – but, Emma, consider how far this is from being the case. She is poor; she has sunk from the comfort she was born to; and if she live to old age must probably sink more. Her situation should secure your compassion. It was badly done, indeed!

(Emma, ch. 43)

For Crabbe, too, personal and social relationships are inextricably linked. Indeed, the last example I am going to take from *The Parish Register* shows how directly Jane Austen is indebted to him. I quote from an episode concerned with attempted seduction:

> Sir *Edward Archer* is an amorous knight,
> And maidens chaste and lovely shun his sight;
> His Bailiff's daughter suited much his taste,
> For *Fanny Price* was lovely and was chaste;
> To her the Knight with gentle looks drew near,
> And timid voice assum'd, to banish fear: –
>   'Hope of my life, dear sovereign of my breast,
> Which, since I knew thee, knows nor joy nor rest:
> Know, thou art all that my delighted eyes,
> My fondest thoughts, my proudest wishes prize . . .
>   Come then, my mistress, and my wife; for she
> Who trusts my honour is the wife for me;
> Your slave, your husband, and your friend employ,
> In search of pleasures we may both enjoy.

In matters of detail that speech is diabolically clever, and though I have not the space to do full justice to Crabbe's art here, I must at least mention the attentive skill with which he shows Sir Edward Archer's tactic of inverting the true nature of his relationship with Fanny Price. Archer pretends that he is hers to command, and given the exactness of the social context his cliché of love becomes a cruel lie. For it is not after all his honour that's at stake, nor is the girl in a position to employ him; but by using such words he tries to confuse the truth about their social relationships, the 'gradations just' which he refuses to honour. Confusion is, indeed, the key to his smooth talk, the reason behind the timid voice he assumes; and in trying to confuse the girl's sense of position he inevitably dishonours the personal claims she has on him. I think it altogether too much of a coincidence to suppose that Jane Austen called the heroine of *Mansfield Park* Fanny Price in ignorance of Crabbe's verses, especially since her heroine, too, resists the offer of marriage from a man socially her superior who pretends this is not so. Again and again, Henry **Crawford** uses words in a way designed to confuse Fanny's awareness of the truth about their relative social standing, and when, after all his efforts, Fanny still resists him, he says, 'My conduct shall speak for me; absence, distance, time shall speak for me. *They* shall prove . . . I do deserve you.' (*Mansfield Park*, ch. 33.)

With sure tact Crabbe can indicate the offensiveness of Archer's behaviour through the impropriety of his speech, just because the strong connections and nice dependencies of the small society make the mode of address a sensitive register of an individual's responsiveness to his social and moral commitments. Outside the small society, the distinctions between propriety and impropriety of speech become blurred; inside they retain the sharpness that Crabbe delights in bringing out.

Since so much of Crabbe's art is directed towards the individual's awareness of social position, it is not surprising that he should enjoy himself at the expense of those who through vanity or self-deceit are blind to the actualities of their situation. He is a master at deflating pretension, often adopting a pompous style that is comically at odds with its subject. A good example of this occurs in the 'Widow's Tale', from the 1812 volume, *Tales in Verse*. The tale deals with a young girl who, having been expensively educated in the city, returns to the rough and ready life of her father's farm and attempts to bring with her the manners of a fine lady for which, as she thinks, her education has intended her. The periphrastic diction that Crabbe employs to describe her joining the kitchen meals is not subtly, but straightforwardly comic.

> The air, surcharged with moisture, flagg'd around,
> And the offended damsel sigh'd and frown'd;
> The swelling fat in lumps conglomerate laid,
> And fancy's sickness seized the loathing maid:
> But when the men beside their station took,
> And maidens with them, and with these the cook;
> When one huge wooden bowl before them stood,
> Filled with huge balls of farinaceous food;
> With bacon, mass saline, where never lean
> Beneath the brown and bristly rind was seen;
> When from a single horn the party drew
> Their copious draughts of heavy ale and new;

When the coarse cloth she saw, with many a stain
Soil'd by rude hinds who cut and came again –
She could not breathe; but with a heavy sigh,
Rein'd the fair neck, and shut th' offended eye;
She minc'd the sanguine flesh in frustums fine,
And wonder'd much to see the creatures dine.

According to the *Oxford English Dictionary*, 'frustums', lovely word, means 'remainder of regular solid whose upper part has been cut off by plane parallel to base'. The word deliciously mocks the precision with which the girl minces her sanguine flesh. There is breeding for you! Moreover to take the word in its line is to see the source of Crabbe's comic method in the passage as a whole. 'She minc'd the sanguine flesh in frustums fine': with its ponderous latinate diction and deliberately insensitive alliteration this parodies the 'sublime' style of a good deal of eighteenth-century poetry. The true founder of this style is James Thomson (1700–48), whose poem *The Seasons*, first published in 1730, and thereafter constantly revised and republished, became one of the most popular and influential works of the century. The style of *The Seasons* is modelled on the more imitable aspects of Milton's *Paradise Lost*, but since Thomson's subject matter has no 'epic' importance he relies on style alone to give it high dignity. Because it was so popular, Thomson's poetry occasioned a host of imitations, the work of minor poets who believed that a sufficiently inflated style would guarantee the authentic worth of their art, and that any triviality of subject matter could be redeemed by the terms in which it was presented.

As the century wore on, the belief that poetic diction ought to be 'sublime' hardened into dogma that came to be widely accepted among men of letters. For example, in his *Elements of Criticism*, which for some time after its appearance in 1762 was regarded as a textbook of poetic theory, Lord Kames said that periphrasis 'hath a happy effect in preventing the familiarity of proper names. The familiarity of a proper name, is communicated to the thing it signifies by means of their intimate connection; and the thing is thereby brought down in our feeling. This bad effect is prevented by using a figurative word instead of one that is proper; as . . . when we express the sky by terming it the *blue vault of heaven*.'

Unfortunately, this disastrous theory found such contented acceptance among poets that even in the most gifted its harmful effects show themselves. William Cowper (1731–1800), at his best a very fine poet indeed, frequently falls foul of the 'sublime' diction, nowhere more ludicrously than in his long poem, *The Task* (1785). For example in Book 3 (ll. 465–7), there is a famous account of the rearing of cucumbers, in the course of which Cowper sees fit to call horse-dung

> a stercoraceous heap,
> Impregnated with quick fermenting salts,
> And potent to resist the freezing blast.

Small wonder that in the Preface to the *Lyrical Ballads* (1800), Wordsworth should protest against poets who 'indulge in arbitrary and capricious habits of expression' and insist that he himself wished to adopt 'the very language of men'. And he promised that in the *Lyrical Ballads*, there would be found 'little of what is usually called poetic diction; I have taken as much pains to avoid it as others ordinarily take to produce it'. Wordsworth's Preface is rightly regarded as one of the most crucial documents in the history of Romanticism. Yet we should beware of seeing the reaction against 'poetic diction' as exclusively Romantic; Crabbe has his own valid contribution to make, one that complements the efforts of Wordsworth.[1] For Wordsworth does not attempt to parody the diction he anathematizes, even if he is betrayed into it on more occasions than he would like to admit. But for Crabbe, concerned with the essentially comic exploration of gaps between pretension and actuality, parody is a valid weapon. The passage from the 'Widow's Tale' is a good example of how he uses it and suggests a further reason for Jane Austen's admiration. The poet who could speak of a young lady mincing her sanguine flesh in frustums fine would readily appeal to the creator of Mr Collins, the vicar who sees no inconsistency between conceited pomposity towards his relatives and servile boot-licking to Lady Catherine de Bourgh, and who as a man of God tells Mr Bennet that 'I condole with you on the grievous affliction you are now suffering under. . . . The death of your daughter would have been a blessing in comparison of this. . . . Let me advise you then, my dear sir, to console yourself as much as possible, to

[1] See *Diction and Imagery*, p. 258.

throw off your unworthy child from your affection for ever, and leave her to reap the fruits of her own heinous offence.' (*Pride and Prejudice*, ch. 38.)

TALES IN VERSE: THE HIGH POINT

And now that I have made mention of *Tales in Verse* it is best to point out why I take this volume to mark the high point of Crabbe's achievement, why, to put it rather differently, it most fully realizes the potentials of *The Parish Register* and *The Borough*. Those two volumes are a great advance on the earlier work, because, as I have said, in them Crabbe no longer feels it necessary to strike the conventionally 'correct' pose as regards his subject matter. A sombrely realistic view controls the art and allows for the unflinching power that is the most remarkable quality of these studies of rural life. After Crabbe's death, John Duncan wrote some commemorative lines in which he declared that in the poet's work

> No dreamy incidents of wild romance,
> With whirling shadows, wilder'd minds entrance;
> But plain realities the mind engage.

Most readers of *The Parish Register* and *The Borough* would, I think, testify to the impressive rendering of plain realities. Yet the phrase suggests limitations, it opens the road to Wordsworth's objection that Crabbe's verse deals in 'mere matters of fact', and it anticipates Ezra Pound's view in *The A.B.C. of Reading* that 'given a curiosity about the social condition of England in 1810, can you find a more condensed account than Crabbe's of the whole social order?' At their finest, *The Parish Register* and *The Borough* deserve more than the faint praise Pound is here according Crabbe. 'Peter Grimes', after all, is one of the masterpieces of our language. Yet Pound's point must partly be conceded. For there is a good deal in *The Parish Register* and *The Borough* that does not rise much above the level of accurate reporting, and though we may find much to admire in the skill with which the facts and observation are deployed, it can hardly be denied that this is not the highest form of poetry and that it does not tap the deepest roots of Crabbe's genius. At least one reviewer of *The Borough* saw where these lay.

Francis Jeffrey (1773–1850), is probably best remembered now for his obtuse refusal to recognize the worth of the great Romantic poets and for his bitter and often ignoble attacks on them in *The Edinburgh Review*, of which he was editor from 1802 to 1829. Yet Jeffrey was by no means a stupid man, as his praise of Crabbe shows. The truth is that he was deeply suspicious of innovation in literature, and while this prevented him from seeing Wordsworth's radical greatness, it put him in a very good position to appreciate Crabbe. Jeffrey was one of Crabbe's warmest admirers, and an extremely acute one; and his diagnosis of Crabbe's essential strengths in his review of *The Borough* remains one of the best we have. Having offered qualified praise of this poem, Jeffrey concludes by admitting that he has 'a very strong desire to see Mr Crabbe apply his great powers to the construction of some interesting and connected story. He has great talents for narration; and that unrivalled gift in the delineation of character which is now used only for the creation of detached portraits, might be turned to admirable account in maintaining the interest, and enhancing the probability of an extended train of adventures.'

Two years after the appearance of *The Borough*, Crabbe published *Tales in Verse*, and in the preface to that volume he took up Jeffrey's suggestion that his gifts would fit him to write something akin to a novel in verse. Crabbe begins by saying that he feels this to be finally beyond the scope of his art, but, he continues: 'if these characters which seemed to be at my disposal were not such as would coalesce into one body, nor were of a nature to be commanded by one mind, so neither on examination did they appear as an unconnected multitude, accidentally collected, to be suddenly dispersed; but rather beings of whom might be formed groups and smaller societies'. And Crabbe goes on to say that though such tales as he has written lack a good deal collectively in 'unity of subject and grandeur of design', they gain by their 'greater variety of incident and more minute display of character, by accuracy of description and diversity of scene'. In these words, Crabbe has indicated the true importance of his volume; for his tales, dealing with different small societies and groups, do manage a minute display of character and an accuracy of description that in their fusion produce major art. True, the phrases Crabbe has used to characterize his work still look in the direction of 'mere matters of fact', but in the preface he himself has made the right reply to hostile critics.

It has been already acknowledged, that these compositions have no pretensions to be estimated with the more lofty and heroic kind of poems; but I feel great reluctance in admitting that they have not a fair and legitimate claim to the poetic character: in vulgar estimation, indeed, all that is not prose passes for poetry; but I have not ambition of so humble a kind as to be satisfied with a concession which requires nothing in the poet except his ability for counting syllables; and I trust something more of the poetic character will be allowed to the succeeding pages than what the heroes of the Dunciad might share with the author; nor was I aware that, by describing, as faithfully as I could, men, manners, and things, I was forfeiting a just title to a name which has been freely granted to many, whom to equal, and even to excel, is but a very stinted commendation.

The words hint still at the uncertainty I mentioned in part one of this introduction; Crabbe will not claim too much for his work: it is not to be compared with 'the more lofty and heroic kind of poems'. Simply, he deals 'faithfully in men, manners, and things', not superficially but with deep and scrupulous attentiveness; we have to take entirely seriously Crabbe's claim to the minute display of character. His art seeks to reconcile, to find the point of balance between social and personal claims, and it does so by examining how far moral precept (the abstract virtue laid down as a social requisite) stands the test of individual experience. Always in his best work there is the acute feeling for the way in which the lives of individuals are shaped by their social circumstances. Indeed it is his very sensitiveness to the complex lives of the 'groups and small societies', the condensed account of the social order for which Pound praised him, that makes him so fine an explorer of the individual consciousness. Some words of Henry James put the point best.

In history it is impossible to view individuals singly, and this point constitutes the chief greatness of the study. We are compelled to look at them in connection with their antecedents, their ancestors, their contemporaries, their circumstances. To judge them morally we are obliged to push our enquiry through a concatenation of causes and effects in which, from their delicate nature, enquiry very soon becomes impracticable and thus we are reduced to talking sentiment. (Review of 'Mr Froude's short studies' in *Literary Reviews and Essays*.)

Of course, the artist has a great advantage over the historian because he can invent the chain of causes and effects which make moral judgment possible, but Crabbe shares with James a deep sense of how complex is the tangle of causes in which individual action is meshed, and much of his finest work is devoted to communicating this sense. For this reason the verse tale is so apt a medium for his art, as the next example, one of the very best, shows.

'PROCRASTINATION'

In outline this tale is extremely simple. Rupert and Dinah, a pair of young lovers too poor to marry, are dependent on the girl's aunt leaving them money. The aunt, seeing that this way she can make Dinah her companion for the rest of her life, promises them she will, and makes them more contentedly accept the arrangement by hinting that she has not long to live. But after several years she is still very much alive and, near to desperation, Rupert goes abroad in the hope of making money that will free Dinah of the need to wait for her aunt's death before they can marry. He fares badly, however, and though the aunt does eventually die, it is not before she has managed to awaken her no longer young niece to the power and attractions of money and possessions. The result is that when Rupert finally returns, Dinah rejects him. The money they had originally needed for marriage, she now chooses instead of marriage. Set down so barely 'Procrastination' reads as one of life's little ironies; it might come from Thomas Hardy's 'Time's Laughingstocks'. But there is in fact nothing shallow about this poem; it does not exist to make a neat point, but to examine the vulnerability of a strong human tie to considerations grouped round money which appropriate to themselves terms of such moral weight as 'care' and 'prudence'. The opening lines reveal a kinship with Jane Austen:

> Love will expire, the gay, the happy dream,
> Will turn to scorn, indiff'rence, or esteem

We note immediately the civilized authority of the wit that governs Crabbe's choice of the word 'esteem'; it reverses the resigned cynicism for which the second line had seemed to be settling; it is unexpected, yet as a rhyme word takes its place so confidently that it challenges any feelings of inevitability about the course of human relationships: better esteem, with its realistic sense of honest regard, than the illusionary dream of love. The curve of thought through these two lines forbids us from attempting an easy certainty of judgment. It introduces us to the gravely subtle enquiry into the 'concatenation of causes and effects' which makes judgment by precept so vulnerable to the actualities of human experience.

'Care' is the key word of the poem, and at each stage of Dinah's progress towards contentment with spinsterhood it is invoked; as a precept it is responsible for the disasters of her life. Dinah, introduced to us as a 'prudent maid', has of necessity become so used to being 'careful' that care – for which prudence is a moral synonym – takes tyrannous hold on her; she lets it operate in all her affairs without seeing that it is often irrelevant. But this is not simple hypocrisy or obtuseness. We are dealing with a poem whose psychological probings are extremely acute, and in which Crabbe explores the processes by which Dinah comes to reject Rupert, armoured always by her controlling 'care'. Early on, the aunt tells the young couple, 'You now are young, and for this brief delay | And Dinah's *care*, what I bequeath will pay'. The word here is operating at a simple level, though even so it suggests that the servant role Dinah plays, in which her own wishes are subservient to those of others, makes for a pliancy that can be exploited. Later, when Rupert is abroad, the aunt begins the process of exploitation when she persists in showing Dinah her wealth,

> With the kind notice – 'They will be your own.'
> This hope, these comforts, cherish'd day by day,
> To Dinah's bosom made a gradual way . . .
> With lively joy those comforts she survey'd,
> And love grew languid in the careful maid.

Here 'careful' is ominously positioned to suggest that it is *because* she is so careful that Dinah's love grows languid. The word is invoked to suggest a prudence that is related to something like financial greed. But Crabbe does not allow us to make the accusation with any shrillness; he makes us aware of the aunt's guilt and the girl's loneliness. For her lover is abroad and hence her immediate hope of marriage and the comfort of his love are denied her. 'Comforts' itself is an ambiguous word, emotional and material in connotation, referring both to the warmth of human relations and the more solid safety of possessions that will guard Dinah against disaster should Rupert not return. And something like a substitution is taking place in her mind, of former emotional comforts for present material ones. Only this means that 'care' becomes transferred from what was worth while to what may not be so. Thus a little later we have the lines

> Sometimes the past would on her mind intrude,
> And then a conflict full of *care* ensued;
> The thoughts of Rupert on her mind would press,
> His worth she knew, but doubted his success.

We need to note about this use of the word how Dinah suppresses the anguish that hovers in her mind by a prudential 'balancing' judgment: 'His worth she knew, but doubted his success'.

Of all the *Tales in Verse*, 'Arabella' is the one where the balancing judgments of dispassionate prudence most centrally show themselves:

> On Captain *Bligh* her mind in balance hung –
> Though valiant, modest; and reserved, though young:
> Against these merits must defects be set –
> Though poor, imprudent; and though proud, in debt.

Dinah's mind similarly hangs in balance, but what we notice in 'Procrastination' is the sheer irrelevance of her judgment, for since the aunt is now dead Rupert does not need to succeed. Therefore, because she goes through with the judging game, we are inevitably drawn to notice Crabbe's brilliant play with the word 'care'; the 'conflict full of care' implies a sense of guilt on Dinah's part that she can evade only by converting it into a prudential reflection which will muffle her sense of 'conflict'. That the evasion is successful we know when we meet Dinah's reflection that Rupert 'oft had . . . lost the chance that care would seize'. Thinking this enables her to transfer her guilt to Rupert; it is all his own fault, for not having been as careful as herself. So timely a thought brings her relief, and we learn that

'Month after month was pass'd, and all were spent | In quiet comfort, and in rich content'. The word 'comfort' has re-entered with a savage twist to suggest that Dinah has bought it by shrugging off the relationship that had previously been her only comfort; now her comfort is in 'rich content', a phrase which would be cliché if it referred to her emotional life, but in implying the opposite – she is content only because rich – is masterly.

Dinah's life has now become uselessly controlled by material possession; 'quiet comfort' hints not only at her growing insensitivity to Rupert's claims on her, but literally at the near sterility of her life. The hint is picked up in the superb lines that elaborate on her possessions.

> Within a costly case of varnish'd wood,
> In level rows, her polish'd volumes stood;
> Shown as a favour to a chosen few,
> To prove what beauty for a book could do:
> A silver urn with curious work was fraught;
> A silver lamp from Grecian pattern wrought:
> Above her head, all gorgeous to behold,
> A time-piece stood on feet of burnish'd gold;
> A stag's head crest adorn'd the pictur'd case,
> Through the pure crystal shone the enamel'd face;
> And while on brilliants moved the hands of steel,
> It click'd from pray'r to pray'r, from meal to meal.

By its absorption in matters of detail, this equivocal celebration of Dinah's wealth makes clear how her comforts have now taken full control of a life which no longer has an impulse of its own; and indeed the last couplet shows the degree to which her life has been emptied of other comforts, with its feeling for a routine of time that is fully measured by the mechanical click of her costly time-piece. In Philip Larkin's fine phrase, this is 'a time unrecommended by event'.

Rupert's return is the one event that threatens to disrupt the quiet comfort and rich content of Dinah's existence. But though momentarily taken aback by his coming to her house, she quickly recovers. 'Meantime the prudent Dinah had contriv'd | Her soul to question, and she then reviv'd.' Prudence now means thinking up the best answer to give Rupert so that she shall be free from his claims on her. We note, too, the cool irony of the word 'contriv'd', indicating that Dinah asks of her soul only that it shall supply her with good arguments, not that it shall tell her the truth about herself. The progress from 'prudent maid' to 'prudent Dinah' here reaches its end-point; prudence can go no farther: percept has become at final odds with the human experience it should serve, and in the act of behaving morally 'well', Dinah tries totally to deceive herself about how morally bad she has become – through whose fault can hardly be established.

Yet for all the blanketings of self-deceit, self-knowledge does intermittently thrust itself on Dinah. We have already seen it at work in the moment when she has to convert 'a conflict full of care' into something else; and constantly Crabbe brings to our attention the force with which guilty knowledge breaks through Dinah's care. Most beautifully this is managed when some friends mention to her that in these 'degen'rate times' 'what was once our pride is now our shame'.

> Dinah was musing, as her friends discoursed,
> When these last words a sudden entrance forced
> Upon her mind, and what was once her pride
> And now her shame, some painful views supplied;
> Thoughts of the past within her bosom press'd,
> And there a change was felt, and was confess'd.

We might note here the way the couplet form almost breaks as the sudden entrance of the unlooked-for thoughts destroys Dinah's content, the care with which she has surrounded her life. Because of the enjambment, 'forced' enacts the power with which the ideas break through Dinah's shield of prudence, and the anarchy they cause shows itself in the disruption of the couplet form, so that when order restores itself in the last couplet it reinforces the inescapable weight of the self-confession to which Dinah is brought. But note how self-knowledge has still to struggle against self-deceit; the passive verbs reveal the fact of the struggle, as does the indirection of the word *change*. It admits to a difference between the feelings Dinah once had for Rupert and her present ones; it admits, too, to a change from *innocence* to something approaching acknowledgment of guilt. And note also how carefully the diction tracks Dinah's awakening to self-knowledge: *press'd, was felt, was confess'd*. The thoughts have an urgent power about them that cannot be resisted; thus Dinah *has* to feel what is happening to her, and therefore, however unwillingly, she is forced to acknowledge it. We move from emotional to intellectual response. The art in this is at one with Jane Austen's in writing about Emma's final awakening: 'Emma's eyes were instantly withdrawn; and she sat silently meditating in a fixed attitude, for a few minutes. A few minutes were sufficient for making her acquainted with her own heart. A mind like hers, once opening to suspicion, made rapid progress; she touched, she admitted, she acknowledged the whole truth.' (*Emma* ch. 47.)

Not all Crabbe's work approaches the level maintained almost throughout *Tales in Verse*. *Tales of the Hall* seems to me a distinct falling-away, and few of the *Posthumous Tales* improve on that volume. In both I find too much narrative, too little of that psychological subtlety and steady intelligence that pulse through the best of his art. Yet even in the late work, though nothing in it moves me as most of *Tales in Verse* does, there is the plainer delight of reading a poet who writes very little that can confidently be called bad. But the major period is between 1807 and 1812, and it is on the work of those years that the reputation must stand. I have already cited Ezra Pound on Crabbe, and I end with another remark of his. In this he links our poet with Jane Austen, and clearly intends that what he says of the one should apply to the other. Pound has been complaining that the poetry of the nineteenth century threw away a great heritage. But, he goes on, 'some day when Arthur's tomb is no longer an object for metrical research, and when the Albert Memorial is no longer regilded, Crabbe's people will still remain vivid. People will read Miss Austen because of her knowledge of the human heart, and not solely for her refinement.' (*Literary Essays.*) The vividness of their people, their knowledge of the human heart: Crabbe and Jane Austen share the accomplishment. Pound, great critic that he is, makes with unerring ease exactly the right, the central point.

Inebriety; A Poem

The mighty spirit, and its power, which stains
The bloodless cheek, and vivifies the brains,
I sing. Say, ye, its fiery vot'ries true,
The jovial curate, and the shrill-tongued shrew;
Ye, in the floods of limpid poison nurst,
Where bowl the second charms like bowl the first;
Say how, and why, the sparkling ill is shed,
The heart which hardens, and which rules the head.
    When winter stern his gloomy front uprears,
10 A sable void the barren earth appears;
The meads no more their former verdure boast,
Fast bound their streams, and all their beauty lost;
The herds, the flocks, in icy garments mourn,
And wildly murmur for the spring's return;
From snow-topp'd hills the whirlwinds keenly blow,
Howl through the woods, and pierce the vales below;
Through the sharp air a flaky torrent flies,
Mocks the slow sight, and hides the gloomy skies;
The fleecy clouds their chilly bosoms bare,
20 And shed their substance on the floating air;
The floating air their downy substance glides
Through springing waters, and prevents their tides;
Seizes the rolling waves, and, as a god,
Charms their swift race, and stops the refluent flood;
The opening valves, which fill the venal road,
Then scarcely urge along the sanguine flood;
The labouring pulse, a slower motion rules,
The tendons stiffen, and the spirit cools;
Each asks the aid of Nature's sister, Art,
30 To cheer the senses, and to warm the heart.
    The gentle fair on nervous tea relies,
Whilst gay good-nature sparkles in her eyes;

An inoffensive scandal fluttering round,
Too rough to tickle, and too light to wound;
Champagne the courtier drinks, the spleen to chase,
The colonel burgundy, and port his grace;
Turtle and 'rrac the city rulers charm,
Ale and content the labouring peasants warm:
O'er the dull embers, happy Colin sits,
40 Colin, the prince of joke, and rural wits;
Whilst the wind whistles through the hollow panes,
He drinks, nor of the rude assault complains;
And tells the tale, from sire to son retold,
Of spirits vanishing near hidden gold;
Of moon-clad imps that tremble by the dew,
Who skim the air, or glide o'er waters blue:
The throng invisible that, doubtless, float
By mouldering tombs, and o'er the stagnant moat;
Fays dimly glancing on the russet plain,
50 And all the dreadful nothing of the green.
Peace be to such, the happiest and the best,
Who with the forms of fancy urge their jest;
Who wage no war with an avenger's rod,
Nor in the pride of reason curse their God.
     When in the vaulted arch Lucina gleams,
And gaily dances o'er the azure streams;
On silent ether when a trembling sound
Reverberates, and wildly floats around,
Breaking through trackless space upon the ear,
60 Conclude the Bacchanalian rustic near;
O'er hills and vales the jovial savage reels,
Fire in his head and frenzy at his heels;
From paths direct the bending hero swerves,
And shapes his way in ill-proportioned curves.
Now safe arrived, his sleeping rib he calls,
And madly thunders on the muddy walls;
The well-known sounds an equal fury move,
For rage meets rage, as love enkindles love:
In vain the 'waken'd infant's accents shrill,
70 The humble regions of the cottage fill;

In vain the cricket chirps the mansion through,
'Tis war, and blood, and battle must ensue.
As when, on humble stage, him Satan hight
Defies the brazen hero to the fight:
From twanging strokes what dire misfortunes rise,
What fate to maple arms and glassen eyes!
Here lies a leg of elm, and there a stroke
From ashen neck has whirl'd a head of oak.
So drops from either power, with vengeance big,
80   A remnant night-cap and an old cut wig;
Titles unmusical retorted round,
On either ear with leaden vengeance sound;
Till equal valour, equal wounds create,
And drowsy peace concludes the fell debate;
Sleep in her woollen mantle wraps the pair,
And sheds her poppies on the ambient air;
Intoxication flies, as fury fled,
On rooky pinions quits the aching head;
Returning reason cools the fiery blood,
90   And drives from memory's seat the rosy god.
Yet still he holds o'er some his maddening rule,
Still sways his sceptre, and still knows his fool;
Witness the livid lip, and fiery front,
With many a smarting trophy placed upon't;
The hollow eye, which plays in misty springs,
And the hoarse voice, which rough and broken rings;
These are his triumphs, and o'er these he reigns,
The blinking deity of reeling brains.
    See Inebriety! her wand she waves,
100   And lo! her pale, and lo! her purple slaves!
Sots in embroidery, and sots in crape,
Of every order, station, rank, and shape:
The king, who nods upon his rattle throne;
The staggering peer, to midnight revel prone;
The slow-tongued bishop, and the deacon sly,
The humble pensioner, and gownsman dry;
The proud, the mean, the selfish, and the great,
Swell the dull throng, and stagger into state.

Lo! proud Flaminius at the splendid board,
The easy chaplain of an atheist lord,
Quaffs the bright juice, with all the gust of sense,
And clouds his brain in torpid elegance;
In china vases, see! the sparkling ill,
From gay decanters view the rosy rill;
The neat-carved pipes in silver settle laid,
The screw by mathematic cunning made:
Oh, happy priest! whose God, like Egypt's, lies,
At once the deity and sacrifice.
But is Flaminius then the man alone
To whom the joys of swimming brains are known?
Lo! the poor toper whose untutor'd sense,
Sees bliss in ale, and can with wine dispense;
Whose head proud fancy never taught to steer,
Beyond the muddy ecstasies of beer;
But simple nature can her longing quench,
Behind the settle's curve, or humbler bench:
Some kitchen fire diffusing warmth around,
The semi-globe by hieroglyphics crown'd;
Where canvass purse displays the brass enroll'd,
Nor waiters rave, nor landlords thirst for gold;
Ale and content his fancy's bounds confine,
He asks no limpid punch, no rosy wine;
But sees, admitted to an equal share,
Each faithful swain the heady potion bear:
Go wiser thou! and in thy scale of taste,
Weigh gout and gravel against ale and rest;
Call vulgar palates what thou judgest so;
Say beer is heavy, windy, cold, and slow;
Laugh at poor sots with insolent pretence,
Yet cry, when tortured, where is Providence?
    In various forms the madd'ning spirit moves,
This drinks and fights, another drinks and loves.
A bastard zeal, of different kinds it shows,
And now with rage, and now religion glows:
The frantic soul bright reason's path defies,
Now creeps on earth, now triumphs in the skies;

Swims in the seas of error, and explores,
Through midnight mists, the fluctuating shores;
From wave to wave in rocky channel glides,
150 And sinks in woe, or on presumption slides;
In pride exalted, or by shame deprest,
An angel-devil, or a human-beast.
Some rage in all the strength of folly mad;
Some love stupidity, in silence clad,
Are never quarrelsome, are never gay,
But sleep, and groan, and drink the night away;
Old Torpio nods, and as the laugh goes round,
Grunts through the nasal duct, and joins the sound,
Then sleeps again, and, as the liquors pass,
160 Wakes at the friendly jog, and takes his glass;
Alike to him who stands, or reels, or moves,
The elbow chair, good wine, and sleep he loves;
Nor cares of state disturb his easy head,
By grosser fumes, and calmer follies fed;
Nor thoughts of when, or where, or how to come,
The canvass general, or the general doom:
Extremes ne'er reach'd one passion of his soul,
A villain tame, and an unmettled fool,
To half his vices he has but pretence,
170 For they usurp the place of common sense;
To half his little merits has no claim,
For very indolence has raised his name;
Happy in this, that, under Satan's sway,
His passions tremble, but will not obey.
The vicar at the table's front presides,
Whose presence a monastic life derides;
The reverend wig, in sideway order placed,
The reverend band, by rubric stains disgraced,
The leering eye, in wayward circles roll'd,
180 Mark him the pastor of a jovial fold,
Whose various texts excite a loud applause,
Favouring the bottle, and the good old cause.
See! the dull smile which fearfully appears,
When gross indecency her front uprears,

39

The joy conceal'd, the fiercer burns within,
As masks afford the keenest gust to sin;
Imagination helps the reverend sire,
And spreads the sails of sub-divine desire;
But when the gay immoral joke goes round,
190   When shame and all her blushing train are drown'd,
Rather than hear his God blasphemed, he takes
The last loved glass, and then the board forsakes.
Not that religion prompts the sober thought,
But slavish custom has the practice taught;
Besides, this zealous son of warm devotion
Has a true Levite bias for promotion.
Vicars must with discretion go astray,
Whilst bishops may be damn'd the nearest way:
So puny robbers individuals kill,
200   When hector-heroes murder as they will.

    Good honest Curio elbows the divine,
And strives a social sinner how to shine;
The dull quaint tale is his, the lengthen'd tale,
That Wilton farmers give you with their ale,
How midnight ghosts o'er vaults terrific pass,
Dance o'er the grave, and slide along the grass;
Or how pale Cicely within the wood
Call'd Satan forth, and bargain'd with her blood:
These, honest Curio, are thine, and these
210   Are the dull treasures of a brain at peace;
No wit intoxicates thy gentle skull,
Of heavy, native, unwrought folly full:
Bowl upon bowl in vain exert their force,
The breathing spirit takes a downward course,
Or vainly soaring upwards to the head,
Meets an impenetrable fence of lead.

    Hast thou, oh reader! search'd o'er gentle Gay,
Where various animals their powers display?
In one strange group a chattering race are hurl'd,
220   Led by the monkey who had seen the world.
Like him Fabricio steals from guardian's side,
Swims not in pleasure's stream, but sips the tide:

He hates the bottle, yet but thinks it right
To boast next day the honours of the night;
None like your coward can describe a fight.
See him as down the sparkling potion goes,
Labour to grin away the horrid dose;
In joy-feign'd gaze his misty eyeballs float,
Th' uncivil spirit gurgling at his throat;
230 So looks dim Titan through a wintry scene,
And faintly cheers the woe foreboding swain.
　　Timon, long practised in the school of art,
Has lost each finer feeling of the heart;
Triumphs o'er shame, and, with delusive wiles,
Laughs at the idiot he himself beguiles:
So matrons past the awe of censure's tongue,
Deride the blushes of the fair and young.
Few with more fire on every subject spoke,
But chief he loved the gay immoral joke;
240 The words most sacred, stole from holy writ,
He gave a newer form, and call'd them wit.
Vice never had a more sincere ally,
So bold no sinner, yet no saint so sly;
Learn'd, but not wise, and without virtue brave,
A gay, deluding, philosophic knave.
When Bacchus' joys his airy fancy fire,
They stir a new, but still a false desire;
And to the comfort of each untaught fool,
Horace in English vindicates the bowl.
250 'The man,' says Timon, 'who is drunk is blest,
'No fears disturb, no cares destroy his rest;
'In thoughtless joy he reels away his life,
'Nor dreads that worst of ills, a noisy wife.
'Oh! place me, Jove, where none but women come,
'And thunders worse than thine afflict the room,
'Where one eternal nothing flutters round,
'And senseless titt'ring sense of mirth confound;
'Or lead me bound to garret, Babel-high,
'Where frantic poet rolls his crazy eye,
260 'Tiring the ear with oft-repeated chimes,

41

'And smiling at the never-ending rhymes:
'E'en here, or there, I'll be as blest as Jove,
'Give me tobacco, and the wine I love.'
Applause from hands the dying accents break,
Of stagg'ring sots who vainly try to speak;
From Milo, him who hangs upon each word,
And in loud praises splits the tortured board,
Collects each sentence, ere it's better known,
And makes the mutilated joke his own,
At weekly club to flourish, where he rules,
The glorious president of grosser fools,
    But cease, my Muse! of those, or these enough,
The fools who listen, and the knaves who scoff;
The jest profane, that mocks th' offended God,
Defies his power, and sets at nought his rod;
The empty laugh, discretion's vainest foe,
From fool to fool re-echoed to and fro;
The sly indecency, that slowly springs
From barren wit, and halts on trembling wings:
Enough of these, and all the charms of wine,
Be sober joys, and social evenings mine;
Where peace and reason, unsoil'd mirth improve
The powers of friendship and the joys of love;
Where thought meets thought ere words its form array,
And all is sacred, elegant, and gay:
Such pleasure leaves no sorrow on the mind,
Too great to fall, to sicken too refined;
Too soft for noise, and too sublime for art,
The social solace of the feeling heart,
For sloth too rápid, and for wit too high,
'Tis VIRTUE's pleasure, and can never die!

The Village

BOOK I

The Village Life, and every care that reigns
O'er youthful peasants and declining swains;
What labour yields, and what, that labour past,
Age, in its hour of languor, finds at last;
What form the real Picture of the Poor,
Demand a song – the Muse can give no more.
   Fled are those times, when, in harmonious strains,
The rustic poet praised his native plains:
No shepherds now, in smooth alternate verse,
10   Their country's beauty or their nymphs' rehearse;
Yet still for these we frame the tender strain,
Still in our lays fond Corydons complain,
And shepherds' boys their amorous pains reveal,
The only pains, alas! they never feel.

   On Mincio's banks, in Cæsar's bounteous reign,
If Tityrus found the Golden Age again,
Must sleepy bards the flattering dream prolong,
Mechanic echoes of the Mantuan song?
From Truth and Nature shall we widely stray,
20   Where Virgil, not where Fancy, leads the way?

   Yes, thus the Muses sing of happy swains,
Because the Muses never knew their pains:
They boast their peasants' pipes; but peasants now
Resign their pipes and plod behind the plough;
And few, amid the rural-tribe, have time
To number syllables, and play with rhyme;
Save honest DUCK, what son of verse could share
The poet's rapture and the peasant's care?
Or the great labours of the field degrade,
30   With the new peril of a poorer trade?
   From this chief cause these idle praises spring,
That themes so easy few forbear to sing;

For no deep thought the trifling subjects ask;
To sing of shepherds is an easy task:
The happy youth assumes the common strain,
A nymph his mistress, and himself a swain;
With no sad scenes he clouds his tuneful prayer,
But all, to look like her, is painted fair.

I grant indeed that fields and flocks have charms
40 For him that grazes or for him that farms;
But when amid such pleasing scenes I trace
The poor laborious natives of the place,
And see the mid-day sun, with fervid ray,
On their bare heads and dewy temples play;
While some, with feebler heads and fainter hearts,
Deplore their fortune, yet sustain their parts –
Then shall I dare these real ills to hide
In tinsel trappings of poetic pride?

No; cast by Fortune on a frowning coast,
50 Which neither groves nor happy valleys boast;
Where other cares than those the Muse relates,
And other shepherds dwell with other mates;
By such examples taught, I paint the Cot,
As Truth will paint it, and as Bards will not:
Nor you, ye Poor, of letter'd scorn complain,
To you the smoothest song is smooth in vain;
O'ercome by labour, and bow'd down by time,
Feel you the barren flattery of a rhyme?
Can poets soothe you, when you pine for bread,
60 By winding myrtles round your ruin'd shed?
Can their light tales your weighty griefs o'erpower,
Or glad with airy mirth the toilsome hour?

Lo! where the heath, with withering brake grown o'er,
Lends the light turf that warms the neighbouring poor;
From thence a length of burning sand appears,
Where the thin harvest waves its wither'd ears;
Rank weeds, that every art and care defy,
Reign o'er the land, and rob the blighted rye:
There thistles stretch their prickly arms afar,
70 And to the ragged infant threaten war;

There poppies nodding, mock the hope of toil;
There the blue bugloss paints the sterile soil;
Hardy and high, above the slender sheaf,
The slimy mallow waves her silky leaf;
O'er the young shoot the charlock throws a shade,
And clasping tares cling round the sickly blade;
With mingled tints the rocky coasts abound,
And a sad splendour vainly shines around.
So looks the nymph whom wretched arts adorn,
80 Betray'd by man, then left for man to scorn;
Whose cheek in vain assumes the mimic rose,
While her sad eyes the troubled breast disclose;
Whose outward splendour is but folly's dress,
Exposing most, when most it gilds distress.

　　Here joyless roam a wild amphibious race,
With sullen woe display'd in every face;
Who, far from civil arts and social fly,
And scowl at strangers with suspicious eye.

　　Here too the lawless merchant of the main
90 Draws from his plough th' intoxicated swain;
What only claim'd the labour of the day,
But vice now steals his nightly rest away.

　　Where are the swains, who, daily labour done,
With rural games play'd down the setting sun;
Who struck with matchless force the bounding ball,
Or made the pond'rous quoit obliquely fall;
While some huge Ajax, terrible and strong,
Engaged some artful stripling of the throng,
And fell beneath him, foil'd, while far around
100 Hoarse triumph rose, and rocks return'd the sound?
Where now are these? – Beneath yon cliff they stand,
To show the freighted pinnace where to land;
To load the ready steed with guilty haste,
To fly in terror o'er the pathless waste,
Or, when detected, in their straggling course,
To foil their foes by cunning or by force;
Or, yielding part (which equal knaves demand),
To gain a lawless passport through the land.

Here, wand'ring long, amid these frowning fields,
I sought the simple life that Nature yields;
Rapine and Wrong and Fear usurp'd her place,
And a bold, artful, surly, savage race;
Who, only skill'd to take the finny tribe,
The yearly dinner, or septennial bribe,
Wait on the shore, and, as the waves run high,
On the tost vessel bend their eager eye,
Which to their coast directs its vent'rous way;
Theirs, or the ocean's, miserable prey.

As on their neighbouring beach yon swallows stand,
And wait for favouring winds to leave the land;
While still for flight the ready wing is spread:
So waited I the favouring hour, and fled;
Fled from these shores where guilt and famine reign,
And cried, Ah! hapless they who still remain;
Who still remain to hear the ocean roar,
Whose greedy waves devour the lessening shore;
Till some fierce tide, with more imperious sway,
Sweeps the low hut and all it holds away;
When the sad tenant weeps from door to door,
And begs a poor protection from the poor!

But these are scenes where Nature's niggard hand
Gave a spare portion to the famish'd land;
Her's is the fault, if here mankind complain
Of fruitless toil and labour spent in vain;
But yet in other scenes more fair in view,
When Plenty smiles – alas! she smiles for few–
And those who taste not, yet behold her store,
Are as the slaves that dig the golden ore –
The wealth around them makes them doubly poor.

Or will you deem them amply paid in health,
Labour's fair child, that languishes with wealth?
Go then! and see them rising with the sun,
Through a long course of daily toil to run;
See them beneath the dog-star's raging heat,
When the knees tremble and the temples beat;
Behold them, leaning on their scythes, look o'er

The labour past, and toils to come explore;
See them alternate suns and showers engage,
And hoard up aches and anguish for their age;
150 Through fens and marshy moors their steps pursue,
When their warm pores imbibe the evening dew;
Then own that labour may as fatal be
To these thy slaves, as thine excess to thee.

Amid this tribe too oft a manly pride
Strives in strong toil the fainting heart to hide;
There may you see the youth of slender frame
Contend with weakness, weariness, and shame;
Yet, urged along, and proudly loth to yield,
He strives to join his fellows of the field:
160 Till long-contending nature droops at last,
Declining health rejects his poor repast,
His cheerless spouse the coming danger sees,
And mutual murmurs urge the slow disease.

Yet grant them health, 'tis not for us to tell,
Though the head droops not, that the heart is well;
Or will you praise that homely, healthy fare,
Plenteous and plain, that happy peasants share!
Oh! trifle not with wants you cannot feel,
Nor mock the misery of a stinted meal;
170 Homely, not wholesome, plain, not plenteous, such
As you who praise would never deign to touch.

Ye gentle souls, who dream of rural ease,
Whom the smooth stream and smoother sonnet please;
Go! if the peaceful cot your praises share,
Go look within, and ask if peace be there;
If peace be his – that drooping weary sire,
Or theirs, that offspring round their feeble fire;
Or hers, that matron pale, whose trembling hand
Turns on the wretched hearth th' expiring brand!
180 Nor yet can Time itself obtain for these
Life's latest comforts, due respect and ease;
For yonder see that hoary swain, whose age
Can with no cares except its own engage;
Who, propt on that rude staff, looks up to see

The bare arms broken from the withering tree,
On which, a boy, he climb'd the loftiest bough,
Then his first joy, but his sad emblem now.
    He once was chief in all the rustic trade;
His steady hand the straightest furrow made;
Full many a prize he won, and still is proud
To find the triumphs of his youth allow'd;
A transient pleasure sparkles in his eyes,
He hears and smiles, then thinks again and sighs:
For now he journeys to his grave in pain;
The rich disdain him; nay, the poor disdain:
Alternate masters now their slave command,
Urge the weak efforts of his feeble hand,
And, when his age attempts its task in vain,
With ruthless taunts, of lazy poor complain.
    Oft may you see him, when he tends the sheep,
His winter charge, beneath the hillock weep;
Oft hear him murmur to the winds that blow
O'er his white locks and bury them in snow,
When, roused by rage and muttering in the morn,
He mends the broken edge with icy thorn: –
    'Why do I live, when I desire to be
'At once from life and life's long labour free?
'Like leaves in spring, the young are blown away,
'Without the sorrows of a slow decay;
'I, like yon wither'd leaf, remain behind,
'Nipt by the frost, and shivering in the wind;
'There it abides till younger buds come on,
'As I, now all my fellow-swains are gone;
'Then, from the rising generation thrust,
'It falls, like me, unnoticed to the dust.
    'These fruitful fields, these numerous flocks I see,
'Are others' gain, but killing cares to me;
'To me the children of my youth are lords,
'Cool in their looks, but hasty in their words:
'Wants of their own demand their care; and who
'Feels his own want and succours others too?
'A lonely, wretched man, in pain I go,

'None need my help, and none relieve my woe;
'Then let my bones beneath the turf be laid,
'And men forget the wretch they would not aid.'
   Thus, groan the old, till, by disease oppress'd,
They taste a final woe, and then they rest.
   Theirs is yon House that holds the parish poor,
230   Whose walls of mud scarce bear the broken door;
There, where the putrid vapours, flagging, play,
And the dull wheel hums doleful through the day; –
There children dwell who know no parents' care;
Parents, who know no children's love, dwell there!
Heart-broken matrons on their joyless bed,
Forsaken wives, and mothers never wed;
Dejected widows with unheeded tears,
And crippled age with more than childhood fears;
The lame, the blind, and, far the happiest they!
240   The moping idiot, and the madman gay.
   Here too the sick their final doom receive,
Here brought, amid the scenes of grief, to grieve,
Where the loud groans from some sad chamber flow,
Mixt with the clamours of the crowd below;
Here, sorrowing, they each kindred sorrow scan,
And the cold charities of man to man:
Whose laws indeed for ruin'd age provide,
And strong compulsion plucks the scrap from pride;
But still that scrap is bought with many a sigh,
250   And pride embitters what it can't deny.
   Say, ye, opprest by some fantastic woes,
Some jarring nerve that baffles your repose;
Who press the downy couch, while slaves advance
With timid eye to read the distant glance;
Who with sad prayers the weary doctor tease,
To name the nameless ever-new disease;
Who with mock patience dire complaints endure,
Which real pain and that alone can cure;
How would ye bear in real pain to lie,
260   Despised, neglected, left alone to die?
How would ye bear to draw your latest breath,

49

Where all that's wretched paves the way for death?
    Such is that room which one rude beam divides,
And naked rafters form the sloping sides;
Where the vile bands that bind the thatch are seen,
And lath and mud are all that lie between;
Save one dull pane, that, coarsely patch'd, gives way·
To the rude tempest, yet excludes the day:
Here, on a matted flock, with dust o'erspread,
270   The drooping wretch reclines his languid head;
For him no hand the cordial cup applies,
Or wipes the tear that stagnates in his eyes;
No friends with soft discourse his pain beguile,
Or promise hope, till sickness wears a smile.
    But soon a loud and hasty summons calls,
Shakes the thin roof, and echoes round the walls;
Anon, a figure enters, quaintly neat,
All pride and business, bustle and conceit;
With looks unalter'd by these scenes of woe,
280   With speed that, entering, speaks his haste to go,
He bids the gazing throng around him fly,
And carries fate and physic in his eye:
A potent quack, long versed in human ills,
Who first insults the victim whom he kills;
Whose murd'rous hand a drowsy Bench protect,
And whose most tender mercy is neglect.
    Paid by the parish for attendance here,
He wears contempt upon his sapient sneer;
In haste he seeks the bed where Misery lies,
290   Impatience mark'd in his averted eyes;
And, some habitual queries hurried o'er,
Without reply, he rushes on the door:
His drooping patient, long inured to pain,
And long unheeded, knows remonstrance vain;
He ceases now the feeble help to crave
Of man; and silent sinks into the grave.
    But ere his death some pious doubts arise,
Some simple fears, which 'bold bad' men despise;
Fain would he ask the parish priest to prove

300 His title certain to the joys above:
For this he sends the murmuring nurse, who calls
The holy stranger to these dismal walls:
And doth not he, the pious man, appear,
He, 'passing rich with forty pounds a year?'
Ah! no; a shepherd of a different stock,
And far unlike him, feeds this little flock:
A jovial youth, who thinks his Sunday's task
As much as God or man can fairly ask;
The rest he gives to loves and labours light,
310 To fields the morning, and to feasts the night;
None better skill'd the noisy pack to guide,
To urge their chase, to cheer them or to chide;
A sportsman keen, he shoots through half the day,
And, skill'd at whist, devotes the night to play:
Then, while such honours bloom around his head,
Shall he sit sadly by the sick man's bed,
To raise the hope he feels not, or with zeal
To combat fears that e'en the pious feel?
    Now once again the gloomy scene explore,
320 Less gloomy now; the bitter hour is o'er,
The man of many sorrows sighs no more. –
Up yonder hill, behold how sadly slow
The bier moves winding from the vale below:
There lie the happy dead, from trouble free,
And the glad parish pays the frugal fee:
No more, O Death! thy victim starts to hear
Churchwarden stern, or kingly overseer;
No more the farmer claims his humble bow,
Thou art his lord, the best of tyrants thou!
330   Now to the church behold the mourners come,
Sedately torpid and devoutly dumb;
The village children now their games suspend,
To see the bier that bears their ancient friend:
For he was one in all their idle sport,
And like a monarch ruled their little court;
The pliant bow he form'd, the flying ball,
The bat, the wicket, were his labours all;

Him now they follow to his grave, and stand,
Silent and sad, and gazing, hand in hand;
340   While bending low, their eager eyes explore
The mingled relics of the parish poor.
The bell tolls late, the moping owl flies round,
Fear marks the flight and magnifies the sound;
The busy priest, detain'd by weightier care,
Defers his duty till the day of prayer;
And, waiting long, the crowd retire distrest,
To think a poor man's bones should lie unblest.

BOOK II

No longer truth, though shown in verse, disdain,
But own the Village Life a life of pain:
350   I too must yield, that oft amid these woes
Are gleams of transient mirth and hours of sweet repose,
Such as you find on yonder sportive Green,
The 'squire's tall gate and churchway-walk between;
Where loitering stray a little tribe of friends,
On a fair Sunday when the sermon ends:
Then rural beaux their best attire put on,
To win their nymphs, as other nymphs are won;
While those long wed go plain, and by degrees,
Like other husbands, quit their care to please.
360   Some of the sermon talk, a sober crowd,
And loudly praise, if it were preach'd aloud;
Some on the labours of the week look round,
Feel their own worth, and think their toil renown'd;
While some, whose hopes to no renown extend,
Are only pleased to find their labours end.

Thus, as their hours glide on, with pleasure fraught,
Their careful masters brood the painful thought;
Much in their mind they murmur and lament,
That one fair day should be so idly spent;
370   And think that Heaven deals hard, to tithe their store
And tax their time for preachers and the poor.

Yet still, ye humbler friends, enjoy your hour,

This is your portion, yet unclaim'd of power;
This is Heaven's gift to weary men oppress'd,
And seems the type of their expected rest:
But yours, alas! are joys that soon decay;
Frail joys, begun and ended with the day;
Or yet, while day permits those joys to reign,
The village vices drive them from the plain.
380   See the stout churl, in drunken fury great,
Strike the bare bosom of his teeming mate!
His naked vices, rude and unrefined,
Exert their open empire o'er the mind;
But can we less the senseless rage despise,
Because the savage acts without disguise?

Yet here Disguise, the city's vice, is seen,
And Slander steals along and taints the Green:
At her approach domestic peace is gone,
Domestic broils at her approach come on;
390   She to the wife the husband's crime conveys,
She tells the husband when his consort strays;
Her busy tongue, through all the little state,
Diffuses doubt, suspicion, and debate;
Peace, tim'rous goddess! quits her old domain,
In sentiment and song content to reign.

Nor are the nymphs that breathe the rural air
So fair as Cynthia's, nor so chaste as fair;
These to the town afford each fresher face,
And the clown's trull receives the peer's embrace;
400   From whom, should chance again convey her down,
The peer's disease in turn attacks the clown.

Here too the 'squire, or 'squire-like farmer, talk,
How round their regions nightly pilferers walk;
How from their ponds the fish are borne, and all
The rip'ning treasures from their lofty wall;
How meaner rivals in their sports delight,
Just right enough to claim a doubtful right;
Who take a licence round their fields to stray,
A mongrel race! the poachers of the day.

410   And hark! the riots of the Green begin,

That sprang at first from yonder noisy inn;
What time the weekly pay was vanish'd all,
And the slow hostess scored the threat'ning wall;
What time they ask'd, their friendly feast to close,
A final cup, and that will make them foes;
When blows ensue that break the arm of toil,
And rustic battle ends the boobies' broil.

Save when to yonder Hall they bend their way,
Where the grave Justice ends the grievous fray;
420 He who recites, to keep the poor in awe,
The law's vast volume – for he knows the law: –
To him with anger or with shame repair
The injured peasant and deluded fair.

Lo! at his throne the silent nymph appears,
Frail by her shape, but modest in her tears;
And while she stands abash'd, with conscious eye,
Some favourite female of her judge glides by,
Who views with scornful glance the strumpet's fate,
And thanks the stars that made her keeper great:
430 Near her the swain, about to bear for life
One certain evil, doubts 'twixt war and wife;
But, while the falt'ring damsel takes her oath,
Consents to wed, and so secures them both.

Yet why, you ask, these humble crimes relate,
Why make the Poor as guilty as the Great?
To show the great, those mightier sons of pride,
How near in vice the lowest are allied;
Such are their natures and their passions such,
But these disguise too little, those too much:
440 So shall the man of power and pleasure see
In his own slave as vile a wretch as he;
In his luxurious lord the servant find
His own low pleasures and degenerate mind:
And each in all the kindred vices trace,
Of a poor, blind, bewilder'd, erring race,
Who, a short time in varied fortune past,
Die, and are equal in the dust at last.

And you, ye Poor, who still lament your fate,

Forbear to envy those you call the Great;
And know, amid those blessings they possess,
They are, like you, the victims of distress;
While Sloth with many a pang torments her slave,
Fear waits on guilt, and Danger shakes the brave.
        Oh! if in life one noble chief appears,
Great in his name, while blooming in his years;
Born to enjoy whate'er delights mankind,
And yet to all you feel or fear resign'd;
Who gave up joys and hopes to you unknown,
For pains and dangers greater than your own:
If such there be, then let your murmurs cease,
Think, think of him, and take your lot in peace.
        And such there was:—Oh! grief, that checks our pride,
Weeping we say there was, — for MANNERS died:
Beloved of Heaven, these humble lines forgive,
That sing of Thee, and thus aspire to live.
        As the tall oak, whose vigorous branches form
An ample shade and brave the wildest storm,
High o'er the subject wood is seen to grow,
The guard and glory of the trees below;
Till on its head the fiery bolt descends,
And o'er the plain the shatter'd trunk extends;
Yet then it lies, all wond'rous as before,
And still the glory, though the guard no more:
        So THOU, when every virtue, every grace,
Rose in thy soul, or shone within thy face;
When, though the son of GRANBY, thou wert known
Less by thy father's glory than thy own;
When Honour loved and gave thee every charm,
Fire to thy eye and vigour to thy arm;
Then from our lofty hopes and longing eyes,
Fate and thy virtues call'd thee to the skies;
Yet still we wonder at thy tow'ring fame,
And, losing thee, still dwell upon thy name.
        Oh! ever honour'd, ever valued! say,
What verse can praise thee, or what work repay?
Yet verse (in all we can) thy worth repays,

Nor trusts the tardy zeal of future days; –
Honours for thee thy country shall prepare,
Thee in their hearts, the good, the brave shall bear;
490 To deeds like thine shall noblest chiefs aspire,
The Muse shall mourn thee, and the world admire.

In future times, when smit with Glory's charms,
The untried youth first quits a father's arms; –
'Oh! be like him,' the weeping sire shall say;
'Like MANNERS walk, who walk'd in Honour's way;
'In danger foremost, yet in death sedate,
'Oh! be like him in all things, but his fate!'

If for that fate such public tears be shed,
That Victory seems to die now THOU art dead;
500 How shall a friend his nearer hope resign,
That friend a brother, and whose soul was thine?
By what bold lines shall we his grief express,
Or by what soothing numbers make it less?

'T is not, I know, the chiming of a song,
Nor all the powers that to the Muse belong,
Words aptly cull'd, and meaning well express'd,
Can calm the sorrows of a wounded breast;
But Virtue, soother of the fiercest pains,
Shall heal that bosom, RUTLAND, where she reigns.

510 Yet hard the task to heal the bleeding heart,
To bid the still-recurring thoughts depart.
Tame the fierce grief and stem the rising sigh,
And curb rebellious passion, with reply;
Calmly to dwell on all that pleased before,
And yet to know that all shall please no more; –
Oh! glorious labour of the soul, to save
Her captive powers, and bravely mourn the brave.

To such these thoughts will lasting comfort give –
Life is not measured by the time we live:
520 'T is not an even course of threescore years, –
A life of narrow views and paltry fears,
Grey hairs and wrinkles and the cares they bring,
That take from Death the terrors or the sting;
But 't is the gen'rous spirit, mounting high

Above the world, that native of the sky;
The noble spirit, that, in dangers brave,
Calmly looks on, or looks beyond the grave: –
Such MANNERS was, so he resign'd his breath,
If in a glorious, then a timely death.

530   Cease then that grief, and let those tears subside;
If Passion rule us, be that passion pride;
If Reason, reason bids us strive to raise
Our fallen hearts, and be like him we praise;
Or if Affection still the soul subdue,
Bring all his virtues, all his worth in view,
And let Affection find its comfort too:
For how can Grief so deeply wound the heart,
When Admiration claims so large a part?

Grief is a foe – expel him then thy soul;
540   Let nobler thoughts the nearer views control!
Oh! make the age to come thy better care,
See other RUTLANDS, other GRANBYS there!
And, as thy thoughts through streaming ages glide,
See other heroes die as MANNERS died:
And from their fate, thy race shall nobler grow,
As trees shoot upwards that are pruned below;
Or as old Thames, borne down with decent pride,
Sees his young streams run warbling at his side;
Though some, by art cut off, no longer run,
550   And some are lost beneath the summer sun –
Yet the pure stream moves on, and, as it moves,
Its power increases and its use improves;
While plenty round its spacious waves bestow,
Still it flows on, and shall for ever flow.

Sir Eustace Grey

Scene: A Mad-House

Persons: Visitor, Physician, and Patient

VISITOR

I'll know no more; – the heart is torn
    By views of woe we cannot heal;
Long shall I see these things forlorn,
    And oft again their griefs shall feel,
    As each upon the mind shall steal;
That wan projector's mystic style,
    That lumpish idiot leering by,
That peevish idler's ceaseless wile,
And that poor maiden's half-form'd smile,
    While struggling for the full-drawn sigh! –
I'll know no more.

PHYSICIAN

              – Yes, turn again;
Then speed to happier scenes thy way,
    When thou hast view'd, what yet remain,
The ruins of Sir Eustace Grey,
    The sport of madness, misery's prey:
But he will no historian need,
    His cares, his crimes, will he display,
And show (as one from frenzy freed)
    The proud lost mind, the rash-done deed.

That cell to him is Greyling Hall: –
    Approach; he'll bid thee welcome there;
Will sometimes for his servant call,
    And sometimes point the vacant chair;
He can, with free and easy air,
    Appear attentive and polite;
Can veil his woes in manners fair,
    And pity with respect excite.

Who comes? – Approach! – 'tis kindly done: –
My learn'd physician, and a friend,
Their pleasures quit, to visit one
Who cannot to their ease attend,
Nor joys bestow, nor comforts lend,
As when I lived so blest, so well,
And dreamt not I must soon contend
With those malignant powers of hell.

PHYSICIAN

'Less warmth, Sir Eustace, or we go.' –

PATIENT

See! I am calm as infant-love,
A very child, but one of woe,
Whom you should pity, not reprove: –
But men at ease, who never strove
With passions wild, will calmly show
How soon we may their ills remove,
And masters of their madness grow.

Some twenty years, I think, are gone, –
(Time flies, I know not how, away,)
The sun upon no happier shone,
Nor prouder man, than Eustace Grey.
Ask where you would, and all would say,
The man admired and praised of all,
By rich and poor, by grave and gay,
Was the young lord of Greyling Hall.

Yes! I had youth and rosy health;
Was nobly form'd, as man might be;
For sickness, then, of all my wealth,
I never gave a single fee:
The ladies fair, the maidens free,
Were all accustom'd then to say,

Who would a handsome figure see
    Should look upon Sir Eustace Grey.

60 He had a frank and pleasant look,
        A cheerful eye and accent bland;
    His very speech and manner spoke
        The generous heart, the open hand;
    About him all was gay or grand,
        He had the praise of great and small;
    He bought, improved, projected, plann'd,
        And reign'd a prince at Greyling Hall.

    My lady! – she was all we love;
        All praise (to speak her worth) is faint;
70 Her manners show'd the yielding dove,
        Her morals, the seraphic saint:
    She never breath'd nor look'd complaint;
        No equal upon earth had she: –
    Now, what is this fair thing I paint?
        Alas! as all that live shall be.

    There was, beside, a gallant youth,
        And him my bosom's friend, I had; –
    Oh! I was rich in very truth,
        It made me proud – it made me mad! –
80 Yes, I was lost – but there was cause! –
        Where stood my tale? – I cannot find –
    But I had all mankind's applause,
        And all the smiles of womankind.

    There were two cherub-things beside,
        A gracious girl, a glorious boy;
    Yet more to swell my full-blown pride,
        To varnish higher my fading joy,
    Pleasures were ours without alloy,
        Nay, Paradise, – till my frail Eve
90 Our bliss was tempted to destroy –
        Deceived and fated to deceive.

60

But I deserved; – for all that time,
　　When I was loved, admired, caress'd,
There was within, each secret crime,
　　Unfelt, uncancell'd, unconfess'd:
I never then my God address'd,
　　In grateful praise or humble prayer;
And if His Word was not my jest –
　　(Dread thought!) it never was my care.

100　I doubted: – fool I was to doubt!
　　If that all-piercing eye could see, –
If He who looks all worlds throughout,
　　Would so minute and careful be,
As to perceive and punish me: –
　　With man I would be great and high,
But with my God so lost, that He,
　　In his large view, should pass me by.

Thus blest with children, friend, and wife,
　　Blest far beyond the vulgar lot;
110　Of all that gladdens human life,
　　Where was the good that I had not?
But my vile heart had sinful spot,
　　And Heaven beheld its deep'ning stain;
Eternal justice I forgot,
　　And mercy sought not to obtain.

Come near, – I'll softly speak the rest! –
　　Alas! 'tis known to all the crowd,
Her guilty love was all confess'd;
　　And his, who so much truth avow'd,
120　My faithless friend's. – In pleasure proud
　　I sat, when these cursed tidings came;
Their guilt, their flight was told aloud,
　　And Envy smiled to hear my shame!

I call'd on Vengeance; at the word
   She came: – Can I the deed forget?
I held the sword – the accursed sword
   The blood of his false heart made wet;
   And that fair victim paid her debt,
   She pined, she died, she loath'd to live; –
130   I saw her dying – see her yet:
   Fair fallen thing! my rage forgive!

Those cherubs still, my life to bless,
   Were left; could I my fears remove,
Sad fears that check'd each fond caress,
   And poison'd all parental love?
Yet that with jealous feelings strove,
   And would at last have won my will,
Had I not, wretch! been doom'd to prove
   Th' extremes of mortal good and ill.

140 In youth! health! joy! in beauty's pride!
   They droop'd – as flowers when blighted bow;
The dire infection came: – they died,
   And I was cursed – as I am now –
Nay, frown not, angry friend, – allow
   That I was deeply, sorely tried;
Hear then, and you must wonder how
   I could such storms and strifes abide.

Storms! – not that clouds embattled make,
   When they afflict this earthly globe;
150 But such as with their terrors shake
   Man's breast, and to the bottom probe;
They make the hypocrite disrobe,
   They try us all, if false or true;
For this one Devil had power on Job;
   And I was long the slave of two.

PHYSICIAN

Peace, peace, my friend; these subjects fly;
Collect thy thoughts – go calmly on.–

And shall I then the fact deny?
　I was, – thou know'st, – I was begone,
160　Like him who fill'd the eastern throne,
　　To whom the Watcher cried aloud;
　That royal wretch of Babylon,
　　Who was so guilty and so proud.

Like him, with haughty, stubborn mind,
　I, in my state, my comforts sought;
Delight and praise I hôped to find,
　In what I builded, planted, bought!
Oh! arrogance! by misery taught –
　Soon came a voice! I felt it come;
170　'Full be his cup, with evil fraught,
　　'Demons his guides, and death his doom!'

Then was I cast from out my state;
　Two fiends of darkness led my way;
They waked me early, watch'd me late,
　My dread by night, my plague by day!
Oh! I was made their sport, their play,
　Through many a stormy troubled year;
And how they used their passive prey
　Is sad to tell: – but you shall hear.

180　And first before they sent me forth,
　　Through this unpitying world to run,
They robb'd Sir Eustace of his worth,
　Lands, manors, lordships, every one;
So was that gracious man undone,
　Was spurn'd as vile, was scorn'd as poor,
Whom every former friend would shun,
　And menials drove from every door.

Then those ill-favour'd Ones, whom none
　But my unhappy eyes could view,
190　Led me, with wild emotion, on,
　　And, with resistless terror, drew.

Through lands we fled, o'er seas we flew,
    And halted on a boundless plain;
Where nothing fed, nor breathed, nor grew,
    But silence ruled the still domain.

Upon that boundless plain, below,
    The setting sun's last rays were shed,
And gave a mild and sober glow,
    Where all were still, asleep, or dead;
200 Vast ruins in the midst were spread,
    Pillars and pediments sublime,
Where the grey moss had form'd a bed,
    And clothed the crumbling spoils of time.

There was I fix'd, I know not how,
    Condemn'd for untold years to stay:
Yet years were not; – one dreadful *Now*
    Endured no change of night or day;
The same mild evening's sleeping ray
    Shone softly solemn and serene,
210 And all that time I gazed away,
    The setting sun's sad rays were seen.

At length a moment's sleep stole on, –
    Again came my commission'd foes;
Again through sea and land we're gone,
    No peace, no respite, no repose:
Above the dark broad sea we rose,
    We ran through bleak and frozen land;
I had no strength their strength t'oppose,
    An infant in a giant's hand.

220 They placed me where those streamers play,
    Those nimble beams of brilliant light;
It would the stoutest heart dismay,
    To see, to feel, that dreadful sight:

So swift, so pure, so cold, so bright,
　　They pierced my frame with icy wound;
And all that half-year's polar night,
　　Those dancing streamers wrapp'd me round.

Slowly that darkness pass'd away,
　　When down upon the earth I fell, –
230　　Some hurried sleep was mine by day;
　　But, soon as toll'd the evening bell,
They forced me on, where ever dwell
　　Far-distant men in cities fair,
Cities of whom no travellers tell,
　　Nor feet but mine were wanderers there.

Their watchmen stare, and stand aghast,
　　As on we hurry through the dark;
The watch-light blinks as we go past,
　　The watch-dog shrinks and fears to bark;
240　　The watch-tower's bell sounds shrill; and, hark!
The free wind blows – we've left the town –
A wide sepulchral ground I mark,
　　And on a tombstone place me down.

What monuments of mighty dead!
　　What tombs of various kind are found!
And stones erect their shadows shed
　　On humble graves, with wickers bound,
Some risen fresh, above the ground,
　　Some level with the native clay:
250　　What sleeping millions wait the sound,
　　'Arise, ye dead, and come away!'

Alas! they stay not for that call;
　　Spare me this woe! ye demons, spare! –
They come! the shrouded shadows all, –
　　'Tis more than mortal brain can bear;

Rustling they rise, they sternly glare
　　At men upheld by vital breath;
Who, led by wicked fiends, should dare
　　To join the shadowy troops of death!

260 Yes, I have felt all man can feel,
　　Till he shall pay his nature's debt;
Ills that no hope has strength to heal,
　　No mind the comfort to forget:
Whatever cares the heart can fret,
　　The spirits wear, the temper gall,
Woe, want, dread, anguish, all beset
　　My sinful soul! – together all!

Those fiends upon a shaking fen
　　Fix'd me, in dark tempestuous night;
270 There never trod the foot of men,
　　There flock'd the fowl in wint'ry flight;
There danced the moor's deceitful light
　　Above the pool where sedges grow;
And when the morning-sun shone bright,
　　It shone upon a field of snow.

They hung me on a bough so small,
　　The rook could build her nest no higher;
They fix'd me on the trembling ball
　　That crowns the steeple's quiv'ring spire;
280 They set me where the seas retire,
　　But drown with their returning tide;
And made me flee the mountain's fire,
　　When rolling from its burning side.

I've hung upon the ridgy steep
　　Of cliffs, and held the rambling brier;
I've plunged below the billowy deep,
　　Where air was sent me to respire;

I've been where hungry wolves retire;
  And (to complete my woes) I've ran
290 Where Bedlam's crazy crew conspire
  Against the life of reasoning man.

I've furl'd in storms the flapping sail,
  By hanging from the topmast-head;
I've served the vilest slaves in jail,
  And pick'd the dunghill's spoil for bread;
I've made the badger's hole my bed,
  I've wander'd with a gipsy crew;
I've dreaded all the guilty dread,
  And done what they would fear to do.

300 On sand, where ebbs and flows the flood,
  Midway they placed and bade me die;
Propt on my staff, I stoutly stood
  When the swift waves came rolling by;
And high they rose, and still more high,
  Till my lips drank the bitter brine;
I sobb'd convulsed, then cast mine eye,
  And saw the tide's re-flowing sign.

And then, my dreams were such as nought
  Could yield but my unhappy case;
310 I've been of thousand devils caught,
  And thrust into that horrid place,
Where reign dismay, despair, disgrace;
  Furies with iron fangs were there,
To torture that accursed race,
  Doom'd to dismay, disgrace, despair.

Harmless I was; yet hunted down
  For treasons, to my soul unfit;
I've been pursued through many a town,
  For crimes that petty knaves commit;

320   I've been adjudged t' have lost my wit,
          Because I preach'd so loud and well;
      And thrown into the dungeon's pit,
          For trampling on the pit of hell.

      Such were the evils, man of sin,
          That I was fated to sustain;
      And add to all, without – within,
          A soul defiled with every stain
      That man's reflecting mind can pain;
          That pride, wrong, rage, despair, can make;
330   In fact, they'd nearly touch'd my brain,
          And reason on her throne would shake.

      But pity will the vilest seek,
          If punish'd guilt will not repine, –
      I heard a heavenly Teacher speak,
          And felt the SUN OF MERCY shine:
      I hail'd the light! the birth divine!
          And then was seal'd among the few;
      Those angry fiends beheld the sign,
          And from me in an instant flew.

340   Come hear how thus the charmers cry
          To wandering sheep, the strays of sin,
      While some the wicket-gate pass by,
          And some will knock and enter in:
      Full joyful 'tis a soul to win,
          For he that winneth souls is wise;
      Now hark! the holy strains begin,
          And thus the sainted preacher cries: –

      'Pilgrim, burthen'd with thy sin,
      'Come the way to Zion's gate,
350   'There, till Mercy let thee in,
      'Knock and weep and watch and wait.

'Knock! – He knows the sinner's cry:
'Weep! – He loves the mourner's tears:
'Watch! – for saving grace is nigh:
'Wait, – till heavenly light appears.

'Hark! it is the Bridegroom's voice;
'Welcome, pilgrim, to thy rest;
'Now within the gate rejoice,
'Safe and seal'd and bought and blest!
   'Safe – from all the lures of vice,
   'Seal'd – by signs the chosen know,
   'Bought – by love and life the price,
   'Blest – the mighty debt to owe.

'Holy Pilgrim! what for thee
'In a world like this remain?
'From thy guarded breast shall flee
'Fear and shame, and doubt and pain.
   'Fear – the hope of Heaven shall fly,
   'Shame – from glory's view retire,
   'Doubt – in certain rapture die,
   'Pain – in endless bliss expire.'

But though my day of grace was come,
   Yet still my days of grief I find;
The former clouds' collected gloom
   Still sadden the reflecting mind;
The soul, to evil things consign'd,
   Will of their evil some retain;
The man will seem to earth inclined,
   And will not look erect again.

Thus, though elect, I feel it hard
   To lose what I possess'd before,
To be from all my wealth debarr'd, –
   The brave Sir Eustace is no more:

But old I wax and passing poor,
　　Stern, rugged men my conduct view;
They chide my wish, they bar my door,
　　'Tis hard – I weep – you see I do.–

Must you, my friends, no longer stay?
　　Thus quickly all my pleasures end;
But I'll remember, when I pray,
　　My kind physician and his friend;
And those sad hours, you deign to spend
　　With me, I shall requite them all;
Sir Eustace for his friends shall send,
　　And thank their love at Greyling Hall.

The poor Sir Eustace! – Yet his hope
　　Leads him to think of joys again;
And when his earthly visions droop,
　　His views of heavenly kind remain: –
But whence that meek and humbled strain,
　　That spirit wounded, lost, resign'd?
Would not so proud a soul disdain
　　The madness of the poorest mind?

No! for the more he swell'd with pride,
　　The more he felt misfortune's blow;
Disgrace and grief he could not hide,
　　And poverty had laid him low:
Thus shame and sorrow working slow,
　　At length this humble spirit gave;
Madness on these began to grow,
　　And bound him to his fiends a slave.

Though the wild·thoughts had touch'd his brain,
　　Then was he free: – So, forth he ran;
To soothe or threat, alike were vain:
　　He spake of fiends; look'd wild and wan;

Year after year, the hurried man
　　Obey'd those fiends from place to place;
Till his religious change began
　　To form a frenzied child of grace.

For, as the fury lost its strength,
　　The mind reposed; by slow degrees
Came lingering hope, and brought at length,
　　To the tormented spirit, ease:
This slave of sin, whom fiends could seize
　　Felt or believed their power had end: –
' 'Tis faith,' he cried, 'my bosom frees,
　'And now my SAVIOUR is my friend.'

But ah! though time can yield relief,
　　And soften woes it cannot cure;
Would we not suffer pain and grief,
　　To have our reason sound and sure?
Then let us keep our bosoms pure,
　　Our fancy's favourite flights suppress;
Prepare the body to endure,
　　And bend the mind to meet distress;
And then HIS guardian care implore,
　　Whom demons dread and men adore.

Phoebe Dawson

Two summers since I saw at Lammas Fair,
The sweetest flower that ever blossom'd there,
When *Phoebe Dawson* gaily cross'd the Green,
In haste to see and happy to be seen:
Her air, her manners, all who saw admired;
Courteous though coy, and gentle though retired;
The joy of youth and health her eyes display'd,
And ease of heart her every look convey'd;

A native skill her simple robes express'd,
10 As with untutor'd elegance she dress'd;
The lads around admired so fair a sight,
And Phoebe felt, and felt she gave, delight.
Admirers soon of every age she gain'd,
Her beauty won them and her worth retain'd;
Envy itself could no contempt display,
They wish'd her well, whom yet they wish'd away.
Correct in thought, she judged a servant's place
Preserved a rustic beauty from disgrace;
But yet on Sunday-eve, in freedom's hour,
20 With secret joy she felt that beauty's power,
When some proud bliss upon the heart would steal,
That, poor or rich, a beauty still must feel. –
    At length the youth ordain'd to move her breast,
Before the swains with bolder spirit press'd;
With looks less timid made his passion known,
And pleased by manners most unlike her own;
Loud though in love, and confident though young;
Fierce in his air, and voluble of tongue;
By trade a tailor, though, in scorn of trade,
30 He served the 'Squire, and brush'd the coat he made.
Yet now, would Phoebe her consent afford,
Her slave alone, again he'd mount the board;
With her should years of growing love be spent,
And growing wealth: – she sigh'd and look'd consent.
    Now, through the lane, up hill, and 'cross the green,
(Seen by but few, and blushing to be seen –
Dejected, thoughtful, anxious, and afraid,)
Led by the lover, walk'd the silent maid,
Slow through the meadows roved they, many a mile,
40 Toy'd by each bank, and trifled at each stile;
Where, as he painted every blissful view,
And highly colour'd what he strongly drew,
The pensive damsel, prone to tender fears,
Dimm'd the false prospect with prophetic tears. –
Thus pass'd th' allotted hours, till lingering late,
The lover loiter'd at the master's gate;

There he pronounced adieu! and yet would stay,
Till chidden – soothed – entreated – forced away;
He would of coldness, though indulged, complain,
50   And oft retire, and oft return again;
When, if his teasing vex'd her gentle mind,
The grief assumed, compell'd her to be kind!
For he would proof of plighted kindness crave,
That she resented first and then forgave,
And to his grief and penance yielded more
Than his presumption had required before. –
    Ah! fly temptation, youth; refrain! refrain!
    Each yielding maid and each presuming swain!

    Lo! now with red rent cloak and bonnet black,
60   And torn green gown loose hanging at her back,
One who an infant in her arms sustains,
And seems in patience striving with her pains;
Pinch'd are her looks, as one who pines for bread,
Whose cares are growing and whose hopes are fled;
Pale her parch'd lips, her heavy eyes sunk low,
And tears unnoticed from their channels flow;
Serene her manner, till some sudden pain
Frets the meek soul, and then she's calm again; –
Her broken pitcher to the pool she takes,
70   And every step with cautious terror makes;
For not alone that infant in her arms,
But nearer cause, her anxious soul alarms,
With water burthen'd, then she picks her way,
Slowly and cautious, in the clinging clay;
Till, in mid-green, she trusts a place unsound,
And deeply plunges in th' adhesive ground;
Thence, but with pain, her slender foot she takes,
While hope the mind as strength the frame forsakes:
For when so full the cup of sorrow grows,
80   Add but a drop, it instantly o'erflows.
And now her path but not her peace she gains,
Safe from her task, but shivering with her pains;
Her home she reaches, open leaves the door,

And placing first her infant on the floor,
She bares her bosom to the wind, and sits,
And sobbing struggles with the rising fits:
In vain, they come, she feels the inflating grief,
That shuts the swelling bosom from relief;
That speaks in feeble cries a soul distress'd,
90 Or the sad laugh that cannot be repress'd.
The neighbour-matron leaves her wheel and flies
With all the aid her poverty supplies;
Unfee'd, the calls of Nature she obeys,
Not led by profit, not allured by praise;
And waiting long, till these contentions cease,
She speaks of comfort, and departs in peace.
    Friend of distress! the mourner feels thy aid,
She cannot pay thee, but thou wilt be paid.

    But who this child of weakness, want, and care?
100 'Tis *Phoebe Dawson*, pride of Lammas Fair:
Who took her lover for his sparkling eyes,
Expressions warm, and love-inspiring lies:
Compassion first assail'd her gentle heart,
For all his suffering, all his bosom's smart:
'And then his prayers! they would a savage move,
'And win the coldest of the sex to love:' –
But ah! too soon his looks success declared,
Too late her loss the marriage-rite repair'd;
The faithless flatterer then his vows forgot,
110 A captious tyrant or a noisy sot:
If present, railing, till he saw her pain'd;
If absent, spending what their labours gain'd;
Till that fair form in want and sickness pined,
And hope and comfort fled that gentle mind.
    Then fly temptation, youth; resist, refrain!
    Nor let me preach for ever and in vain!

Sir Edward Archer

Last on my list appears a match of love,
And one of virtue; – happy may it prove! –
Sir *Edward Archer* is an amorous knight,
And maidens chaste and lovely shun his sight;
His bailiff's daughter suited much his taste,
For *Fanny Price* was lovely and was chaste;
To her the Knight with gentle looks drew near,
And timid voice assumed, to banish fear: –
    'Hope of my life, dear sovereign of my breast,
10 'Which, since I knew thee, knows not joy nor rest;
'Know, thou art all that my delighted eyes,
'My fondest thoughts, my proudest wishes prize;
'And is that bosom – (what on earth so fair!)
'To cradle some coarse peasant's sprawling heir,
'To be that pillow which some surly swain
'May treat with scorn and agonize with pain?
'Art thou, sweet maid, a ploughman's wants to share,
'To dread his insult, to support his care;
'To hear his follies, his contempt to prove,
20 'And (oh! the torment!) to endure his love;
'Till want and deep regret those charms destroy,
'That time would spare, if time were pass'd in joy?
'With him, in varied pains, from morn till night,
'Your hours shall pass; yourself a ruffian's right;
'Your softest bed shall be the knotted wool;
'Your purest drink the waters of the pool;
'Your sweetest food will but your life sustain,
'And your best pleasure be a rest from pain;
'While, through each year, as health and strength abate,
30 'You'll weep your woes and wonder at your fate;
'And cry, "Behold," as life's last cares come on,
' "My burthens growing when my strength is gone."
    'Now turn with me, and all the young desire,
'That taste can form, that fancy can require;
'All that excites enjoyment, or procures
'Wealth, health, respect, delight, and love, are yours:

75

'Sparkling, in cups of gold, your wines shall flow,
'Grace that fair hand, in that dear bosom glow;
'Fruits of each clime, and flowers, through all the year,
40 'Shall on your walls and in your walks appear:
'Where all beholding, shall your praise repeat,
'No fruit so tempting and no flower so sweet:
'The softest carpets in your rooms shall lie,
'Pictures of happiest loves shall meet your eye,
'And tallest mirrors, reaching to the floor,
'Shall show you all the object I adore;
'Who, by the hands of wealth and fashion dress'd,
'By slaves attended and by friends caress'd,
'Shall move, a wonder, through the public ways,
50 'And hear the whispers of adoring praise.
'Your female friends, though gayest of the gay,
'Shall see you happy, and shall, sighing, say,
'While smother'd envy rises in the breast, –
' "Oh! that we lived so beauteous and so blest."

'Come, then, my mistress, and my wife; for she
'Who trusts my honour is the wife for me;
'Your slave, your husband, and your friend employ,
'In search of pleasures we may both enjoy.'

To this the Damsel, meekly firm, replied:
60 'My mother loved, was married, toil'd, and died;
'With joys she'd griefs, had troubles in her course,
'But not one grief was pointed by remorse;
'My mind is fix'd, to Heaven I resign,
'And be her love, her life, her comforts mine.'

Tyrants have wept; and those with hearts of steel,
Unused the anguish of the heart to heal,
Have yet the transient power of virtue known,
And felt th' imparted joy promote their own.

Our Knight relenting, now befriends a youth,
70 Who to the yielding maid had vow'd his truth;
And finds in that fair deed a sacred joy,
That will not perish, and that cannot cloy; –
A living joy, that shall its spirit keep,
When every beauty fades, and all the passions sleep.

Lady of the Hall

Next died the Lady who yon Hall possess'd;
And here they brought her noble bones to rest.
In Town she dwelt; – forsaken stood the Hall:
Worms ate the floors, the tap'stry fled the wall:
No fire the kitchen's cheerless grate display'd;
No cheerful light the long-closed sash convey'd;
The crawling worm, that turns a summer-fly,
Here spun his shroud and laid him up to die
The winter-death: – upon the bed of state,
10   The bat shrill shrieking woo'd his flickering mate;
To empty rooms the curious came no more,
From empty cellars turn'd the angry poor,
And surly beggars cursed the ever-bolted door.
To one small room the steward found his way,
Where tenants follow'd to complain and pay;
Yet no complaint before the *Lady* came,
The feeling servant spared the feeble dame;
Who saw her farms with his observing eyes,
And answer'd all requests with his replies: –
20   She came not down, her falling groves to view;
Why should she know, what one so faithful knew?
Why come, from many clamorous tongues to hear,
What one so just might whisper in her ear?
Her oaks or acres, why with care explore;
Why learn the wants, the sufferings of the poor;
When one so knowing all their worth could trace,
And one so piteous govern'd in her place?
    Lo! now, what dismal Sons of Darkness come,
To bear this Daughter of Indulgence home;
30   Tragedians all, and well-arranged in black!
Who nature, feeling, force, expression lack;
Who cause no tear, but gloomily pass by,
And shake their sables in the wearied eye,
That turns disgusted from the pompous scene,
Proud without grandeur, with profusion, mean!
The tear for kindness past affection owes;

For worth deceased the sigh from reason flows;
E'en well-feign'd passion for our sorrows call,
And real tears for mimic miseries fall:
40   But this poor farce has neither truth nor art,
To please the fancy or to touch the heart;
Unlike the darkness of the sky, that pours
On the dry ground its fertilizing showers;
Unlike to that which strikes the soul with dread,
When thunders roar and forky fires are shed;
Dark but not awful, dismal but yet mean,
With anxious bustle moves the cumbrous scene;
Presents no objects tender or profound,
But spreads its cold unmeaning gloom around.
50   When woes are feign'd, how ill such forms appear,
And oh! how needless, when the woe's sincere.

    Slow to the vault they come, with heavy tread,
Bending beneath the Lady and her lead;
A case of elm surrounds that ponderous chest,
Close on that case the crimson velvet's press'd;
Ungenerous this, that to the worm denies,
With niggard-caution, his appointed prize;
For now, ere yet he works his tedious way,
Through cloth and wood and metal to his prey,
60   That prey dissolving shall a mass remain,
That fancy loathes and worms themselves disdain.

    But see! the master-mourner makes his way,
To end his office for the coffin'd clay;
Pleased that our rustic men and maids behold
His plate like silver, and his studs like gold,
As they approach to spell the age, the name,
And all the titles of th' illustrious dame. –
This as (my duty done) some scholar read,
A Village-father look'd disdain and said:
70   'Away, my friends! why take such pains to know
'What some brave marble soon in Church shall show?
'Where not alone her gracious name shall stand,
'But how she lived – the blessing of the land;
'How much we all deplored the noble dead,

'What groans we utter'd and what tears we shed;
'Tears, true as those, which in the sleepy eyes
'Of weeping cherubs on the stone shall rise;
'Tears, true as those which, ere she found her grave,
'The noble Lady to our sorrows gave.'

The Borough

'Describe the Borough' – though our idle tribe
May love description, can we so describe,
That you shall fairly streets and buildings trace,
And all that gives distinction to a place?
This cannot be; yet, moved by your request,
A part I paint – let Fancy form the rest.
    Cities and towns, the various haunts of men,
Require the pencil; they defy the pen:
Could he, who sang so well the Grecian fleet,
So well have sung of alley, lane, or street?
Can measured lines these various buildings show,
The Town-Hall Turning, or the Prospect Row?
Can I the seats of wealth and want explore,
And lengthen out my lays from door to door?
    Then let thy Fancy aid me – I repair
From this tall mansion of our last-year's Mayor,
Till we the outskirts of the Borough reach,
And these half-buried buildings next the beach;
Where hang at open doors the net and cork,
While squalid sea-dames mend the meshy work;
Till comes the hour, when fishing through the tide
The weary husband throws his freight aside;
A living mass, which now demands the wife,
Th' alternate labours of their humble life.
    Can scenes like these withdraw thee from thy wood,
Thy upland forest or thy valley's flood?

Seek then thy garden's shrubby bound, and look,
As it steals by, upon the bordering brook;
That winding streamlet, limpid, lingering, slow,
Where the reeds whisper when the zephyrs blow;
Where in the midst, upon her throne of green,
Sits the large Lily as the water's queen;
And makes the current, forced awhile to stay,
Murmur and bubble as it shoots away;
Draw then the strongest contrast to that stream,
And our broad river will before thee seem.

With ceaseless motion comes and goes the tide,
Flowing, it fills the channel vast and wide;
Then back to sea, with strong majestic sweep
It rolls, in ebb yet terrible and deep;
Here Samphire-banks and Salt-wort bound the flood,
There stakes and sea-weeds withering on the mud;
And higher up, a ridge of all things base,
Which some strong tide has roll'd upon the place.

Thy gentle river boasts its pigmy boat,
Urged on by pains, half grounded, half afloat;
While at her stern an angler takes his stand,
And marks the fish he purposes to land;
From that clear space, where, in the cheerful ray
Of the warm sun, the scaly people play.

Far other craft our prouder river shows,
Hoys, pinks and sloops; brigs, brigantines and snows:
Nor angler we on our wide stream descry,
But one poor dredger where his oysters lie:
He, cold and wet, and driving with the tide,
Beats his weak arms against his tarry side,
Then drains the remnant of diluted gin,
To aid the warmth that languishes within;
Renewing oft his poor attempts to beat
His tingling fingers into gathering heat.

He shall again be seen when evening comes,
And social parties crowd their favourite rooms:
Where on the table pipes and papers lie,
The steaming bowl or foaming tankard by;

'Tis then, with all these comforts spread around,
They hear the painful dredger's welcome sound;
And few themselves the savoury boon deny,
The food that feeds, the living luxury.
   Yon is our Quay! those smaller hoys from town,
70 Its various ware, for country-use, bring down;
Those laden waggons, in return, impart
The country-produce to the city mart;
Hark! to the clamour in that miry road,
Bounded and narrow'd by yon vessel's load;
The lumbering wealth she empties round the place,
Package, and parcel, hogshead, chest, and case:
While the loud seaman and the angry hind,
Mingling in business, bellow to the wind.
   Near these a crew amphibious, in the docks,
80 Rear, for the sea, those castles on the stocks:
See! the long keel, which soon the waves must hide;
See! the strong ribs which form the roomy side;
Bolts yielding slowly to the sturdiest stroke,
And planks which curve and crackle in the smoke.
Around the whole rise cloudy wreaths, and far
Bear the warm pungence of o'er-boiling tar.
   Dabbling on shore half-naked sea-boys crowd,
Swim round a ship, or swing upon the shroud;
Or in a boat purloin'd, with paddles play,
90 And grow familiar with the watery way:
Young though they be, they feel whose sons they are,
They know what British seamen do and dare;
Proud of that fame, they raise and they enjoy
The rustic wonder of the village-boy.
   Before you bid these busy scenes adieu,
Behold the wealth that lies in public view,
Those far-extended heaps of coal and coke,
Where fresh-fill'd lime-kilns breathe their stifling smoke.
This shall pass off, and you behold, instead,
100 The night-fire gleaming on its chalky bed;
When from the Light-house brighter beams will rise,
To show the shipman where the shallow lies.

Thy walks are ever pleasant; every scene
Is rich in beauty, lively, or serene –
Rich – is that varied view with woods around,
Seen from the seat, within the shrubb'ry bound;
Where shines the distant lake, and where appear
From ruins bolting, unmolested deer;
Lively – the village-green, the inn, the place,
110 Where the good widow schools her infant-race.
Shops, whence are heard the hammer and the saw,
And village-pleasures unreproved by law:
Then how serene! when in your favourite room,
Gales from your jasmine soothe the evening gloom;
When from your upland paddock you look down,
And just perceive the smoke which hides the town;
When weary peasants at the close of day
Walk to their cots, and part upon the way;
When cattle slowly cross the shallow brook,
120 And shepherds pen their folds, and rest upon their crook.
  We prune our hedges, prime our slender trees,
And nothing looks untutor'd and at ease,
On the wide heath, or in the flow'ry vale,
We scent the vapours of the sea-born gale;
Broad-beaten paths lead on from stile to stile,
And sewers from streets, the road-side banks defile;
Our guarded fields a sense of danger show,
Where garden-crops with corn and clover grow;
Fences are form'd of wreck and placed around,
130 (With tenters tipp'd) a strong repulsive bound;
Wide and deep ditches by the gardens run,
And there in ambush lie the trap and gun;
Or yon broad board, which guards each tempting prize,
'Like a tall bully, lifts its head and lies.'
  There stands a cottage with an open door,
Its garden undefended blooms before:
Her wheel is still, and overturn'd her stool,
While the lone Widow seeks the neighb'ring pool:
This gives us hope, all views of town to shun –
140 No! here are tokens of the Sailor-son;

That old blue jacket, and that shirt of check,
And silken kerchief for the seaman's neck;
Sea-spoils and shells from many a distant shore,
And furry robe from frozen Labrador.
　　Our busy streets and sylvan-walks between,
Fen, marshes, bog and heath all intervene;
Here pits of crag, with spongy, plashy base,
To some enrich th' uncultivated space:
For there are blossoms rare, and curious rush,
150　The gale's rich balm, and sun-dew's crimson blush,
Whose velvet leaf with radiant beauty dress'd,
Forms a gay pillow for the plover's breast.
　　Not distant far, a house commodious made,
(Lonely yet public stands) for Sunday-trade;
Thither, for this day free, gay parties go,
Their tea-house walk, their tippling rendezvous;
There humble couples sit in corner-bowers,
Or gaily ramble for th'allotted hours;
Sailors and lasses from the town attend,
160　The servant-lover, the apprentice-friend;
With all the idle social tribes who seek
And find their humble pleasures once a week.
　　Turn to the watery world! – but who to thee
(A wonder yet unview'd) shall paint – the Sea?
Various and vast, sublime in all its forms,
When lull'd by zephyrs, or when roused by storms,
Its colours changing, when from clouds and sun
Shades after shades upon the surface run;
Embrown'd and horrid now, and now serene,
170　In limpid blue, and evanescent green;
And oft the foggy banks on ocean lie,
Lift the fair sail, and cheat th' experienced eye.
　　Be it the Summer-noon: a sandy space
The ebbing tide has left upon its place;
Then just the hot and stony beach above,
Light twinkling streams in bright confusion move;
(For heated thus, the warmer air ascends,
and with the cooler in its fall contends) –

Then the broad bosom of the ocean keeps
180 An equal motion; swelling as it sleeps,
Then slowly sinking; curling to the strand,
Faint, lazy waves o'ercreep the ridgy sand,
Or tap the tarry boat with gentle blow,
And back return in silence, smooth and slow.
Ships in the calm seem anchor'd; for they glide
On the still sea, urged solely by the tide:
Art thou not present, this calm scene before,
Where all beside is pebbly length of shore,
And far as eye can reach, it can discern no more?
190 Yet sometimes comes a ruffling cloud to make
The quiet surface of the ocean shake;
As an awaken'd giant with a frown
Might show his wrath, and then to sleep sink down.
View now the Winter-storm! above, one cloud,
Black and unbroken, all the skies o'ershroud;
Th' unwieldy porpoise through the day before
Had roll'd in view of boding men on shore;
And sometimes hid and sometimes show'd his form,
Dark as the cloud, and furious as the storm.
200 All where the eye delights, yet dreads to roam,
The breaking billows cast the flying foam
Upon the billows rising – all the deep
Is restless change; the waves so swell'd and steep,
Breaking and sinking, and the sunken swells,
Nor one, one moment, in its station dwells:
But nearer land you may the billows trace,
As if contending in their watery chase;
May watch the mightiest till the shoal they reach,
Then break and hurry to their utmost stretch;
210 Curl'd as they come, they strike with furious force,
And then re-flowing, take their grating course,
Raking the rounded flints, which ages past
Roll'd by their rage, and shall to ages last.
Far off the Petrel in the troubled way
Swims with her brood, or flutters in the spray;
She rises often, often drops again,

And sports at ease on the tempestuous main.
   High o'er the restless deep, above the reach
Of gunner's hope, vast flights of Wild-ducks stretch;
220 Far as the eye can glance on either side,
In a broad space and level line they glide;
All in their wedge-like figures from the north,
Day after day, flight after flight, go forth.
In-shore their passage tribes of Sea-gulls urge,
And drop for prey within the sweeping surge;
Oft in the rough opposing blast they fly
Far back, then turn, and all their force apply,
While to the storm they give their weak complaining cry;
Or clap the sleek white pinion to the breast,
230 And in the restless ocean dip for rest.
   Darkness begins to reign; the louder wind
Appals the weak and awes the firmer mind;
But frights not him, whom evening and the spray
In part conceal – yon Prowler on his way:
Lo! he has something seen; he runs apace,
As if he fear'd companion in the chase;
He sees his prize, and now he turns again,
Slowly and sorrowing – 'Was your search in vain?'
Gruffly he answers, ''Tis a sorry sight!
240 'A seaman's body: there'll be more to-night!'
   Hark! to those sounds! they're from distress at sea:
How quick they come! What terrors may there be!
Yes, 'tis a driven vessel: I discern
Lights, signs of terror, gleaming from the stern;
Others behold them too, and from the town
In various parties seamen hurry down;
Their wives pursue, and damsels urged by dread,
Lest men so dear be into danger led;
Their head the gown has hooded, and their call
250 In this sad night is piercing like the squall;
They feel their kinds of power, and when they meet,
Chide, fondle, weep, dare, threaten, or entreat.
   See one poor girl, all terror and alarm,
Has fondly seized upon her lover's arm;

'Thou shalt not venture;' and he answers 'No!
'I will not' – still she cries, 'Thou shalt not go.'
   No need of this; not here the stoutest boat
Can through such breakers, o'er such billows float,
Yet may they view these lights upon the beach,
Which yield them hope, whom help can never reach.
   From parted clouds the moon her radiance throws
On the wild waves, and all the danger shows;
But shows them beaming in her shining vest,
Terrific splendour! gloom in glory dress'd!
This for a moment, and then clouds again
Hide every beam, and fear and darkness reign.
   But hear we now those sounds? Do lights appear?
I see them not! the storm alone I hear:
And lo! the sailors homeward take their way;
Man must endure – let us submit and pray.
   Such are our Winter-views: but night comes on –
Now business sleeps, and daily cares are gone;
Now parties form, and some their friends assist
To waste the idle hours at sober whist;
The tavern's pleasure or the concert's charm
Unnumber'd moments of their sting disarm;
Play-bills and open doors a crowd invite,
To pass off one dread portion of the night;
And show and song and luxury combined,
Lift off from man this burthen of mankind.
   Others advent'rous walk abroad and meet
Returning parties pacing through the street,
When various voices, in the dying day,
Hum in our walks, and greet us on our way;
When tavern-lights flit on from room to room,
And guide the tippling sailor staggering home:
There as we pass, the jingling bells betray
How business rises with the closing day:
Now walking silent, by the river's side,
The ear perceives the rippling of the tide;
Or measured cadence of the lads who tow
Some enter'd hoy, to fix her in her row;

86

Or hollow sound, which from the parish-bell
To some departed spirit bids farewell!
  Thus shall you something of our BOROUGH know,
Far as a verse, with Fancy's aid, can show;
Of Sea or River, of a Quay or Street,
The best description must be incomplete;
But when a happier theme succeeds, and when
300 Men are our subjects and the deeds of men;
Then may we find the Muse in happier style,
And we may sometimes sigh and sometimes smile.

Ellen Orford

Observe yon tenement, apart and small,
Where the wet pebbles shine upon the wall;
Where the low benches lean beside the door,
And the red paling bounds the space before;
Where thrift and lavender, and lad's love bloom, –
That humble dwelling is the widow's home;
There live a pair, for various fortunes known,
But the blind *Ellen* will relate her own; –
Yet ere we hear the story she can tell,
10 On prouder sorrows let us briefly dwell.

  I've often marvel'd, when, by night, by day,
I've marked the manners moving in my way,
And heard the language and beheld the lives
Of lass and lover, goddesses and wives,
That books, which promise much of life to give,
Should show so little how we truly live.

  To me it seems, their females and their men
Are but the creatures of the author's pen;
Nay, creatures borrow'd and again convey'd

20 From book to book – the shadows of a shade:
Life, if they'd search, would show them many a change;
The ruin sudden, and the misery strange!
With more of grievous, base, and dreadful things,
Than novelists relate or poet sings:
But they, who ought to look the world around,
Spy out a single spot in fairy-ground;
Where all, in turn, ideal forms behold,
And plots are laid and histories are told.

Time have I lent – I would their debt were less –
30 To flow'ry pages of sublime distress;
And to the heroine's soul-distracting fears
I early gave my sixpences and tears:
Oft have I travell'd in these tender tales,
To *Darnley-Cottages* and *Maple-Vales*,
And watch'd the fair-one from the first-born sigh,
When Henry pass'd and gazed in passing by;
Till I beheld them pacing in the park,
Close by a coppice where 'twas cold and dark;
When such affection with such fate appear'd,
40 Want and a father to be shunn'd and fear'd,
Without employment, prospect, cot, or cash;
That I have judged th' heroic souls were rash.

Now shifts the scene, – the fair in tower confined,
In all things suffers but in change of mind;
Now woo'd by greatness to a bed of state,
Now deeply threaten'd with a dungeon's grate;
Till, suffering much, and being tried enough,
She shines, triumphant maid! – temptation-proof.

Then was I led to vengeful monks, who mix
50 With nymphs and swains, and play unpriestly tricks;
Then view'd banditti who in forest wide,
And cavern vast, indignant virgins hide;
Who, hemm'd with bands of sturdiest rogues about,
Find some strange succour, and come virgins out.

88

I've watch'd a wint'ry night on castle-walls,
I've stalk'd by moonlight through deserted halls,
And when the weary world was sunk to rest,
I've had such nights as – may not be express'd.

Lo! that château, the western tower decay'd,
60   The peasants shun it, – they are all afraid;
For there was done a deed! – could walls reveal,
Or timbers tell it, how the heart would feel!
Most horrid was it: – for, behold, the floor
Has stain of blood, and will be clean no more:
Hark to the winds! which through the wide saloon
And the long passage send a dismal tune, –
Music that ghosts delight in; – and now heed
Yon beauteous nymph, who must unmask the deed;
See! with majestic sweep she swims alone,
70   Through rooms, all dreary, guided by a groan:
Though windows rattle, and though tap'stries shake,
And the feet falter every step they take,
'Mid moans and gibing sprights she silent goes,
To find a something, which will soon expose
The villainies and wiles of her determined foes:
And, having thus adventured, thus endured,
Fame, wealth, and lover are for life secured.
   Much have I fear'd, but am no more afraid,
When some chaste beauty, by some wretch betray'd,
80   Is drawn away with such distracted speed,
That she anticipates a dreadful deed:
Not so do I – Let solid walls impound
The captive fair, and dig a moat around;
Let there be brazen locks and bars of steel,
And keepers cruel, such as never feel;
With not a single note the purse supply,
And when she begs, let men and maids deny;
Be windows those from which she dares not fall,
And help so distant, 'tis in vain to call;
90   Still means of freedom will some power devise,
And from the baffled ruffian snatch his prize.

To Northern Wales, in some sequester'd spot,
I've follow'd fair *Louisa* to her cot;
Where, then a wretched and deserted bride,
The injured fair-one wished from man to hide;
Till by her fond repenting Belville found,
By some kind chance – the straying of a hound,
He at her feet craved mercy, nor in vain,
For the relenting dove flew back again.

100   There's something rapturous in distress, or, oh!
Could *Clementina* bear her lot of woe?
Or what she underwent could maiden undergo?
The day was fix'd; for so the lover sigh'd,
So knelt and craved, he couldn't be denied;
When, tale most dreadful! every hope adieu, –
For the fond lover is the brother too:
All other griefs abate; this monstrous grief
Has no remission, comfort, or relief;
Four ample volumes, through each page disclose, –
110   Good Heaven protect us! only woes on woes;
Till some strange means afford a sudden view
Of some vile plot, and every woe adieu!

     Now, should we grant these beauties all endure
Severest pangs, they've still the speediest cure;
Before one charm be wither'd from the face,
Except the bloom, which shall again have place,
In wedlock ends each wish, in triumph all disgrace;
And life to come, we fairly may suppose.
One light, bright contrast to these wild dark woes.

120   These let us leave, and at her sorrows look,
Too often seen, but seldom in a book;
Let her who felt, relate them; – on her chair
The heroine sits – in former years, the fair,
Now aged and poor; but *Ellen Orford* knows
That we should humbly take what Heav'n bestows.

'My father died – again my mother wed,
'And found the comforts of her life were fled;
'Her angry husband, vex'd through half his years
'By loss and troubles, fill'd her soul with fears:
130 'Their children many, and 't was my poor place
'To nurse and wait on all the infant-race;
'Labour and hunger were indeed my part,
'And should have strengthen'd an erroneous heart.

'Sore was the grief to see him angry come,
'And teased with business, make distress at home:
'The father's fury and the children's cries
'I soon could bear, but not my mother's sighs;
'For she look'd back on comforts, and would say,
' "I wrong'd thee, Ellen," and then turn away:
140 'Thus, for my age's good, my youth was tried,
'And this my fortune till my mother died.

'So, amid sorrow much and little cheer –
'A common case – I pass'd my twentieth year;
'For these are frequent evils; thousands share
'An equal grief – the like domestic care.

'Then in my days of bloom, of health and youth,
'One, much above me, vow'd his love and truth:
'We often met, he dreading to be seen,
'And much I question'd what such dread might mean;
150 'Yet I believed him true; my simple heart
'And undirected reason took his part.

'Can he who loves me, whom I love, deceive?
'Can I such wrong of one so kind believe,
'Who lives but in my smile, who trembles when I grieve?

'He dared not marry, but we met to prove
'What sad encroachments and deceits has love:
'Weak that I was, when he, rebuked, withdrew,
'I let him see that I was wretched too;

'When less my caution, I had still the pain
160 'Of his or mine own weakness to complain.

'Happy the lovers class'd alike in life,
'Or happier yet the rich endowing wife;
'But most aggrieved the fond believing maid,
'Of her rich lover tenderly afraid:
'You judge th' event; for grievous was my fate,
'Painful to feel, and shameful to relate:
'Ah! sad it was my burthen to sustain,
'When the least misery was the dread of pain;
'When I have grieving told him my disgrace,
170 'And plainly mark'd indifference in his face.

'Hard! with these fears and terrors to behold
'The cause of all, the faithless lover, cold;
'Impatient grown at every wish denied,
'And barely civil, soothed and gratified;
'Peevish when urged to think of vows so strong,
'And angry when I spake of crime and wrong.
'All this I felt, and still the sorrow grew,
'Because I felt that I deserved it too,
'And begg'd my infant stranger to forgive
180 'The mother's shame, which in herself must live.

'When known that shame, I, soon expell'd from home,
'With a frail sister shared a hovel's gloom;
'There barely fed – (what could I more request?)
'My infant slumberer sleeping at my breast,
'I from my window saw his blooming bride,
'And my seducer smiling at her side;
'Hope lived till then; I sank upon the floor,
'And grief and thought and feeling were no more:
'Although revived, I judged that life would close,
190 'And went to rest, to wonder that I rose;
'My dreams were dismal, – wheresoe'er I stray'd,
'I seem'd ashamed, alarm'd, despised, betray'd;
'Always in grief, in guilt, disgraced, forlorn,

'Mourning that one so weak, so vile, was born;
'The earth a desert, tumult in the sea,
'The birds affrighten'd fled from tree to tree,
'Obscured the setting sun, and every thing like me:
'But Heav'n had mercy, and my need at length
'Urged me to labour, and renew'd my strength.
200 'I strove for patience as a sinner must,
'Yet felt th' opinion of the world unjust:
'There was my lover, in his joy esteem'd,
'And I, in my distress, as guilty deem'd;
'Yet sure, not all the guilt and shame belong
'To her who feels and suffers for the wrong:
'The cheat at play may use the wealth he's won,
'But is not honour'd for the mischief done;
'The cheat in love may use each villain art,
'And boast the deed that breaks the victim's heart.

210 'Four years were past; I might again have found
'Some erring wish, but for another wound:
'Lovely my daughter grew, her face was fair,
'But no expression ever brighten'd there;
'I doubted long, and vainly strove to make
'Some certain meaning of the words she spake;
'But meaning there was none, and I survey'd
'With dread the beauties of my idiot-maid.
'Still I submitted; – Oh! 'tis meet and fit
'In all we feel to make the heart submit;
220 'Gloomy and calm my days, but I had then,
'It seem'd, attractions for the eyes of men:
'The sober master of a decent trade
'O'erlook'd my errors, and his offer made;
'Reason assented: – true, my heart denied,
' "But thou," I said, "shalt be no more my guide."

'When wed, our toil and trouble, pains and care,
'Of means to live procured us humble share;
'Five were our sons, – and we, though careful, found
'Our hopes declining as the year came round:

93

230 'For I perceived, yet would not soon perceive,
'My husband stealing from my view to grieve:
'Silent he grew, and when he spoke he sigh'd,
'And surly look'd, and peevishly replied:
'Pensive by nature, he had gone of late
'To those who preach'd of destiny and fate,
'Of things fore-doom'd, and of election-grace,
'And how in vain we strive to run our race;
'That all by works and moral worth we gain
'Is to perceive our care and labour vain;
240 'That still the more we pay, our debts the more remain:
'That he who feels not the mysterious call,
'Lies bound in sin, till grov'ling from the fall.
'My husband felt not: – our persuasion, prayer,
'And our best reason darken'd his despair;
'His very nature changed; he now reviled
'My former conduct, – he reproach'd my child:
'He talked of bastard slips, and cursed his bed,
'And from our kindness to concealment fled;
  'For ever to some evil change inclined,
250 'To every gloomy thought he lent his mind,
'Nor rest would give to us, nor rest himself could find;
'His son suspended saw him, long bereft
'Of life, nor prospect of revival left.

  'With him died all our prospects, and once more
'I shared th' allotments of the parish poor;
'They took my children too, and this I know
'Was just and lawful, but I felt the blow:
'My idiot-maid and one unhealthy boy
'Were left, a mother's misery and her joy.

260   'Three sons I follow'd to the grave, and one –
'Oh! can I speak of that unhappy son?
'Would all the memory of that time were fled,
'And all those horrors, with my child, were dead!
'Before the world seduced him, what a grace
'And smile of gladness shone upon his face!

'Then, he had knowledge; finely would he write;
'Study to him was pleasure and delight;
'Great was his courage, and but few could stand
'Against the sleight and vigour of his hand;
270 'The maidens loved him; – when he came to die,
'No, not the coldest could suppress a sigh:
'Here I must cease – how can I say, my child
'Was by the bad of either sex beguiled?
'Worst of the bad – they taught him that the laws
'Made wrong and right; there was no other cause,
'That all religion was the trade of priests,
'And men, when dead, must perish like the beasts: –
'And he, so lively and so gay before –
'Ah! spare a mother – I can tell no more.

280   'Int'rest was made that they should not destroy
'The comely form of my deluded boy –
'But pardon came not; damp the place and deep
'Where he was kept, as they'd a tiger keep;
'For he, unhappy! had before them all
'Vow'd he'd escape, whatever might befall.

'He'd means of dress, and dress'd beyond his means,
'And so to see him in such dismal scenes,
'I cannot speak of it – cannot bear to tell
'Of that sad hour – I heard the passing bell!

290   'Slowly they went; he smiled, and look'd so smart,
'Yet sure he shudder'd when he saw the cart,
'And gave a look – until my dying day,
'That look will never from my mind away:
'Oft as I sit, and ever in my dreams,
'I see that look, and they have heard my screams.

'Now let me speak no more – yet all declared
'That one so young, in pity, should be spared,
'And one so manly; – on his graceful neck,
'That chains of jewels may be proud to deck,

300 'To a small mole a mother's lips have press'd, –
'And there the cord – my breath is sore oppress'd.

    'I now can speak again: – my elder boy
'Was that year drown'd, – a seaman in a hoy:
'He left a numerous race; of these would some
'In their young troubles to my cottage come,
'And these I taught – an humble teacher I –
'Upon their heavenly Parent to rely.

    'Alas! I needed such reliance more:
'My idiot-girl, so simply gay before,
310 'Now wept in pain; some wretch had found a time,
'Depraved and wicked, for that coward-crime;
'I had indeed my doubt, but I suppress'd
'The thought that day and night disturb'd my rest;
'She and that sick-pale brother – but why strive
'To keep the terrors of that time alive?

    'The hour arrived, the new, th' undreaded pain,
'That came with violence, and yet came in vain.
'I saw her die: her brother too is dead;
'Nor own'd such crime – what is it that I dread?

320   'The parish aid withdrawn, I look'd around,
'And in my school a bless'd subsistence found –
'My winter-calm of life: to be of use
'Would pleasant thoughts and heavenly hopes produce;
'I loved them all; it soothed me to presage
'The various trials of their riper age,
'Then dwell on mine, and bless the Power who gave
'Pains to correct us, and remorse to save.

    'Yes! these were days of peace, but they are past, –
'A trial came, I will believe, a last;
330 'I lost my sight, and my employment gone,
'Useless I live, but to the day live on;
'Those eyes, which long the light of heaven enjoy'd,

'Were not by pain, by agony destroy'd:
'My senses fail not all; I speak, I pray;
'By night my rest, my food I take by day;
'And, as my mind looks cheerful to my end,
'I love mankind, and call my GOD my friend.'

Peter Grimes

Old *Peter Grimes* made fishing his employ,
His wife he cabin'd with him and his boy,
And seem'd that life laborious to enjoy:
To town came quiet Peter with his fish,
And had of all a civil word and wish.
He left his trade upon the Sabbath-day,
And took young Peter in his hand to pray:
But soon the stubborn boy from care broke loose,
At first refused, then added his abuse:
His father's love he scorn'd, his power defied,   10
But being drunk, wept sorely when he died.

Yes! then he wept, and to his mind there came
Much of his conduct, and he felt the shame, –
How he had oft the good old man reviled,
And never paid the duty of a child;
How, when the father in his Bible read,
He in contempt and anger left the shed;
'It is the word of life,' the parent cried;
– 'This is the life itself,' the boy replied;
And while old Peter in amazement stood,   20
Gave the hot spirit to his boiling blood: –
How he, with oath and furious speech, began
To prove his freedom and assert the man;
And when the parent check'd his impious rage,
How he had cursed the tyranny of age, –

*

Nay, once had dealt the sacrilegious blow
On his bare head, and laid his parent low;
The father groan'd – 'If thou art old,' said he,
'And hast a son – thou wilt remember me:
30 'Thy mother left me in a happy time,
'Thou kill'dst not her – Heav'n spares the double crime.'

On an inn-settle, in his maudlin grief,
This he resolved, and drank for his relief.

Now lived the youth in freedom, but debarr'd
From constant pleasure, and he thought it hard;
Hard that he could not every wish obey,
But must awhile relinquish ale and play;
Hard! that he could not to his cards attend,
But must acquire the money he would spend.

40 With greedy eye he look'd on all he saw,
He knew not justice, and he laugh'd at law;
On all he mark'd, he stretch'd his ready hand;
He fish'd by water and he filch'd by land:
Oft in the night has Peter dropp'd his oar,
Fled from his boat, and sought for prey on shore;
Oft up the hedge-row glided, on his back
Bearing the orchard's produce in a sack,
Or farm-yard load, tugg'd fiercely from the stack;
And as these wrongs to greater numbers rose,
50 The more he look'd on all men as his foes.

He built a mud-wall'd hovel, where he kept
His various wealth, and there he oft-times slept;
But no success could please his cruel soul,
He wish'd for one to trouble and control;
He wanted some obedient boy to stand
And bear the blow of his outrageous hand;
And hoped to find in some propitious hour
A feeling creature subject to his power.

98

Peter had heard there were in London then, –
60 Still have they being! – workhouse-clearing men,
Who, undisturb'd by feelings just or kind,
Would parish-boys to needy tradesmen bind:
They in their want a trifling sum would take,
And toiling slaves of piteous orphans make.

Such Peter sought, and when a lad was found,
The sum was dealt him, and the slave was bound.
Some few in town observed in Peter's trap
A boy, with jacket blue and woollen cap;
But none enquired how Peter used the rope,
70 Or what the bruise, that made the stripling stoop;
None could the ridges on his back behold,
None sought him shiv'ring in the winter's cold;
None put the question, – 'Peter, dost thou give
'The boy his food? – What, man! the lad must live:
'Consider, Peter, let the child have bread,
'He'll serve thee better if he's stroked and fed.'
None reason'd thus – and some, on hearing cries,
Said calmly, 'Grimes is at his exercise.'

Pinn'd, beaten, cold, pinch'd, threaten'd, and abused –
80 His efforts punish'd and his food refused, –
Awake tormented, – soon aroused from sleep, –
Struck if he wept, and yet compell'd to weep,
The trembling boy dropp'd down and strove to pray,
Received a blow, and trembling turn'd away,
Or sobb'd and hid his piteous face; – while he,
The savage master, grinn'd in horrid glee:
He'd now the power he ever loved to show,
A feeling being subject to his blow.

Thus lived the lad, in hunger, peril, pain,
90 His tears despised, his supplications vain:
Compell'd by fear to lie, by need to steal,
His bed uneasy and unbless'd his meal,
For three sad years the boy his tortures bore,
And then his pains and trials were no more.

'How died he, Peter?' when the people said,
He growl'd – 'I found him lifeless in his bed;'
Then tried for softer tone, and sigh'd, 'Poor Sam is dead.'
Yet murmurs were there, and some questions ask'd –
How he was fed, how punish'd, and how task'd?
100 Much they suspected, but they little proved,
And Peter pass'd untroubled and unmoved.

Another boy with equal ease was found,
The money granted, and the victim bound;
And what his fate? – One night it chanced he fell
From the boat's mast and perish'd in her well.
Where fish were living kept, and where the boy
(So reason'd men) could not himself destroy: –

'Yes! so it was,' said Peter, 'in his play,
'(For he was idle both by night and day,)
110 'He climb'd the main-mast and then fell below;' –
Then show'd his corpse, and pointed to the blow:
'What said the jury?' – they were long in doubt,
But sturdy Peter faced the matter out:
So they dismiss'd him, saying at the time,
'Keep fast your hatchway when you've boys who climb.'
This hit the conscience, and he colour'd more
Than for the closest questions put before.

Thus all his fears the verdict set aside,
And at the slave-shop Peter still applied.

120 Then came a boy, of manners soft and mild, –
Our seamen's wives with grief beheld the child;
All thought (the poor themselves) that he was one
Of gentle blood, some noble sinner's son,
Who had, belike, deceived some humble maid,
Whom he had first seduced and then betray'd: –
However this, he seem'd a gracious lad,
In grief submissive and with patience sad.

Passive he labour'd, till his slender frame
Bent with his loads, and he at length was lame:
130 Strange that a frame so weak could bear so long
The grossest insult and the foulest wrong;
But there were causes – in the town they gave
Fire, food, and comfort, to the gentle slave;
And though stern Peter, with a cruel hand,
And knotted rope, enforced the rude command,
Yet he consider'd what he'd lately felt,
And his vile blows with selfish pity dealt.

One day such draughts the cruel fisher made,
He could not vend them in his borough-trade,
140 But sail'd for London-mart: the boy was ill,
But ever humbled to his master's will;
And on the river, where they smoothly sail'd,
He strove with terror and awhile prevail'd;
But new to danger on the angry sea,
He clung affrighten'd to his master's knee:
The boat grew leaky and the wind was strong,
Rough was the passage and the time was long;
His liquor fail'd, and Peter's wrath arose, –
No more is known – the rest we must suppose,
150 Or learn of Peter: – Peter says, he 'spied
'The stripling's danger and for harbour tried;
'Meantime the fish, and then th' apprentice died.'

The pitying women raised a clamour round,
And weeping said, 'Thou hast thy 'prentice drown'd.'

Now the stern man was summon'd to the hall,
To tell his tale before the burghers all:
He gave th' account; profess'd the lad he loved,
And kept his brazen features all unmoved.

The mayor himself with tone severe replied, –
160 'Henceforth with thee shall never boy abide;
'Hire thee a freeman, whom thou durst not beat,
'But who, in thy despite, will sleep and eat:

'Free thou art now! – again shouldst thou appear,
'Thou'lt find thy sentence, like thy soul, severe.'

Alas! for Peter not a helping hand,
So was he hated, could he now command;
Alone he row'd his boat, alone he cast
His nets beside, or made his anchor fast;
To hold a rope or hear a curse was none, –
170 He toil'd and rail'd; he groan'd and swore alone.

Thus by himself compell'd to live each day,
To wait for certain hours the tide's delay;
At the same time the same dull views to see,
The bounding marsh-bank and the blighted tree;
The water only, when the tides were high,
When low, the mud half-cover'd and half-dry;
The sun-burnt tar that blisters on the planks,
And bank-side stakes in their uneven ranks;
Heaps of entangled weeds that slowly float,
180 As the tide rolls by the impeded boat.

When tides were neap, and, in the sultry day,
Through the tall bounding mud-banks made their way,
Which on each side rose swelling, and below
The dark warm flood ran silently and slow;
There anchoring, Peter chose from man to hide,
There hang his head, and view the lazy tide
In its hot slimy channel slowly glide;
Where the small eels that left the deeper way
For the warm shore, within the shallows play;
190 Where gaping muscles, left upon the mud,
Slope their slow passage to the fallen flood; –
Here dull and hopeless he'd lie down and trace
How sidelong crabs had scrawl'd their crooked race;
Or sadly listen to the tuneless cry
Of fishing gull or clanging golden-eye;
What time the sea-birds to the marsh would come,
And the loud bittern, from the bull-rush home,

Gave from the salt-ditch side the bellowing boom:
He nursed the feelings these dull scenes produce,
200 And loved to stop beside the opening sluice;
Where the small stream, confined in narrow bound,
Ran with a dull, unvaried, sadd'ning sound;
Where all, presented to the eye or ear,
Oppress'd the soul with misery, grief, and fear.

Besides these objects, there were places three,
Which Peter seem'd with certain dread to see;
When he drew near them he would turn from each,
And loudly whistle till he pass'd the reach.

A change of scene to him brought no relief,
210 In town, 't was plain, men took him for a thief:
The sailors' wives would stop him in the street,
And say, 'Now, Peter, thou'st no boy to beat:'
Infants at play, when they perceived him, ran,
Warning each other – 'That's the wicked man:'
He growl'd an oath, and in an angry tone
Cursed the whole place and wish'd to be alone.

Alone he was, the same dull scenes in view,
And still more gloomy in his sight they grew:
Though man he hated, yet employ'd alone
220 At bootless labour, he would swear and groan,
Cursing the shoals that glided by the spot,
And gulls that caught them when his arts could not.

Cold nervous tremblings shook his sturdy frame,
And strange disease – he couldn't say the name;
Wild were his dreams, and oft he rose in fright,
Waked by his view of horrors in the night, –
Horrors that would the sternest minds amaze,
Horrors that demons might be proud to raise:
And though he felt forsaken, grieved at heart,
230 To think he lived from all mankind apart;
Yet, if a man approach'd, in terrors he would start.

A winter pass'd since Peter saw the town,
And summer lodgers were again come down;
These, idly curious, with their glasses spied
The ships in bay as anchor'd for the tide, –
The river's craft, – the bustle of the quay, –
And sea-port views, which landmen love to see.

One, up the river, had a man and boat
Seen day by day, now anchor'd, now afloat;
240   Fisher he seem'd, yet used no net nor hook;
Of sea-fowl swimming by no heed he took,
But on the gliding waves still fix'd his lazy look:
At certain stations he would view the stream,
As if he stood bewilder'd in a dream,
Or that some power had chain'd him for a time,
To feel a curse or meditate on crime.

This known, some curious, some in pity went,
And others question'd – 'Wretch, dost thou repent?'
He heard, he trembled, and in fear resign'd
250   His boat: new terror fill'd his restless mind;
Furious he grew, and up the country ran,
And there they seized him – a distemper'd man: –
Him we received, and to a parish-bed,
Follow'd and cursed, the groaning man was led.

Here when they saw him, whom they used to shun,
A lost, lone man, so harass'd and undone;
Our gentle females, ever prompt to feel,
Perceived compassion on their anger steal;
His crimes they could not from their memories blot,
260   But they were grieved, and trembled at his lot.

A Priest too came, to whom his words are told;
And all the signs they shudder'd to behold.

'Look! look!' they cried; 'his limbs with horror shake,
'And as he grinds his teeth, what noise they make!
'How glare his angry eyes, and yet he's not awake:
'See! what cold drops upon his forehead stand,
'And how he clenches that broad bony hand.'

The Priest attending, found he spoke at times
As one alluding to his fears and crimes;
270 'It was the fall,' he mutter'd, 'I can show
'The manner how, – I never struck a blow:' –
And then aloud, – 'Unhand me, free my chain;
'On oath he fell – it struck him to the brain: –
'Why ask my father? – that old man will swear
'Against my life; besides, he wasn't there: –
'What, all agreed? – Am I to die to-day? –
'My Lord, in mercy give me time to pray.'

Then as they watch'd him, calmer he became,
And grew so weak he couldn't move his frame,
280 But murmuring spake – while they could see and hear
The start of terror and the groan of fear;
See the large dew-beads on his forehead rise,
And the cold death-drop glaze his sunken eyes;
Nor yet he died, but with unwonted force
Seem'd with some fancied being to discourse;
He knew not us, or with accustom'd art
He hid the knowledge, yet exposed his heart;
'T was part confession and the rest defence,
A madman's tale, with gleams of waking sense.

290   'I'll tell you all,' he said, 'the very day
'When the old man first placed them in my way:
'My father's spirit – he who always tried
'To give me trouble, when he lived and died –
'When he was gone he could not be content
'To see my days in painful labour spent,
'But would appoint his meetings, and he made
'Me watch at these, and so neglect my trade.

  ' 'Twas one hot noon, all silent, still, serene,
  'No living being had I lately seen;
300 'I paddled up and down and dipp'd my net,
  'But (such his pleasure) I could nothing get, –
  'A father's pleasure, when his toil was done,
  'To plague and torture thus an only son!
  'And so I sat and look'd upon the stream,
  'How it ran on, and felt as in a dream:
  'But dream it was not: No! – I fix'd my eyes
  'On the mid stream and saw the spirits rise:
  'I saw my father on the water stand,
  'And hold a thin pale boy in either hand;
310 'And there they glided ghastly on the top
  'Of the salt flood, and never touch'd a drop:
  'I would have struck them, but they knew th' intent,
  'And smiled upon the oar, and down they went.

  'Now, from that day, whenever I began
  'To dip my net, there stood the hard old man –
  'He and those boys: I humbled me and pray'd
  'They would be gone; – they heeded not, but stay'd:
  'Nor could I turn, nor would the boat go by,
  'But, gazing on the spirits, there was I:
320 'They bade me leap to death, but I was loth to die:
  'And every day, as sure as day arose,
  'Would these three spirits meet me ere the close;
  'To hear and mark them daily was my doom,
  'And "Come," they said, with weak, sad voices, "come."
  'To row away, with all my strength I tried,
  'But there were they, hard by me in the tide,
  'The three unbodied forms – and "Come," still "come,"
    they cried.

  'Fathers should pity – but this old man shook
  'His hoary locks, and froze me by a look:
330 'Thrice, when I struck them, through the water came
  'A hollow groan, that weaken'd all my frame:
  ' "Father!" said I, "have mercy:" – he replied,

'I know not what – the angry spirit lied, –
' "Didst thou not draw thy knife?" said he: – 'T was true,
'But I had pity and my arm withdrew:
'He cried for mercy, which I kindly gave,
'But he has no compassion in his grave.

'There were three places, where they ever rose, –
'The whole long river has not such as those –
340 'Places accursed, where, if a man remain,
'He'll see the things which strike him to the brain;
'And there they made me on my paddle lean,
'And look at them for hours; – accursed scene!
'When they would glide to that smooth eddy-space,
'Then bid me leap and join them in the place;
'And at my groans each little villain sprite
'Enjoy'd my pains and vanish'd in delight.

'In one fierce summer-day, when my poor brain
'Was burning hot, and cruel was my pain,
350 'Then came this father-foe, and there he stood
'With his two boys again upon the flood:
'There was more mischief in their eyes, more glee,
'In their pale faces when they glared at me:
'Still did they force me on the oar to rest,
'And when they saw me fainting and oppress'd,
'He, with his hand, the old man, scoop'd the flood,
'And there came flame about him mix'd with blood;
'He bade me stoop and look upon the place,
'Then flung the hot-red liquor in my face;
360 'Burning it blazed, and then I roar'd for pain,
'I thought the demons would have turn'd my brain.

'Still there they stood, and forced me to behold
'A place of horrors – they can not be told –
'Where the flood open'd, there I heard the shriek
'Of tortured guilt – no earthly tongue can speak:
' "All days alike! for ever!" did they say,
' "And unremitted torments every day" –

'Yes, so they said' – But here he ceased, and gazed
On all around, affrighten'd and amazed;
370 And still he tried to speak, and look'd his dread
Of frighten'd females gathering round his bed;
Then dropp'd exhausted, and appear'd at rest,
Till the strong foe the vital powers possess'd;
Then with an inward, broken voice he cried,
'Again they come,' and mutter'd as he died.

Prisons

'T is well – that Man to all the varying states
Of good and ill his mind accommodates;
He not alone progressive grief sustains,
But soon submits to unexperienced pains:
Change after change, all climes his body bears;
His mind repeated shocks of changing cares:
Faith and fair Virtue arm the nobler breast;
Hope and mere want of feeling aid the rest.

Or who could bear to lose the balmy air
10 Of summer's breath, from all things fresh and fair,
With all that man admires or loves below;
All earth and water, wood and vale bestow,
Where rosy pleasures smile, whence real blessings flow;
With sight and sound of every kind that lives,
And crowning all with joy that freedom gives?

Who could from these, in some unhappy day,
Bear to be drawn by ruthless arms away,
To the vile nuisance of a noisome room,
Where only insolence and misery come?
20 (Save that the curious will by chance appear,
Or some in pity drop a fruitless tear;)

To a damp Prison, where the very sight
Of the warm sun is favour and not right;
Where all we hear or see the feelings shock,
The oath and groan, the fetter and the lock?

Who could bear this and live? – Oh! many a year
All this is borne, and miseries more severe;
And some there are, familiar with the scene,
Who live in mirth, though few become serene.

30   Far as I might the inward man perceive,
There was a constant effort – not to grieve:
Not to despair, for better days would come,
And the freed debtor smile again at home:
Subdued his habits, he may peace regain,
And bless the woes that were not sent in vain.

Thus might we class the Debtors here confined,
The more deceived, the more deceitful kind;
Here are the guilty race, who mean to live
On credit, that credulity will give;
40   Who purchase, conscious they can never pay;
Who know their fate, and traffic to betray;
On whom no pity, fear, remorse, prevail,
Their aim a statute, their resource a jail; –
These as the public spoilers we regard,
No dun so harsh, no creditor so hard.

A second kind are they, who truly strive
To keep their sinking credit long alive;
Success, nay prudence, they may want, but yet
They would be solvent, and deplore a debt;
50   All means they use, to all expedients run,
And are by slow, sad steps, at last undone:
Justly, perhaps, you blame their want of skill,
But mourn their feelings and absolve their will.

There is a Debtor, who his trifling *all*
Spreads in a shop; it would not fill a stall;
There at one window his temptation lays,
And in new modes disposes and displays:
Above the door you shall his name behold,
And what he vends in ample letters told,
60 The words 'Repository,' 'Warehouse,' all
He uses to enlarge concerns so small:
He to his goods assigns some beauty's name,
Then in her reign, and hopes they'll share her fame,
And talks of credit, commerce, traffic, trade,
As one important by their profit made;
But who can paint the vacancy, the gloom,
And spare dimensions of one backward room?
Wherein he dines, if so 't is fit to speak
Of one day's herring and the morrow's steak:
70 An anchorite in diet, all his care
Is to display his stock and vend his ware.

Long waiting hopeless, then he tries to meet
A kinder fortune in a distant street;
There he again displays, increasing yet
Corroding sorrow and consuming debt:
Alas! he wants the requisites to rise –
The true connections, the availing ties;
They who proceed on certainties advance,
These are not times when men prevail by chance:
80 But still he tries, till, after years of pain,
He finds, with anguish, he has tried in vain.
Debtors are these on whom 't is hard to press,
'T is base, impolitic, and merciless.

To these we add a miscellaneous kind,
By pleasure, pride, and indolence confined;
Those whom no calls, no warnings could divert,
The unexperienced and the inexpert;
The builder, idler, schemer, gamester, sot, –
The follies different, but the same their lot;

90 Victims of horses, lasses, drinking, dice,
　 Of every passion, humour, whim, and vice.

　 See! that sad Merchant, who but yesterday
　 Had a vast household in command and pay;
　 He now entreats permission to employ
　 A boy he needs, and then entreats the boy.

　 And there sits one, improvident but kind,
　 Bound for a friend, whom honour could not bind;
　 Sighing, he speaks to any who appear,
　 'A treach'rous friend – 't was that which sent me here:
100 'I was too kind, – I thought I could depend
　 'On his bare word – he was a treach'rous friend.'

　 A Female too! – it is to her a home,
　 She came before – and she again will come:
　 Her friends have pity; when their anger drops,
　 They take her home; – she's tried her schools and shops –
　 Plan after plan; – but fortune would not mend,
　 She to herself was still the treach'rous friend;
　 And wheresoe'er began, all here was sure to end:
　 And there she sits, as thoughtless and as gay
110 As if she'd means, or not a debt to pay –
　 Or knew to-morrow she'd be call'd away –
　 Or felt a shilling and could dine to-day.

　 While thus observing, I began to trace
　 The sober'd features of a well-known face –
　 Looks once familiar, manners form'd to please,
　 And all illumined by a heart at ease:
　 But fraud and flattery ever claim'd a part
　 (Still unresisted) of that easy heart;
　 But he at length beholds me – 'Ah! my friend!
120 'And have thy pleasures this unlucky end?

　 'Too sure,' he said, and smiling as he sigh'd;
　 'I went astray, though Prudence seem'd my guide;

'All she proposed I in my heart approved,
'And she was honour'd but my pleasure loved –
'Pleasure, the mistress to whose arms I fled,
'From wife-like lectures angry Prudence read.

'Why speak the madness of a life like mine,
'The powers of beauty, novelty, and wine?
'Why paint the wanton smile, the venal vow,
130 'Or friends whose worth I can appreciate now;
'Oft I perceived my fate, and then could say,
'I'll think to-morrow, I must live to-day:
'So am I here – I own the laws are just –
'And here, where thought is painful, think I must:
'But speech is pleasant; this discourse with thee
'Brings to my mind the sweets of liberty,
'Breaks on the sameness of the place, and gives
'The doubtful heart conviction that it lives.

'Let me describe my anguish in the hour
140 'When law detain'd me and I felt its power.

'When, in that shipwreck, this I found my shore,
'And join'd the wretched, who were wreck'd before;
'When I perceived each feature in the face,
'Pinch'd through neglect or turbid by disgrace;
'When in these wasting forms affliction stood
'In my afflicted view, it chill'd my blood; –
'And forth I rush'd, a quick retreat to make,
'Till a loud laugh proclaim'd the dire mistake:
'But when the groan had settled to a sigh,
150 'When gloom became familiar to the eye,
'When I perceive how others seem to rest,
'With every evil rankling in my breast, –
'Led by example, I put on the man,
'Sing off my sighs, and trifle as I can.

'Homer! nay Pope! (for never will I seek
'Applause for learning – nought have I with Greek)

112

'Gives us the secrets of his pagan hell,
'Where ghost with ghost in sad communion dwell;
'Where shade meets shade, and round the gloomy meads
160 'They glide, and speak of old heroic deeds, –
'What fields they conquer'd, and what foes they slew,
'And sent to join the melancholy crew,
'When a new spirit in that world was found,
'A thousand shadowy forms came flitting round;
'Those who had known him, fond enquiries made, –
' "Of all we left, inform us, gentle shade
' "Now as we lead thee in our realms to dwell,
' "Our twilight groves, and meads of asphodel."

'What paints the poet, is our station here,
170 'Where we like ghosts and flitting shades appear:
'This is the hell he sings, and here we meet,
'And former deeds to new-made friends repeat;
'Heroic deeds, which here obtain us fame,
'And are in fact the causes why we came:
'Yes! this dim region is old Homer's hell,
'Abate but groves and meads of asphodel.
'Here, when a stranger from your world we spy,
'We gather round him and for news apply;
'He hears unheeding, nor can speech endure,
180 'But shivering gazes on the vast obscure:
'We smiling pity, and by kindness show
'We felt his feelings and his terrors know;
'Then speak of comfort – time will give him sight,
'Where now 't is dark; where now 't is woe – delight.

' "Have hope," we say, "and soon the place to thee
' "Shall not a prison but a castle be:
' "When to the wretch whom care and guilt confound,
' "The world's a prison, with a wider bound;
' "Go where he may, he feels himself confined,
190 ' "And wears the fetters of an abject mind.

'But now adieu! those giant-keys appear,
'Thou art not worthy to be inmate here:

113

'Go to thy world, and to the young declare
'What we, our spirits and employments, are;
'Tell them how we the ills of life endure,
'Our empire stable, and our state secure;
'Our dress, our diet, for their use describe,
'And bid them haste to join the gen'rous tribe:
'Go to thy world, and leave us here to dwell,
200 'Who to its joys and comforts bid farewell.'

Farewell to these; but other scenes I view,
And other griefs, and guilt of deeper hue;
Where Conscience gives to outward ills her pain,
Gloom to the night, and pressure to the chain:
Here separate cells awhile in misery keep
Two doom'd to suffer: there they strive for sleep;
By day indulged, in larger space they range,
Their bondage certain, but their bounds have change.

One was a female, who had grievous ill
210 Wrought in revenge, and she enjoy'd it still:
With death before her, and her fate in view,
Unsated vengeance in her bosom grew:
Sullen she was and threat'ning; in her eye
Glared the stern triumph that she dared to die:
But first a being in the world must leave –
'T was once reproach; 't was now a short reprieve.

She was a pauper bound, who early gave
Her mind to vice and doubly was a slave:
Upbraided, beaten, held by rough control,
220 Revenge sustain'd, inspired, and fill'd her soul:
She fired a full-stored barn, confess'd the fact,
And laugh'd at law and justified the act:
Our gentle Vicar tried his powers in vain,
She answer'd not, or answer'd with disdain;
Th' approaching fate she heard without a sigh,
And neither cared to live nor fear'd to die.

Not so he felt, who with her was to pay
The forfeit, life – with dread he view'd the day,
And that short space which yet for him remain'd,
230 Till with his limbs his faculties were chain'd:
He paced his narrow bounds some ease to find,
But found it not, – no comfort reach'd his mind:
Each sense was palsied; when he tasted food,
He sigh'd and said, 'Enough – 't is very good.'
Since his dread sentence, nothing seem'd to be
As once it was – he seeing could not see,
Nor hearing, hear aright; – when first I came
Within his view, I fancied there was shame,
I judged resentment; I mistook the air, –
240 These fainter passions live not with despair;
Or but exist and die: – Hope, fear, and love,
Joy, doubt, and hate, may other spirits move,
But touch not his, who every waking hour
Has one fix'd dread, and always feels its power.

'But will not Mercy?' – No! she cannot plead
For such an outrage; – 't was a cruel deed:
He stopp'd a timid traveller; – to his breast,
With oaths and curses, was the danger press'd: –
No! he must suffer; pity we may find
250 For one man's pangs, but must not wrong mankind.

Still I behold him, every thought employ'd
On one dire view! – all others are destroy'd;
This makes his features ghastly, gives the tone
Of his few words resemblance to a groan;
He takes his tasteless food, and when 't is done,
Counts up his meals, now lessen'd by that one;
For expectation is on time intent,
Whether he brings us joy or punishment.

Yes! e'en in sleep the impressions all remain,
260 He hears the sentence and he feels the chain;

He sees the judge and jury, when he shakes,
And loudly cries, 'Not guilty,' and awakes:
Then chilling tremblings o'er his body creep,
Till worn-out nature is compell'd to sleep.

Now comes the dream again: it shows each scene,
With each small circumstance that comes between –
The call to suffering and the very deed –
There crowds go with him, follow, and precede;
Some heartless shout, some pity, all condemn,
270 While he in fancied envy looks at them:
He seems the place for that sad act to see,
And dreams the very thirst which then will be:
A priest attends – it seems, the one he knew
In his best days, beneath whose care he grew.

At this his terrors take a sudden flight,
He sees his native village with delight;
The house, the chamber, where he once array'd
His youthful person; where he knelt and pray'd:
Then too the comforts he enjoy'd at home,
280 The days of joy; the joys themselves are come; –
The hours of innocence; – the timid look
Of his loved maid, when first her hand he took,
And told his hope; her trembling joy appears,
Her forced reserve and his retreating fears.

All now is present; – 't is a moment's gleam
Of former sunshine – stay, delightful dream!
Let him within his pleasant garden walk,
Give him her arm, of blessings let them talk.

Yes! all are with him now, and all the while
290 Life's early prospects and his Fanny's smile:
Then come his sister and his village-friend,
And he will now the sweetest moments spend
Life has to yield; – No! never will he find
Again on earth such pleasure in his mind:

He goes through shrubby walks these friends among,
Love in their looks and honour on the tongue:
Nay, there's a charm beyond what nature shows,
The bloom is softer and more sweetly glows; –
Pierced by no crime, and urged by no desire
300 For more than true and honest hearts require,
They feel the calm delight, and thus proceed
Through the green land, – then linger in the mead, –
Stray o'er the heath in all its purple bloom, –
And pluck the blossom where the wild bees hum;
Then through the broomy bound with ease they pass,
And press the sandy sheep-walk's slender grass,
Where dwarfish flowers among the gorse are spread,
And the lamb browses by the linnet's bed;
Then 'cross the bounding brook they make their way
310 O'er its rough bridge – and there behold the bay! –
The ocean smiling to the fervid sun –
The waves that faintly fall and slowly run –
The ships at distance and the boats at hand;
And now they walk upon the sea-side sand,
Counting the number and what kind they be,
Ships softly sinking in the sleepy sea:
Now arm in arm, now parted, they behold
The glitt'ring waters on the shingles roll'd:
The timid girls, half dreading their design,
320 Dip the small foot in the retarded brine,
And search for crimson weeds, which spreading flow,
Or lie like pictures on the sand below:
With all those bright red pebbles, that the sun
Through the small waves so softly shines upon;
And those live lucid jellies which the eye
Delights to trace as they swim glittering by:
Pearl-shells and rubied star-fish they admire,
And will arrange above the parlour-fire, –
Tokens of bliss! – 'Oh! horrible! a wave
330 'Roars as it rises – save me, Edward! save!'
She cries: – Alas! the watchman on his way
Calls, and lets in – truth, terror, and the day!

Procrastination

Love will expire – the gay, the happy dream
Will turn to scorn, indiff'rence, or esteem:
Some favour'd pairs, in this exchange, are blest,
Nor sigh for raptures in a state of rest;
Others, ill match'd, with minds unpair'd, repent
At once the deed, and know no more content;
From joy to anguish they, in haste, decline,
And, with their fondness, their esteem resign;
More luckless still their fate, who are the prey
10 Of long-protracted hope and dull delay:
'Mid plans of bliss the heavy hours pass on,
Till love is wither'd, and till joy is gone.

This gentle flame two youthful hearts possess'd,
The sweet disturber of unenvied rest:
The prudent *Dinah* was the maid beloved,
And the kind *Rupert* was the swain approved:
A wealthy Aunt her gentle niece sustain'd,
He, with a father, at his desk remain'd;
The youthful couple, to their vows sincere,
20 Thus loved expectant; year succeeding year,
With pleasant views and hopes, but not a prospect near.
Rupert some comfort in his station saw,
But the poor virgin lived in dread and awe;
Upon her anxious looks the widow smiled,
And bade her wait, 'for she was yet a child.'
She for her neighbour had a due respect,
Nor would his son encourage or reject;
And thus the pair, with expectations vain,
Beheld the seasons change and change again:
30 Meantime the nymph her tender tales perused,
Where cruel aunts impatient girls refused:
While hers, though teasing, boasted to be kind,
And she, resenting, to be all resign'd.

The dame was sick, and when the youth applied
For her consent, she groan'd, and cough'd and cried,
Talk'd of departing, and again her breath
Drew hard, and cough'd and talk'd again of death:
'Here you may live, my Dinah! here the boy
'And you together my estate enjoy:'
40   Thus to the lovers was her mind express'd,
Till they forbore to urge the fond request.

Servant, and nurse, and comforter, and friend,
Dinah had still some duty to attend;
But yet their walk, when Rupert's evening call
Obtain'd an hour, made sweet amends for all;
So long they now each other's thoughts had known,
That nothing seem'd exclusively their own:
But with the common wish, the mutual fear,
They now had travell'd to their thirtieth year.

50   At length a prospect open'd – but alas!
Long time must yet, before the union, pass:
Rupert was call'd, in other clime, t' increase
Another's wealth, and toil for future peace.
Loth were the lovers; but the aunt declared
'T was fortune's call, and they must be prepared:
'You now are young, and for this brief delay,
'And Dinah's care, what I bequeath will pay;
'All will be yours; nay, love, suppress that sigh;
'The kind must suffer, and the best must die:'
60   Then came the cough, and strong the signs it gave
Of holding long contention with the grave.

The lovers parted with a gloomy view,
And little comfort, but that both were true;
He for uncertain duties doom'd to steer,
While hers remain'd too certain and severe.

Letters arrived, and Rupert fairly told
'His cares were many, and his hopes were cold:

'The view more clouded, that was never fair,
'And love alone preserved him from despair:'
70   In other letters brighter hopes he drew,
'His friends were kind and he believed them true.'

When the sage widow Dinah's grief descried,
She wonder'd much why one so happy sigh'd:
Then bade her see how her poor aunt sustain'd
The ills of life, nor murmur'd nor complain'd.
To vary pleasures, from the lady's chest
Were drawn the pearly string and tabby vest;
Beads, jewels, laces, all their value shown,
With the kind notice – 'They will be your own.'

80   This hope, these comforts, cherish'd day by day,
To Dinah's bosom made a gradual way;
Till love of treasure had as large a part,
As love of Rupert, in the virgin's heart.
Whether it be that tender passions fail,
From their own nature, while the strong prevail:
Or whether av'rice, like the poison-tree,
Kills all beside it, and alone will be;
Whatever cause prevail'd, the pleasure grew
In Dinah's soul, – she loved the hoards to view;
90   With lively joy those comforts she survey'd,
And love grew languid in the careful maid.

Now the grave niece partook the widow's cares,
Look'd to the great, and ruled the small affairs:
Saw clean'd the plate, arranged the china-show,
And felt her passion for a shilling grow:
Th' indulgent aunt increased the maid's delight,
By placing tokens of her wealth in sight;
She loved the value of her bonds to tell,
And spake of stocks, and how they rose and fell.

100   This passion grew, and gain'd at length such sway,
That other passions shrank to make it way;

Romantic notions now the heart forsook,
She read but seldom, and she changed her book;
And for the verses she was wont to send,
Short was her prose, and she was Rupert's friend.
Seldom she wrote, and then the widow's cough,
And constant call, excused her breaking off;
Who, now oppress'd, no longer took the air,
But sate and dozed upon an easy chair.
110 The cautious doctor saw the case was clear,
But judged it best to have companions near;
They came, they reason'd, they prescribed, – at last,
Like honest men, they said their hopes were past;
Then came a priest – 't is comfort to reflect
When all is over, there was no neglect:
And all was over – By her husband's bones,
The widow rests beneath the sculptured stones,
That yet record their fondness and their fame,
While all they left, the virgin's care became;
120 Stock, bonds, and buildings; – it disturb'd her rest,
To think what load of troubles she possess'd:
Yet, if a trouble, she resolved to take
Th' important duty for the donor's sake;
She too was heiress to the widow's taste,
Her love of hoarding, and her dread of waste.

Sometimes the past would on her mind intrude,
And then a conflict full of care ensued;
The thoughts of Rupert on her mind would press,
His worth she knew, but doubted his success:
130 Of old she saw him heedless; what the boy
Forbore to save, the man would not enjoy;
Oft had he lost the chance that care would seize,
Willing to live, but more to live at ease:
Yet could she not a broken vow defend,
And Heav'n, perhaps, might yet enrich her friend.

Month after month was pass'd, and all were spent
In quiet comfort and in rich content:

Miseries there were, and woes the world around,
But these had not her pleasant dwelling found;
140   She knew that mothers grieved, and widows wept,
And she was sorry, said her prayers, and slept:
Thus pass'd the seasons, and to Dinah's board
Gave what the seasons to the rich afford;
For she indulged, nor was her heart so small,
That one strong passion should engross it all.

    A love of splendour now with av'rice strove,
And oft appear'd to be the stronger love:
A secret pleasure fill'd the Widow's breast,
When she reflected on the hoards possess'd;
150   But livelier joy inspired th' ambitious Maid,
When she the purchase of those hoards display'd:
In small but splendid room she loved to see
That all was placed in view and harmony;
There, as with eager glance she look'd around,
She much delight in every object found;
While books devout were near her – to destroy,
Should it arise, an overflow of joy.

    Within that fair apartment guests might see
The comforts cull'd for wealth by vanity:
160   Around the room an Indian paper blazed,
With lively tint and figures boldly raised;
Silky and soft upon the floor below,
Th' elastic carpet rose with crimson glow;
All things around implied both cost and care,
What met the eye was elegant or rare:
Some curious trifles round the room were laid,
By hope presented to the wealthy Maid;
Within a costly case of varnish'd wood,
In level rows, her polish'd volumes stood;
170   Shown as a favour to a chosen few,
To prove what beauty for a book could do:
A silver urn with curious work was fraught;
A silver lamp from Grecian pattern wrought:

Above her head, all gorgeous to behold,
A time-piece stood on feet of burnish'd gold;
A stag's head crest adorn'd the pictured case,
Through the pure crystal shone the enamel'd face;
And while on brilliants moved the hands of steel,
It click'd from pray'r to pray'r, from meal to meal.

180   Here as the lady sat, a friendly pair
Stept in t' admire the view, and took their chair:
They then related how the young and gay
Were thoughtless wandering in the broad highway:
How tender damsels sail'd in tilted boats,
And laugh'd with wicked men in scarlet coats;
And how we live in such degen'rate times,
That men conceal their wants, and show their crimes;
While vicious deeds are screen'd by fashion's name,
And what was once our pride is now our shame.

190   Dinah was musing, as her friends discoursed,
When these last words a sudden entrance forced
Upon her mind, and what was once her pride
And now her shame, some painful views supplied;
Thoughts of the past within her bosom press'd,
And there a change was felt, and was confess'd:
While thus the Virgin strove with secret pain,
Her mind was wandering o'er the troubled main;
Still she was silent, nothing seem'd to see,
But sat and sigh'd in pensive reverie.

200   The friends prepared new subjects to begin,
When tall Susannah, maiden starch, stalk'd in;
Not in her ancient mode, sedate and slow,
As when she came, the mind she knew, to know;
Nor as, when list'ning half an hour before,
She twice or thrice tapp'd gently at the door;
But, all decorum cast in wrath aside,
'I think the devil's in the man!' she cried;

'A huge tall sailor, with his tawny cheek,
'And pitted face, will with my lady speak;
210 'He grinn'd an ugly smile, and said he knew,
'Please you, my lady, 't would be joy to you:
'What must I answer?' – Trembling and distress'd
Sank the pale Dinah by her fears oppress'd;
When thus alarm'd, and brooking no delay,
Swift to her room the stranger made his way.

'Revive, my love!' said he, 'I've done thee harm,
'Give me thy pardon,' and he look'd alarm:
Meantime the prudent Dinah had contrived
Her soul to question, and she then revived.

220 'See! my good friend,' and then she raised her head,
'The bloom of life, the strength of youth is fled;
'Living we die; to us the world is dead;
'We parted bless'd with health, and I am now
'Age-struck and feeble – so I find art thou;
'Thine eye is sunken, furrow'd is thy face,
'And downward look'st thou – so we run our race;
'And happier they whose race is nearly run,
'Their troubles over, and their duties done.'

'True, lady, true – we are not girl and boy,
230 'But time has left us something to enjoy.'

'What! thou hast learn'd my fortune? – yes, I live
'To feel how poor the comforts wealth can give:
'Thou too perhaps art wealthy; but our fate
'Still mocks our wishes, wealth is come too late.'

'To me nor late nor early; I am come
'Poor as I left thee to my native home:
'Nor yet,' said Rupert, 'will I grieve; 't is mine
'To share thy comforts, and the glory thine;
'For thou wilt gladly take that generous part
240 'That both exalts and gratifies the heart;

124

'While mine rejoices' – 'Heavens!' return'd the maid,
'This talk to one so wither'd and decay'd?
'No! all my care is now to fit my mind
'For other spousal, and to die resign'd:
'As friend and neighbour, I shall hope to see
'These noble views, this pious love in thee;
'That we together may the change await,
'Guides and spectators in each other's fate;
'When, fellow-pilgrims, we shall daily crave
250 'The mutual prayer that arms us for the grave.'

Half angry, half in doubt, the lover gazed
On the meek maiden, by her speech amazed;
'Dinah,' said he, 'dost thou respect thy vows?
'What spousal mean'st thou? – thou art Rupert's spouse;
'The chance is mine to take, and thine to give;
'But, trifling this, if we together live:
'Can I believe, that, after all the past,
'Our vows, our loves, thou wilt be false at last?
'Something thou hast – I know not what – in view;
260 'I find thee pious – let me find thee true.'

'Ah! cruel this; but do, my friend, depart;
'And to its feelings leave my wounded heart.'

'Nay, speak at once; and Dinah, let me know,
'Mean'st thou to take me, now I'm wreck'd, in tow?
'Be fair; nor longer keep me in the dark;
'Am I forsaken for a trimmer spark?
'Heaven's spouse thou art not; nor can I believe
'That God accepts her who will man deceive:
'True I am shatter'd, I have service seen,
270 'And service done, and have in trouble been;
'My cheek (it shames me not) has lost its red,
'And the brown buff is o'er my features spread;
'Perchance my speech is rude; for I among
'Th' untamed have been, in temper and in tongue;

'Have been trepann'd, have lived in toil and care,
'And wrought for wealth I was not doom'd to share;
'It touch'd me deeply, for I felt a pride
'In gaining riches for my destined bride:
'Speak then my fate; for these my sorrows past,
280 'Time lost, youth fled, hope wearied, and at last
'This doubt of thee – a childish thing to tell,
'But certain truth – my very throat they swell;
'They stop the breath, and but for shame could I
'Give way to weakness, and with passion cry;
'These are unmanly struggles, but I feel
'This hour must end them, and perhaps will heal.' –

Here Dinah sigh'd, as if afraid to speak –
And then repeated – 'They were frail and weak
'His soul she lov'd, and hoped he had the grace
290 'To fix his thoughts upon a better place.'

She ceased; – with steady glance, as if to see
The very root of this hypocrisy, –
He her small fingers moulded in his hard
And bronzed broad hand; then told her his regard,
His best respect were gone, but love had still
Hold in his heart, and govern'd yet the will –
Or he would curse her: – saying this, he threw
The hand in scorn away, and bade adieu
To every lingering hope, with every care in view.

300 Proud and indignant, suffering, sick, and poor,
He grieved unseen; and spoke of love no more –
Till all he felt in indignation died,
As hers had sunk in avarice and pride.

In health declining, as in mind distress'd,
To some in power his troubles he confess'd,
And shares a parish-gift; – at prayers he sees
The pious Dinah dropp'd upon her knees;

Thence as she walks the street with stately air
As chance directs, oft meet the parted pair;
310 When he, with thickset coat of badge-man's blue,
Moves near her shaded silk of changeful hue;
When his thin locks of grey approach her braid,
A costly purchase made in Beauty's aid;
When his frank air, and his unstudied pace,
Are seen with her soft manner, air, and grace,
And his plain artless look with her sharp meaning face;
It might some wonder in a stranger move,
How these together could have talk'd of love.

Behold them now! – see there a tradesman stands,
320 And humbly hearkens to some fresh commands;
He moves to speak, she interrupts him – 'Stay,'
Her air expresses – 'Hark! to what I say:'
Ten paces off, poor Rupert on a seat
Has taken refuge from the noon-day heat,
His eyes on her intent, as if to find
What were the movements of that subtle mind:
How still! – how earnest is he! – it appears
His thoughts are wand'ring through his earlier years;
Through years of fruitless labour, to the day
330 When all his earthly prospects died away:
'Had I,' he thinks, 'been wealthier of the two,
'Would she have found me so unkind, untrue?
'Or knows not man when poor, what man when rich will
    do?
'Yes, yes! I feel that I had faithful proved,
'And should have soothed and raised her, bless'd and
    loved.'

But Dinah moves – she had observed before,
The pensive Rupert at an humble door:
Some thoughts of pity raised by his distress,
Some feeling touch of ancient tenderness;
340 Religion, duty urged the maid to speak,
In terms of kindness to a man so weak:

But pride forbad, and to return would prove
She felt the shame of his neglected love;
Nor wrapp'd in silence could she pass, afraid
Each eye should see her, and each heart upbraid;
One way remain'd – the way the Levite took,
Who without mercy could on misery look;
(A way perceived by craft, approved by pride),
She cross'd and pass'd him on the other side.

The Frank Courtship

Grave *Jonas Kindred*, Sybil Kindred's sire,
Was six feet high, and look'd six inches higher;
Erect, morose, determined, solemn, slow,
Who knew the man, could never cease to know;
His faithful spouse, when Jonas was not by,
Had a firm presence and a steady eye;
But with her husband dropp'd her look and tone,
And Jonas ruled unquestion'd and alone.

He read, and oft would quote the sacred words,
10 .How pious husbands of their wives were lords;
Sarah call'd Abraham Lord! and who could be,
So Jonas thought, a greater man than he?
Himself he view'd with undisguised respect,
And never pardon'd freedom or neglect.

They had one daughter, and this favourite child
Had oft the father of his spleen beguiled;
Soothed by attention from her early years,
She gain'd all wishes by her smiles or tears:
But *Sybil* then was in that playful time,
20 When contradiction is not held a crime;
When parents yield their children idle praise
For faults corrected in their after days.

Peace in the sober house of Jonas dwelt,
Where each his duty and his station felt:
Yet not that peace some favour'd mortals find,
In equal views and harmony of mind;
Not the soft peace that blesses those who love,
Where all with one consent in union move;
But it was that which one superior will
30 Commands, by making all inferiors still;
Who bids all murmurs, all objections cease,
And with imperious voice announces – Peace!

They were, to wit, a remnant of that crew,
Who, as their foes maintain, their Sovereign slew;
An independent race, precise, correct,
Who ever married in the kindred sect:
No son or daughter of their order wed
A friend to England's king who lost his head;
Cromwell was still their Saint, and when they met,
40 They mourn'd that Saints were not our rulers yet.

Fix'd were their habits; they arose betimes,
Then pray'd their hour, and sang their party-rhymes:
Their meals were plenteous, regular and plain;
The trade of Jonas brought him constant gain;
Vendor of hops and malt, of coals and corn –
And, like his father, he was merchant born:
Neat was their house; each table, chair, and stool,
Stood in its place, or moving moved by rule;
No lively print or picture graced the room;
50 A plain brown paper lent its decent gloom;
But here the eye, in glancing round, survey'd
A small recess that seem'd for china made;
Such pleasing pictures seem'd this pencill'd ware,
That few would search for nobler objects there –
Yet, turn'd by chosen friends, and there appear'd
His stern, strong features, whom they all revered;
For there in lofty air was seen to stand
The bold Protector of the conquer'd land;

Drawn in that look with which he wept and swore,
60 Turn'd out the Members, and made fast the door,
Ridding the House of every knave and drone,
Forced, though it grieved his soul, to rule alone.
The stern still smile each friend approving gave,
Then turn'd the view, and all again were grave.

There stood a clock, though small the owner's need,
For habit told when all things should proceed;
Few their amusements, but when friends appear'd,
They with the world's distress their spirits cheer'd;
The nation's guilt, that would not long endure
70 The reign of men so modest and so pure:
Their town was large, and seldom pass'd a day
But some had fail'd, and others gone astray;
Clerks had absconded, wives eloped, girls flown
To Gretna-Green, or sons rebellious grown;
Quarrels and fires arose; – and it was plain
The times were bad; the Saints had ceased to reign!
A few yet lived, to languish and to mourn
For good old manners never to return.

Jonas had sisters, and of these was one
80 Who lost a husband and an only son:
Twelve months her sables she in sorrow wore,
And mourn'd so long that she could mourn no more.
Distant from Jonas, and from all her race,
She now resided in a lively place;
There, by the sect unseen, at whist she play'd,
Nor was of churchmen or their church afraid:
If much of this the graver brother heard,
He something censured, but he little fear'd;
He knew her rich and frugal; for the rest,
90 He felt no care, or, if he felt, suppress'd:
Nor for companion when she ask'd her Niece,
Had he suspicions that disturb'd his peace;

Frugal and rich, these virtues as a charm
Preserved the thoughtful man from all alarm;
An infant yet, she soon would home return,
Nor stay the manners of the world to learn;
Meantime his boys would all his care engross,
And be his comforts if he felt the loss.

The sprightly *Sybil*, pleased and unconfined,
100 Felt the pure pleasure of the op'ning mind:
All here was gay and cheerful – all at home
Unvaried quiet and unruffled gloom:
There were no changes, and amusements few; –
Here, all was varied, wonderful, and new;
There were plain meals, plain dresses, and grave looks –
Here, gay companions and amusing books;
And the young Beauty soon began to taste
The light vocations of the scene she graced.

A man of business feels it as a crime
110 On calls domestic to consume his time;
Yet this grave man had not so cold a heart,
But with his daughter he was grieved to part:
And he demanded that in every year
The Aunt and Niece should at his house appear.

'Yes! we must go, my child, and by our dress
'A grave conformity of mind express;
'Must sing at meeting, and from cards refrain,
'The more t' enjoy when we return again.'

Thus spake the Aunt, and the discerning child
120 Was pleased to learn how fathers are beguiled.
Her artful part the young dissembler took,
And from the matron caught th' approving look:
When thrice the friends had met, excuse was sent
For more delay, and Jonas was content;
Till a tall maiden by her sire was seen,
In all the bloom and beauty of sixteen;

He gazed admiring; – she, with visage prim,
Glanced an arch look of gravity on him;
For she was gay at heart, but wore disguise,
130 And stood a vestal in her father's eyes;
Pure, pensive, simple, sad; the damsel's heart,
When Jonas praised, reproved her for the part;
For Sybil, fond of pleasure, gay and light,
Had still a secret bias to the right;
Vain as she was – and flattery made her vain –
Her simulation gave her bosom pain.

Again return'd, the Matron and the Niece
Found the late quiet gave their joy increase;
The aunt infirm, no more her visits paid,
140 But still with her sojourn'd the favourite maid.
Letters were sent when franks could be procured,
And when they could not, silence was endured;
All were in health, and if they older grew,
It seem'd a fact that none among them knew;
The aunt and niece still led a pleasant life,
And quiet days had Jonas and his wife.

Near him a Widow dwelt of worthy fame,
Like his her manners, and her creed the same;
The wealth her husband left, her care retain'd
150 For one tall Youth, and widow she remain'd;
His love respectful all her care repaid,
Her wishes watch'd, and her commands obey'd.

Sober he was and grave from early youth,
Mindful of forms, but more intent on truth;
In a light drab he uniformly dress'd,
And look serene th' unruffled mind express'd;
A hat with ample verge his brows o'erspread,
And his brown locks curl'd graceful on his head;
Yet might observers in his speaking eye
160 Some observation, some acuteness spy;

The friendly thought it keen, the treacherous deem'd it
    sly;
    Yet not a crime could foe or friend detect,
His actions all were, like his speech, correct;
And they who jested on a mind so sound,
Upon his virtues must their laughter found;
Chaste, sober, solemn, and devout they named
Him who was thus, and not of *this* ashamed.

    Such were the virtues Jonas found in one
In whom he warmly wish'd to find a son:
170 Three years had pass'd since he had Sybil seen;
But she was doubtless what she once had been,
Lovely and mild, obedient and discreet;
The pair must love whenever they should meet;
Then ere the widow or her son should choose
Some happier maid, he would explain his views:
Now she, like him, was politic and shrewd,
With strong desire of lawful gain embued;
To all he said, she bow'd with much respect,
Pleased to comply, yet seeming to reject;
180 Cool and yet eager, each admired the strength
Of the opponent, and agreed at length:
As a drawn battle shows to each a force,
Powerful as his, he honours it of course;
So in these neighbours, each the power discern'd,
And gave the praise that was to each return'd.

    Jonas now ask'd his daughter – and the Aunt,
Though loth to lose her, was obliged to grant: –
But would not Sybil to the matron cling,
And fear to leave the shelter of her wing?
190 No! in the young there lives a love of change,
And to the easy, they prefer the strange!
Then, too, the joys she once pursued with zeal,
From whist and visits sprung, she ceased to feel:
When with the matrons Sybil first sat down,
To cut for partners and to stake her crown,

This to the youthful maid preferment seem'd,
Who thought what woman she was then esteem'd;
But in few years, when she perceived, indeed,
The real woman to the girl succeed,
No longer tricks and honours fill'd her mind,
But other feelings, not so well defined;
She then reluctant grew, and thought it hard,
To sit and ponder o'er an ugly card;
Rather the nut-tree shade the nymph preferr'd,
Pleased with the pensive gloom and evening bird;
Thither, from company retired, she took
The silent walk, or read the fav'rite book.

The father's letter, sudden, short, and kind,
Awaked her wonder, and disturb'd her mind;
She found new dreams upon her fancy seize,
Wild roving·thoughts and endless reveries:
The parting came; – and when the Aunt perceived
The tears of Sybil, and how much she grieved –
To love for her that tender grief she laid,
That various, soft, contending passions made.

When Sybil rested in her father's arms,
His pride exulted in a daughter's charms;
A maid accomplish'd he was pleased to find,
Nor seem'd the form more lovely than the mind:
But when the fit of pride and fondness fled,
He saw his judgment by his hopes misled;
High were the lady's spirits, far more free
Her mode of speaking than a maid's should be;
Too much, as Jonas thought, she seem'd to know,
And all her knowledge was disposed to show;
'Too gay her dress, like theirs who idly dote
'On a young coxcomb, or a coxcomb's coat;
'In foolish spirits when our friends appear.
'And vainly grave when not a man is near.'

230   Thus Jonas, adding to his sorrow blame,
       And terms disdainful to a Sister's name: –
       'The sinful wretch has by her arts defiled
       'The ductile spirit of my darling child.'

          'The maid is virtuous,' said the dame – Quoth he,
       'Let her give proof, by acting virtuously:
       'Is it in gaping when the Elders pray?
       'In reading nonsense half a summer's day?
       'In those mock forms that she delights to trace,
       'Or her loud laughs in Hezekiah's face?
240   'She – O Susanna! – to the world belongs;
       'She loves the follies of its idle throngs,
       'And reads soft tales of love, and sing's love's soft'ning
              songs.
       'But, as our friend is yet delay'd in town,
       'We must prepare her till the Youth comes down:
       'You shall advise the maiden; I will threat;
       'Her fears and hopes may yield us comfort yet.'

          Now the grave father took the lass aside,
       Demanding sternly, 'Wilt thou be a bride?'
       She answer'd, calling up an air sedate,
250   'I have not vow'd against the holy state.'

          'No folly, Sybil,' said the parent; 'know
       'What to their parents virtuous maidens owe:
       'A worthy, wealthy youth, whom I approve,
       'Must thou prepare to honour and to love.
       'Formal to thee his air and dress may seem,
       'But the good youth is worthy of esteem:
       'Shouldst thou with rudeness treat him; of disdain
       'Should he with justice or of slight complain,
       'Or of one taunting speech give certain proof,
260   'Girl! I reject thee from my sober roof.'

          'My aunt,' said Sybil, 'will with pride protect
       'One whom a father can for this reject;

'Nor shall a formal, rigid, soul-less boy
'My manners alter, or my views destroy!'

.Jonas then lifted up his hands on high,
And, utt'ring something 'twixt a groan and sigh,
Left the determined maid, her doubtful mother by.

'Hear me,' she said; 'incline thy heart, my child,
'And fix thy fancy on a man so mild:
'Thy father, Sybil, never could be moved
'By one who loved him, or by one he loved,
'Union like ours is but a bargain made
'By slave and tyrant – he will be obey'd;
'Then calls the quiet, comfort – but thy Youth
'Is mild by nature, and as frank as truth.'

'But will he love?' said Sybil; 'I am told
'That these mild creatures are by nature cold.'

'Alas!' the matron answer'd, 'much I dread
'That dangerous love by which the young are led!
'That love is earthy; you the creature prize,
'And trust your feelings and believe your eyes:
'Can eyes and feelings inward worth descry?
'No! my fair daughter, on our choice rely!
'Your love, like that display'd upon the stage,
'Indulged is folly, and opposed is rage; –
'More prudent love our sober couples show,
'All that to mortal beings, mortals owe;
'All flesh is grass – before you give a heart,
'Remember, Sybil, that in death you part;
'And should your husband die before your love,
'What needless anguish must a widow prove!
'No! my fair child, let all such visions cease;
'Yield but esteem, and only try for peace.'

'I must be loved,' said Sybil; 'I must see
'The man in terrors who aspires to me;

'At my forbidding frown his heart must ache,
'His tongue must falter, and his frame must shake:
'And if I grant him at my feet to kneel,
'What trembling, fearful pleasure must he feel;
300 'Nay, such the raptures that my smiles inspire,
'That reason's self must for a time retire.'

'Alas! for good *Josiah*,' said the dame,
'These wicked thoughts would fill his soul with shame;
'He kneel and tremble at a thing of dust!
'He cannot, child:' – the Child replied, 'He must.'

They ceased: the matron left her with a frown;
So Jonas met her when the Youth came down:
'Behold,' said he, 'thy future spouse attends;
'Receive him, daughter, as the best of friends;
310 'Observe, respect him – humble be each word,
'That welcomes home thy husband and thy lord.'

Forewarn'd, thought Sybil, with a bitter smile,
I shall prepare my manner and my style.

Ere yet Josiah enter'd on his task,
The father met him – 'Deign to wear a mask
'A few dull days, Josiah, – but a few –
'It is our duty, and the sex's due;
'I wore it once, and every grateful wife
'Repays it with obedience through her life:
320 'Have no regard to Sybil's dress, have none
'To her pert language, to her flippant tone;
'Henceforward thou shalt rule unquestion'd and alone;
'And she thy pleasure in thy looks shall seek –
'How she shall dress, and whether she may speak.'

A sober smile return'd the Youth, and said,
'Can I cause fear, who am myself afraid?'

Sybil, meantime, sat thoughtful in her room,
And often wonder'd – 'Will the creature come?
'Nothing shall tempt, shall force me to bestow
'My hand upon him, – yet I wish to know.'

330

The door unclosed, and she beheld her sire
Lead in the Youth, then hasten to retire;
'Daughter, my friend – my daughter, friend' – he cried,
And gave a meaning look, and stepp'd aside:
That look contain'd a mingled threat and prayer,
'Do take him, child – offend him, if you dare.'

The couple gazed – were silent, and the maid
Look'd in his face, to make the man afraid;
The man, unmoved, upon the maiden cast

340

A steady view – so salutation pass'd:
But in this instant Sybil's eye had seen
The tall fair person, and the still staid mien;
The glow that temp'rance o'er the cheek had spread,
Where the soft down half veil'd the purest red;
And the serene deportment that proclaim'd
A heart unspotted, and a life unblamed:
But then with these she saw attire too plain,
The pale brown coat, though worn without a stain;
The formal air, and something of the pride

350

That indicates the wealth it seems to hide;
And looks that were not, she conceived, exempt
From a proud pity, or a sly contempt.

Josiah's eyes had their employment too,
Engaged and soften'd by so bright a view;
A fair and meaning face, an eye of fire,
That check'd the bold, and made the free retire:
But then with these he mark'd the studied dress
And lofty air, that scorn or pride express;
With that insidious look, that seem'd to hide

360

In an affected smile the scorn and pride;

And if his mind the virgin's meaning caught,
He saw a foe with treacherous purpose fraught –
Captive the heart to take, and to reject it, caught.

Silent they sat – thought Sybil, that he seeks
Something, no doubt; I wonder if he speaks:
Scarcely she wonder'd, when these accents fell
Slow in her ear – 'Fair maiden, art thou well?'
'Art thou physician?' she replied; 'my hand,
'My pulse, at least, shall be at thy command.'

370   She said – and saw, surprised, Josiah kneel,
And gave his lips the offer'd pulse to feel;
The rosy colour rising in her cheek,
Seem'd that surprise unmix'd with wrath to speak;
Then sternness she assumed, and – 'Doctor, tell,
'Thy words cannot alarm me – am I well?'

'Thou are,' said he; 'and yet thy dress so light,
'I do conceive, some danger must excite:'
'In whom?' said Sybil, with a look demure:
'In more,' said he, 'than I expect to cure; –
380   'I, in thy light luxuriant robe, behold
'Want and excess, abounding and yet cold;
'Here needed, there display'd, in many a wanton fold:
'Both health and beauty, learned authors show,
'From a just medium in our clothing flow.'

'Proceed, good doctor; if so great my need,
'What is thy fee? Good doctor! pray proceed.'

'Large is my fee, fair lady, but I take
'None till some progress in my cure I make:
'Thou hast disease, fair maiden; thou art vain;
390   'Within that face sit insult and disdain;
'Thou art enamour'd of thyself; my art
'Can see the naughty malice of thy heart:

139

'With a strong pleasure would thy bosom move,
'Were I to own thy power, and ask thy love;
'And such thy beauty, damsel, that I might,
'But for thy pride, feel danger in thy sight,
'And lose my present peace in dreams of vain delight.'

'And can thy patients,' said the nymph, 'endure
'Physic like this? and will it work a cure?'

400 'Such is my hope, fair damsel; thou, I find,
'Hast the true tokens of a noble mind;
'But the world wins thee, Sybil, and thy joys
'Are placed in trifles, fashions, follies, toys;
'Thou hast sought pleasure in the world around,
'That in thine own pure bosom should be found:
'Did all that world admire thee, praise and love,
'Could it the least of nature's pains remove?
'Could it for errors, follies, sins atone,
'Or give thee comfort, thoughtful and alone?
410 'It has, believe me, maid, no power to charm
'Thy soul from sorrow, or thy flesh from harm:
'Turn then, fair creature, from a world of sin,
'And seek the jewel happiness within.'

'Speak'st thou at meeting?' said the nymph; 'thy speech
'Is that of mortal very prone to teach;
'But wouldst thou, doctor, from the patient learn
'Thine own disease? – The cure is thy concern.'

'Yea, with good will.' – 'Then know 't is thy complaint,
'That, for a sinner, thou'rt too much a saint;
420 'Hast too much show of the sedate and pure,
'And without cause art formal and demure:
'This makes a man unsocial, unpolite;
'Odious when wrong, and insolent if right.
'Thou may'st be good, but why should goodness be
'Wrapt in a garb of such formality?

140

'Thy person well might please a damsel's eye,
'In decent habit with a scarlet dye;
'But, jest apart – what virtue canst thou trace
'In that broad brim that hides thy sober face?
430   'Does that long-skirted drab, that over-nice
'And formal clothing, prove a scorn of vice?
'Then for thine accent – what in sound can be
'So void of grace as dull monotony?
'Love has a thousand varied notes to move
'The human heart: – thou may'st not speak of love,
'Till thou hast cast thy formal ways aside,
'And those becoming youth and nature tried:
'Not till exterior freedom, spirit, ease,
'Prove it thy study and delight to please;
440   'Not till these follies meet thy just disdain,
'While yet thy virtues and thy worth remain.'

'This is severe! – Oh! maiden, wilt not thou
'Something for habits, manners, modes, allow?' –
'Yes! but allowing much, I much require,
'In my behalf, for manners, modes, attire!'

'True, lovely Sybil; and, this point agreed,
'Let me to those of greater weight proceed:
'Thy father!' – 'Nay,' she quickly interposed,
'Good doctor, here our conference is closed!'

450   Then left the Youth, who, lost in his retreat,
Pass'd the good matron on her garden-seat;
His looks were troubled, and his air, once mild
And calm, was hurried: – 'My audacious child!'
Exclaim'd the dame, 'I read what she has done
'In thy displeasure – Ah! the thoughtless one:
'But yet, Josiah, to my stern good man
'Speak of the maid as mildly as you can:
'Can you not seem to woo a little while
'The daughter's will, the father to beguile?
460   'So that his wrath in time may wear away;
'Will you preserve our peace, Josiah? say.'

'Yes! my good neighbour,' said the gentle youth,
'Rely securely on my care and truth;
'And should thy comfort with my efforts cease;
'And only then, – perpetual is thy peace.'

The dame had doubts: she well his virtues knew,
His deeds were friendly, and his words were true;
'But to address this vixen is a task
'He is ashamed to take, and I to ask.'
470 Soon as the father from Josiah learn'd
What pass'd with Sybil, he the truth discern'd.
'He loves,' the man exclaim'd, 'he loves, 't is plain,
'The thoughtless girl, and shall he love in vain?
'She may be stubborn, but she shall be tried,
'Born as she is of wilfulness and pride.'

With anger fraught, but willing to persuade,
The wrathful father met the smiling maid:
'Sybil,' said he, 'I long, and yet I dread
'To know thy conduct – hath Josiah fled?
480 'And, grieved and fretted by thy scornful air,
'For his lost peace, betaken him to prayer?
'Couldst thou his pure and modest mind distress,
'By vile remarks upon his speech, address,
'Attire, and voice?' – 'All this I must confess.' –
'Unhappy child! what labour will it cost
'To win him back!' – 'I do not think him lost.' –
'Courts he then, (trifler!) insult and disdain?' –
'No: but from these he courts me to refrain.' –
'Then hear me, Sybil – should Josiah leave
490 'Thy father's house?' – 'My father's child would grieve:'
'That is of grace, and if he come again
'To speak of love?' – 'I might from grief refrain.'
'Then wilt thou, daughter, our design embrace?' –
'Can I resist it, if it be of grace?' –
'Dear child! in three plains words thy mind express –
'Wilt thou have this good youth?' – 'Dear father! yes.'

The Widow's Tale

To Farmer *Moss*, in Langar Vale came down,
His only Daughter, from her school in town;
A tender, timid maid! who knew not how
To pass a pig-sty, or to face a cow:
Smiling she came, with petty talents graced,
A fair complexion, and a slender waist.

Used to spare meals, disposed in manner pure,
Her father's kitchen she could ill endure:
Where by the steaming beef he hungry sat,
And laid at once a pound upon his plate;
Hot from the field, her eager brother seized
An equal part, and hunger's rage appeased;
The air surcharged with moisture, flagg'd around,
And the offended damsel sigh'd and frown'd;
The swelling fat in lumps conglomerate laid,
And fancy's sickness seized the loathing maid:
But when the men beside their station took,
The maidens with them, and with these the cook:
When one huge wooden bowl before them stood,
Fill'd with huge balls of farinaceous food;
With bacon, mass saline, where never lean
Beneath the brown and bristly rind was seen;
When from a single horn the party drew
Their copious draughts of heavy ale and new;
When the coarse cloth she saw, with many a stain,
Soil'd by rude hinds who cut and came again –
She could not breathe; but with a heavy sigh,
Rein'd the fair neck, and shut th' offended eye;
She minced the sanguine flesh in frustums fine,
And wonder'd much to see the creatures dine:
When she resolved her father's heart to move,
If hearts of farmers were alive to love.

She now entreated by herself to sit
In the small parlour, if papa thought fit,

And there to dine, to read, to work alone: –
'No!' said the Farmer, in an angry tone;
'These are your school-taught airs; your mother's pride
'Would send you there; but I am now your guide. –
'Arise betimes, our early meal prepare,
40 'And, this despatch'd, let business be your care;
'Look to the lasses, let there not be one
'Who lacks attention, till her tasks be done;
'In every household work your portion take,
'And what you make not, see that others make:
'At leisure times attend the wheel, and see
'The whit'ning web be sprinkled on the lea;
'When thus employ'd, should our young neighbour view,
'A useful lass, – you may have more to do.'

Dreadful were these commands; but worse than these
50 The parting hint – a Farmer could not please:
'T is true she had without abhorrence seen
Young *Harry Carr*, when he was smart and clean;
But, to be married – be a farmer's wife, –
A slave! a drudge! – she could not, for her life.

With swimming eyes the fretful nymph withdrew,
And, deeply sighing, to her chamber flew;
There on her knees, to Heaven she grieving pray'd
For change of prospect to a tortured maid.

Harry, a youth whose late-departed sire
60 Had left him all industrious men require,
Saw the pale Beauty, – and her shape and air
Engaged him much, and yet he must forbear:
'For my small farm, what can the damsel do?'
He said, – then stopp'd to take another view:
'Pity so sweet a lass will nothing learn
'Of household cares, – for what can beauty earn
'By those small arts which they at school attain,
That keep them useless, and yet make them vain?'

This luckless Damsel look'd the village round,
70 To find a friend, and one was quickly found:
A pensive Widow, – whose mild air and dress
Pleased the sad nymph, who wish'd her soul's distress
To one so seeming kind, confiding, to confess.

'What Lady that?' the anxious lass inquired,
Who then beheld the one she most admired:
'Here,' said the Brother, 'are no ladies seen –
'That is a widow dwelling on the Green;
'A dainty dame, who can but barely live
'On her poor pittance, yet contrives to give;
80 'She happier days has known, but seems at ease,
'And you may call her Lady, if you please:
'But if you wish, good sister, to improve,
'You shall see twenty better worth your love.'

These *Nancy* met; but, spite of all they taught,
This useless Widow was the one she sought:
The father growl'd; but said he knew no harm
In such connexion that could give alarm;
'And if we thwart the trifler in her course,
' 'T is odds against us she will take a worse.'

90 Then met the friends; the Widow heard the sigh
That ask'd at once compassion and reply: –
'Would you, my child, converse with one so poor,
'Yours were the kindness – yonder is my door:
'And, save the time that we in public pray,
'From that poor cottage I but rarely stray.'

There went the Nymph, and made her strong com-
　　plaints,
Painting her wo as injured feeling paints.

'Oh, dearest friend! do think how one must feel,
'Shock'd all day long, and sicken'd every meal;
100 'Could you behold our kitchen (and to you
'A scene so shocking must indeed be new),

'A mind like yours, with true refinement graced,
'Would let no vulgar scenes pollute your taste:
'And yet, in truth, from such a polish'd mind
'All base ideas must resistance find,
'And sordid pictures from the fancy pass,
'As the breath startles from the polish'd glass.

'Here you enjoy a sweet romantic scene,
'Without so pleasant, and within so clean;
110 'These twining jess'mines, what delicious gloom
'And soothing fragrance yield they to the room!
'What lovely garden! there you oft retire,
'And tales of woe and tenderness admire:
'In that neat case your books, in order placed,
'Soothe the full soul, and charm the cultured taste;
'And thus, while all about you wears a charm,
'How must you scorn the Farmer and the Farm!'

The Widow smiled, and 'Know you not,' said she,
'How much these farmers scorn or pity me;
120 'Who see what you admire, and laugh at all they see?
'True, their opinion alters not my fate,
'By falsely judging of an humble state:
'This garden you with such delight behold,
'Tempts not a feeble dame who dreads the cold;
'These plants, which please so well your livelier sense,
'To mine but little of their sweets dispense:
'Books soon are painful to my failing sight,
'And oftener read from duty than delight;
'(Yet let me own, that I can sometimes find
130 'Both joy and duty in the act combined;)
'But view me rightly, you will see no more
'Than a poor female, willing to be poor;
'Happy indeed, but not in books nor flowers,
'Not in fair dreams, indulged in earlier hours,
'Of never-tasted joys; – such visions shun,
'My youthful friend, nor scorn the Farmer's Son.'

146

'Nay,' said the Damsel, nothing pleased to see
A Friend's advice could like a Father's be,
'Bless'd in your cottage, you must surely smile
140 'At those who live in our detested style:
'To my Lucinda's sympathizing heart
'Could I my prospects and my griefs impart,
'She would console me; but I dare not show
'Ills that would wound her tender soul to know:
'And I confess, it shocks my pride to tell
'The secrets of the prison where I dwell;
'For that dear maiden would be shock'd to feel
'The secrets I should shudder to reveal;
'When told her friend was by a parent ask'd,
150 ' "Fed you the swine?" – Good heaven! how I am task'd! –
'What! can you smile? Ah! smile not at the grief
'That woos your pity and demands relief.'

'Trifles, my love: you take a false alarm;
'Think, I beseech you, better of the Farm:
'Duties in every state demand your care,
'And light are those that will require it there.
'Fix on the Youth a favouring eye, and these,
'To him pertaining, or as his, will please.'

'What words,' the Lass replied, 'offend my ear!
160 'Try you my patience? Can you be sincere?
'And am I told a willing hand to give
'To a rude farmer, and with rustics live?
'Far other fate was yours; – some gentle youth
'Admired your beauty, and avow'd his truth;
'The power of love prevail'd, and freely both
'Gave the fond heart, and pledged the binding oath;
'And then the rival's plot, the parent's power,
'And jealous fears, drew on the happy hour:
'Ah! let not memory lose the blissful view,
170 'But fairly show what Love has done for you.'

'Agreed, my daughter; what my heart has known
'Of Love's strange power, shall be with frankness shown:
'But let me warn you, that experience finds
'Few of the names that lively hope designs.'

'Mysterious all,' said Nancy; 'you, I know,
'Have suffer'd much; now deign the grief to show; –
'I am your friend, and so prepare my heart
'In all your sorrows to receive a part."

The Widow answer'd: 'I had once, like you,
180 'Such thoughts of love; no dream is more untrue;
'You judge it fated, and decreed to dwell
'In youthful hearts, which nothing can expel,
'A passion doom'd to reign, and irresistible.
'The struggling mind, when once subdued, in vain
'Rejects the fury or defies the pain;
'The strongest reason fails the flame t' allay,
'And resolution droops and faints away:
'Hence, when the destined lovers meet, they prove
'At once the force of this all-powerful love;
190 'Each from that period feels the mutual smart,
'Nor seeks to cure it – heart is changed for heart;
'Nor is there peace till they delighted stand,
'And, at the altar – hand is join'd to hand.

'Alas! my child, there are who, dreaming so,
'Waste their fresh youth, and waking feel the woe;
'There is no spirit sent the heart to move
'With such prevailing and alarming love;
'Passion to reason will submit – or why
'Should wealthy maids the poorest swains deny?
200 'Or how could classes and degrees create
'The slightest bar to such resistless fate?
'Yet high and low, you see, forbear to mix;
'No beggars' eyes the heart of kings transfix;
'And who but am'rous peers or nobles sigh,
'When titled beauties pass triumphant by?

'For reason wakes, proud wishes to reprove;
'You cannot hope, and therefore dare not love:
'All would be safe, did we at first inquire –
' "Does reason sanction what our hearts desire?"
210 'But quitting precept, let example show
'What joys from Love uncheck'd by prudence flow.

'A Youth my father in his office placed,
'Of humble fortune, but with sense and taste;
'But he was thin and pale, had downcast looks;
'He studied much, and pored upon his books:
'Confused he was when seen, and, when he saw
'Me or my sisters, would in haste withdraw;
'And had this youth departed with the year,
'His loss had cost us neither sigh nor tear.

220 'But with my father still the Youth remain'd,
'And more reward and kinder notice gain'd:
'He often, reading, to the garden stray'd,
'Where I by books or musing was delay'd;
'This to discourse in summer evenings led,
'Of these same evenings, or of what we read:
'On such occasions we were much alone;
'But, save the look, the manner, and the tone,
'(These might have meaning,) all that we discuss'd
'We could with pleasure to a parent trust.

230 'At length 't was friendship – and my Friend and I
'Said we were happy, and began to sigh:
'My sisters first, and then my father, found
'That we were wandering o'er enchanted ground;
'But he had troubles in his own affairs,
'And would not bear addition to his cares:
'With pity moved, yet angry, "Child," said he,
' "Will you embrace contempt and beggary?
' "Can you endure to see each other cursed
' "By want, of every human woe the worst?
240 ' "Warring for ever with distress, in dread
' "Either of begging or of wanting bread;

149

' "While poverty, with unrelenting force,
' "Will your own offspring from your love divorce;
' "They, through your folly, must be doom'd to pine,
' "And you deplore your passion, or resign;
' "For if it die, what good will then remain?
' "And if it live, it doubles every pain." '

'But you were true,' exclaim'd the Lass, 'and fled
'The tyrant's power who fill'd your soul with dread?'
250 'But,' said the smiling Friend, 'he fill'd my mouth with
bread:
'And in what other place that bread to gain
'We long consider'd, and we sought in vain:
'This was my twentieth year, – at thirty-five
'Our hope was fainter, yet our love alive;
'So many years in anxious doubt had pass'd.'
'Then,' said the Damsel, 'you were bless'd at last?'
A smile again adorn'd the Widow's face,
But soon a starting tear usurp'd its place.

'Slow pass'd the heavy years, and each had more
260 'Pains and vexations than the years before.
'My father fail'd; his family was rent,
'And to new states his grieving daughters sent;
'Each to more thriving kindred found a way,
'Guests without welcome – servants without pay;
'Our parting hour was grievous; still I feel
'The sad, sweet converse at our final meal;
'Our father then reveal'd his former fears,
'Cause of his sternness, and then join'd our tears:
'Kindly he strove our feelings to repress,
270 'But died, and left us heirs to his distress.
'The rich, as humble friends, my sisters chose;
'I with a wealthy widow sought repose;
'Who with a chilling frown her friend received,
'Bade me rejoice, and wonder'd that I grieved:
'In vain my anxious lover tried his skill
'To rise in life, he was dependent still;

'We met in grief, nor can I paint the fears
'Of these unhappy, troubled, trying years:
'Our dying hopes and stronger fears between,
280 'We felt no season peaceful or serene;
'Our fleeting joys, like meteors in the night,
'Shone on our gloom with inauspicious light;
'And then domestic sorrows, till the mind,
'Worn with distresses, to despair inclined;
'Add too the ill that from the passion flows,
'When its contemptuous frown the world bestows,
'The peevish spirit caused by long delay,
'When, being gloomy, we contemn the gay,
'When, being wretched, we inclined to hate
290 'And censure others in a happier state;
'Yet loving still, and still compell'd to move
'In the sad labyrinth of lingering love:
'While you, exempt from want, despair, alarm,
'May wed – oh! take the Farmer and the Farm.'

'Nay,' said the Nymph, 'joy smiled on you at last?'
'Smiled for a moment,' she replied, 'and pass'd:
'My lover still the same dull means pursued,
'Assistant call'd, but kept in servitude;
'His spirits wearied in the prime of life,
300 'By fears and wishes in eternal strife;
'At length he urged impatient – "Now consent;
' "Wish thee united, Fortune may relent."
'I paused, consenting; but a Friend arose,
'Pleased a fair view, though distant, to disclose;
'From the rough ocean we beheld a gleam
'Of joy, as transient as the joys we dream;
'By lying hopes deceived, my friend retired,
'And sail'd – was wounded – reach'd us – and expired!
'You shall behold his grave; and when I die,
310 'There – but 't is folly – I request to lie.'

'Thus,' said the Lass, 'to joy you bade adieu!
'But how a widow? – that cannot be true:

151

'Or was it force, in some unhappy hour,
'That placed you, grieving, in a tyrant's power?'

    'Force, my young friend, when forty years are fled,
'Is what a woman seldom has to dread;
'She needs no brazen locks nor guarding walls,
'And seldom comes a lover though she calls:
'Yet, moved by fancy, one approved my face,
320 'Though time and tears had wrought it much disgrace.

    'The man I married was sedate and meek,
'And spoke of love as men in earnest speak;
'Poor as I was, he ceaseless sought, for years,
'A heart in sorrow and a face in tears:
'That heart I gave not; and 't was long before
'I gave attention, and then nothing more;
'But in my breast some grateful feeling rose,
'For one whose love so sad a subject chose;
'Till long delaying, fearing to repent,
330 'But grateful still, I gave a cold assent.

    'Thus we were wed; no fault had I to find,
'And he but one; my heart could not be kind:
'Alas! of every early hope bereft,
'There was no fondness in my bosom left;
'So had I told him, but had told in vain,
'He lived but to indulge me and complain:
'His was this cottage; he inclosed this ground,
'And planted all these blooming shrubs around;
'He to my room these curious trifles brought,
340 'And with assiduous love my pleasure sought;
'He lived to please me, and I ofttimes strove,
'Smiling, to thank his unrequited love:
' "Teach me," he cried, "that pensive mind to ease,
' "For all my pleasure is the hope to please."

    'Serene, though heavy, were the days we spent,
'Yet kind each word, and gen'rous each intent;

'But his dejection lessen'd every day,
'And to a placid kindness died away:
'In tranquil ease we pass'd our latter years,
350   'By griefs untroubled, unassail'd by fears.

   'Let not romantic views your bosom sway,
'Yield to your duties, and their call obey:
'Fly not a Youth, frank, honest and sincere;
'Observe his merits, and his passion hear!
' 'T is true, no hero, but a farmer sues –
'Slow in his speech, but worthy in his views;
'With him you cannot that affliction prove,
'That rends the bosom of the poor, in love:
'Health, comfort, competence, and cheerful days,
360   'Your friends' approval, and your father's praise,
'Will crown the deed, and you escape *their* fate
'Who plan so wildly, and are wise too late.'

The Damsel heard; at first th' advice was strange,
Yet wrought a happy, nay, a speedy change:
'I have no care,' she said, when next they met,
'But one may wonder, he is silent yet;
'He looks around him with his usual stare,
'And utters nothing – not that I shall care.'

   This pettish humour pleased th' experienced Friend –
370   None need despair, whose silence can offend;
'Should I,' resumed the thoughtful Lass, 'consent
'To hear the man, the man may now repent:
'Think you my sighs shall call him from the plough,
'Or give one hint, that "You may woo me now?" '

   'Persist, my love,' replied the Friend, 'and gain
'A parent's praise, *that* cannot be in vain.'

   The father saw the change, but not the cause,
And gave the alter'd maid his fond applause;
The coarser manners she in part removed,
380   In part endured, improving and improved;

She spoke of household works, she rose betimes,
And said neglect and indolence were crimes;
The various duties of their life she weigh'd,
And strict attention to her dairy paid;
The names of servants now familiar grew,
And fair Lucinda's from her mind withdrew;
As prudent travellers for their ease assume
Their modes and language to whose lands they come:
So to the Farmer this fair Lass inclined,
Gave to the business of the Farm her mind;
To useful arts she turn'd her hand and eye;
And by her manners told him – 'You may try.'

Th' observing Lover more attention paid,
With growing pleasure, to the alter'd maid;
He fear'd to lose her, and began to see
That a slim beauty might a helpmate be:
'Twixt hope and fear he now the lass address'd,
And in his Sunday robe his love express'd:
She felt no chilling dread, no thrilling joy,
Nor was too quickly kind, too slowly coy;
But still she lent an unreluctant ear
To all the rural business of the year;
Till love's strong hopes endured no more delay,
And Harry ask'd, and Nancy named the day.

'A happy change! my Boy,' the father cried:
'How lost your sister all her school-day pride?'
The Youth replied, 'It is the Widow's deed;
'The cure is perfect, and was wrought with speed.' –
'And comes there, Boy, this benefit of books,
'Of that smart dress, and of those dainty looks?
'We must be kind – some offerings from the Farm
'To the White Cot will speak our feelings warm;
'Will show that people, when they know the fact,
'Where they have judged severely, can retract.
'Oft have I smiled, when I beheld her pass
'With cautious step, as if she hurt the grass;

390

400

410

'Where, if a snail's retreat she chanced to storm,
'She look'd as begging pardon of the worm;
'And what, said I, still laughing at the view,
'Have these weak creatures in the world to do?
'But some are made for action, some to speak;
'And, while she looks so pitiful and meek,
'Her words are weighty, though her nerves are weak.'

Soon told the village-bells the rite was done,
That join'd the school-bred Miss and Farmer's Son;
Her former habits some slight scandal raised,
But real worth was soon perceived and praised;
She, her neat taste imparted to the Farm,
And he, th' improving skill and vigorous arm.

Arabella

Of a fair town where Doctor *Rack* was guide,
His only daughter was the boast and pride;
Wise *Arabella*, yet not wise alone,
She like a bright and polish'd brilliant shone;
Her father own'd her for his prop and stay,
Able to guide, yet willing to obey;
Pleased with her learning while discourse could please,
And with her love in languor and disease:
To every mother were her virtues known,
And to their daughters as a pattern shown;
Who in her youth had all that age requires,
And with her prudence, all that youth admires:
These odious praises made the damsels try
Not to obtain such merits, but deny;
For, whatsoever wise mammas might say,
To guide a daughter, this was not the way;
From such applause disdain and anger rise,
And envy lives where emulation dies.

In all his strength, contends the noble horse,
20   With one who just precedes him on the course;
But when the rival flies too far before,
His spirit fails, and he attempts no more.

This reasoning Maid, above her sex's dread,
Had dared to read, and dared to say she read;
Not the last novel, not the new-born play;
Not the mere trash and scandal of the day;
But (though her young companions felt the shock)
She studied Berkeley, Bacon, Hobbes, and Locke:
Her mind within the maze of history dwelt,
30   And of the moral Muse and beauty felt;
The merits of the Roman page she knew,
And could converse with More and Montagu:
Thus she became the wonder of the town,
From that she reap'd, to that she gave renown,
And strangers coming, all were taught t' admire
The learned lady, and the lofty spire.

Thus Fame in public fix'd the Maid where all
Might throw their darts, and see the idol fall:
A hundred arrows came with vengeance keen,
40   From tongues envenom'd, and from arms unseen;
A thousand eyes were fix'd upon the place,
That, if she fell, she might not fly disgrace:
But malice vainly throws the poison'd dart,
Unless our frailty shows the peccant part;
And Arabella still preserved her name
Untouch'd, and shone with undisputed fame;
Her very notice some respect would cause,
And her esteem was honour and applause.

Men she avoided; not in childish fear,
50   As if she thought some savage foe was near;
Not as a prude, who hides that man should seek,
Or who by silence hints that they should speak;
But with discretion all the sex she view'd,
Ere yet engaged pursuing or pursued;

156

Ere love had made her to his vices blind,
Or hid the favourite's failings from her mind.

Thus was the picture of the man portray'd,
By merit destined for so rare a maid;
At whose request she might exchange her state,
Or still be happy in a virgin's fate: –
He must be one with manners like her own,
His life unquestion'd, his opinions known;
His stainless virtue must all tests endure,
His honour spotless, and his bosom pure;
She no allowance made for sex or times,
Of lax opinion – crimes were ever crimes;
No wretch forsaken must his frailty curse,
No spurious offspring drain his private purse;
He at all times his passions must command,
And yet possess – or be refused her hand.

All this without reserve the maiden told,
And some began to weigh the rector's gold;
To ask what sum a prudent man might gain,
Who had such store of virtues to maintain?

A Doctor *Campbell*, north of Tweed, came forth,
Declared his passion, and proclaim'd his worth;
Not unapproved, for he had much to say
On every cause, and in a pleasant way;
Not all his trust was in a pliant tongue,
His form was good, and ruddy he, and young:
But though the doctor was a man of parts,
He read not deeply male or female hearts;
But judged that all whom he esteem'd as wise
Must think alike, though some assumed disguise;
That every reasoning Bramin, Christian, Jew,
Of all religions took their liberal view;
And of her own, no doubt, this learned Maid
Denied the substance, and the forms obey'd:
And thus persuaded, he his thoughts express'd
Of her opinions, and his own profess'd:

60

70

80

90

157

'All states demand this aid, the vulgar need
'Their priests and pray'rs, their sermons and their creed;
'And those of stronger minds should never speak
'(In his opinion) what might hurt the weak:
'A man may smile, but still he should attend
'His hour at church, and be the Church's friend,
'What there he thinks conceal, and what he hears com-
    mend.'

Frank was the speech, but heard with high disdain,
Nor had the doctor leave to speak again;
100 A man who own'd, nay gloried in deceit,
'He might despise her, but he should not cheat.'

The Vicar *Holmes* appear'd: he heard it said
That ancient men best pleased the prudent maid;
And true it was her ancient friends she loved,
Servants when old she favour'd and approved,
Age in her pious parents she revered,
And neighbours were by length of days endear'd;
But, if her husband too must ancient be,
The good old vicar found it was not he.

110 On Captain *Bligh* her mind in balance hung –
Though valiant, modest; and reserved, though young:
Against these merits must defects be set –
Though poor, imprudent; and though proud, in debt:
In vain the captain close attention paid;
She found him wanting, whom she fairly weigh'd.

Then came a youth, and all their friends agreed,
That *Edward Huntly* was the man indeed;
Respectful duty he had paid awhile,
Then ask'd her hand, and had a gracious smile:
120 A lover now declared, he led the fair
To woods and fields, to visits, and to pray'r;
Then whisper'd softly – 'Will you name the day?'
She softly whisper'd – 'If you love me, stay:'

'Oh! try me not beyond my strength,' he cried:
'Oh! be not weak,' the prudent Maid replied;
'But by some trial your affection prove –
'Respect and not impatience argues love:
'And love no more is by impatience known,
'Than ocean's depth is by its tempests shown:
130 'He whom a weak and fond impatience sways,
'But for himself with all his fervour prays,
'And not the maid he woos, but his own will obeys;
'And will she love the being who prefers,
'With so much ardour, his desire to hers?'

Young Edward grieved, but let not grief be seen;
He knew obedience pleased his fancy's queen:
Awhile he waited, and then cried – 'Behold!
'The year advancing, be no longer cold!'
For she had promised – 'Let the flowers appear,
140 'And I will pass with thee the smiling year:'
Then pressing grew the youth; the more he press'd,
The less inclined the maid to his request:
'Let June arrive.' – Alas! when April came,
It brought a stranger, and the stranger, shame;
Nor could the Lover from his house persuade
A stubborn lass whom he had mournful made;
Angry and weak, by thoughtless vengeance moved,
She told her story to the Fair beloved;
In strongest words th' unwelcome truth was shown,
150 To blight his prospects, careless of her own.

Our heroine grieved, but had too firm a heart
For him to soften, when she swore to part;
In vain his seeming penitence and pray'r,
His vows, his tears; she left him in despair:
His mother fondly laid her grief aside,
And to the reason of the nymph applied –

'It well becomes thee, lady, to appear,
'But not to be, in very truth, severe;

'Although the crime be odious in thy sight,
160 'That daring sex is taught such things to slight:
'His heart is thine, although it once was frail;
'Think of his grief, and let his love prevail!' –

'Plead thou no more,' the lofty lass return'd;
'Forgiving woman is deceived and spurn'd:
'Say that the crime is common – shall I take
'A common man my wedded lord to make?
'See! a weak woman by his arts betray'd,
'An infant born his father to upbraid;
'Shall I forgive his vileness, take his name,
170 'Sanction his error, and partake his shame?
'No! this assent would kindred frailty prove,
'A love for him would be a vicious love:
'Can a chaste maiden secret counsel hold
'With one whose crime by every mouth is told?
'Forbid it spirit, prudence, virtuous pride;
'He must despise me, were he not denied:
'The way from vice the erring mind to win
'Is with presuming sinners to begin,
'And show, by scorning them, a just contempt for sin.'

180 The youth repulsed, to one more mild convey'd
His heart, and smiled on the remorseless maid;
The maid, remorseless in her pride, the while
Despised the insult, and return'd the smile.

First to admire, to praise her, and defend,
Was (now in years advanced) a virgin-friend:
Much she preferr'd, she cried, the single state,
'It was her choice' – it surely was her fate;
And much it pleased her in the train to view
A maiden vot'ress, wise and lovely too.

190 Time to the yielding mind his change imparts,
He varies notions, and he alters hearts;
'Tis right, 'tis just to feel contempt for vice,
But he that shows it may be over-nice:

There are who feel, when young, the false sublime,
And proudly love to show disdain for crime;
To whom the future will new thoughts supply,
The pride will soften, and the scorn will die;
Nay, where they still the vice itself condemn,
They bear the vicious, and consort with them:
200 Young Captain Grove, when one had changed his side,
Despised the venal turn-coat, and defied;
Old Colonel Grove now shakes him by the hand,
Though he who bribes may still his vote command:
Why would not Ellen to Belinda speak,
When she had flown to London for a week,
And then return'd, to every friend's surprise,
With twice the spirit, and with half the size?
She spoke not then – but, after years had flown,
A better friend had Ellen never known:
210 Was it the lady her mistake had seen?
Or had she also such a journey been?
No: 'twas the gradual change in human hearts,
That time, in commerce with the world, imparts;
That on the roughest temper throws disguise,
And steals from virtue her asperities.
The young and ardent, who with glowing zeal
Felt wrath for trifles, and were proud to feel,
Now find those trifles all the mind engage,
To soothe dull hours, and cheat the cares of age;
220 As young Zelinda, in her quaker-dress,
Disdain'd each varying fashion's vile excess,
And now her friends on old Zelinda gaze,
Pleased in rich silks and orient gems to blaze:
Changes like these 'tis folly to condemn,
So virtue yields not, nor is changed with them.

Let us proceed: – Twelve brilliant years were past,
Yet each with less of glory than the last:
Whether these years to this fair virgin gave
A softer mind – effect they often have;

230 Whether the virgin-state was not so bless'd
As that good maiden in her zeal profess'd;
Or whether lovers falling from her train,
Gave greater price to those she could retain,
Is all unknown; – but Arabella now
Was kindly listening to a Merchant's vow;
Who offer'd terms so fair, against his love
To strive was folly, so she never strove. –
Man in his earlier days we often find
With a too easy and unguarded mind;
240 But by increasing years and prudence taught,
He grows reserved, and locks up every thought:
Not thus the maiden, for in blooming youth
She hides her thought and guards the tender truth:
This, when no longer young, no more she hides,
But frankly in the favour'd swain confides:
Man, stubborn man, is like the growing tree,
That, longer standing, still will harder be;
And like its fruit, the virgin, first austere,
Then kindly softening with the ripening year.

250 Now was the lover urgent, and the kind
And yielding lady to his suit inclined:
'A little time, my friend, is just, is right;
'We must be decent in our neighbours' sight:'
Still she allow'd him of his hopes to speak,
And in compassion took off week by week;
Till few remain'd, when, wearied with delay,
She kindly meant to take off day by day.

That female Friend who gave our virgin praise
For flying man and all his treacherous ways,
260 Now heard with mingled anger, shame, and fear,
Of one accepted, and a wedding near;
But she resolved again with friendly zeal
To make the maid her scorn of wedlock feel;
For she was grieved to find her work undone,
And like a sister mourn'd the failing nun.

Why are these gentle maidens prone to make
Their sister-doves the tempting world forsake?
Why all their triumph when a maid disdains
The tyrant sex, and scorns to wear its chains?
270 Is it pure joy to see a sister flown
From the false pleasures they themselves have known?
Or do they, as the call-birds in the cage,
Try, in pure envy, others to engage?
And therefore paint their native woods and groves,
As scenes of dangerous joys and naughty loves?

Strong was the maiden's hope; her friend was proud,
And had her notions to the world avow'd;
And, could she find the Merchant weak and frail,
With power to prove it, then she must prevail:
280 For she aloud would publish his disgrace,
And save his victim from a man so base.

When all inquiries had been duly made,
Came the kind Friend her burthen to unlade –
'Alas! my dear! not all our care and art
'Can thread the maze of man's deceitful heart:
'Look not surprise – nor let resentment swell
'Those lovely features, all will yet be well;
'And thou, from love's and man's deceptions free,
'Wilt dwell in virgin-state, and walk to Heaven with me.'

290 The Maiden frown'd, and then conceived 'that wives
'Could walk as well, and lead as holy lives,
'As angry prudes who scorn'd the marriage-chain,
'Or luckless maids, who sought it still in vain.'

The Friend was vex'd – she paused: at length she cried,
'Know your own danger, then your lot decide;
'That taitor Beswell, while he seeks your hand,
'Has, I affirm, a wanton at command;
'A slave, a creature from a foreign place,
The nurse and mother of a spurious race;

'Brown ugly bastards – (Heaven the word forgive,
'And the deed punish!) – in his cottage live;
'To town if business calls him, there he stays
'In sinful pleasures wasting countless days;
'Nor doubt the facts, for I can witness call
'For every crime, and prove them one and all.'

Here ceased th' informer; Arabella's look
Was like a school-boy's puzzled by his book;
Intent she cast her eyes upon the floor,
Paused – then replied –
                                          'I wish to know no more:
'I question not your motive, zeal, or love,
'But must decline such dubious points to prove –
'All is not true, I judge, for who can guess
'Those deeds of darkness men with care suppress?
'He brought a slave perhaps to England's coast,
'And made her free; it is our country's boast!
'And she perchance too grateful – good and ill
'Were sown at first, and grow together still;
'The colour'd infants on the village green,
'What are they more than we have often seen?
'Children half-clothed who round their village stray,
'In sun or rain, now starved, now beaten, they
'Will the dark colour of their fate betray:
'Let us in Christian love for all account,
'And then behold to what such tales amount.'

'His heart is evil,' said th' impatient Friend.
'My duty bids me try that heart to mend,'
Replied the virgin – 'We may be too nice
'And lose a soul in our contempt of vice;
'If false the charge, I then shall show regard
'For a good man, and be his just reward:
'And what for virtue can I better do
'Than to reclaim him, if the charge be true?'

She spoke, nor more her holy work delay'd;
'Twas time to lend an erring mortal aid:

'The noblest way,' she judged, 'a soul to win,
'Was with an act of kindness to begin,
'To make the sinner sure, and then t' attack the sin.'

The Lover's Journey

It is the Soul that sees; the outward eyes
Present the object, but the Mind descries;
And thence delight, disgust, or cool indiff'rence rise:
When minds are joyful, then we look around,
And what is seen is all on fairy ground;
Again they sicken, and on every view
Cast their own dull and melancholy hue;
Or, if absorb'd by their peculiar cares,
The vacant eye on viewless matter glares,
10 Our feelings still upon our views attend,
And their own natures to the objects lend;
Sorrow and joy are in their influence sure,
Long as the passion reigns th' effects endure;
But Love in minds his various changes makes,
And clothes each object with the change he takes;
His light and shade on every view he throws,
And on each object, what he feels, bestows.

Fair was the morning, and the month was June,
When rose a Lover; – love awakens soon:
20 Brief his repose, yet much he dreamt the while
Of that day's meeting, and his *Laura's* smile;
Fancy and love that name assign'd to her,
Call'd Susan in the parish-register;
And he no more was John – his Laura gave
The name *Orlando* to her faithful slave.

Bright shone the glory of the rising day,
When the fond traveller took his favourite way;

He mounted gaily, felt his bosom light,
And all he saw was pleasing in his sight.

30   'Ye hours of expectation, quickly fly,
          'And brings on hours of blest reality;
          'When I shall Laura see, beside her stand,
          'Hear her sweet voice, and press her yielded hand.'

          First o'er a barren heath beside the coast
          Orlando rode, and joy began to boast.

          'This neat low gorse,' said he, 'with golden bloom,
          'Delights each sense, is beauty, is perfume;
          'And this gay ling, with all its purple flowers,
          'A man at leisure might admire for hours;
40   'This green-fringed cup-moss has a scarlet tip,
          'That yields to nothing but my Laura's lip;
          'And then how fine this herbage! men may say
          'A heath is barren; nothing is so gay:
          'Barren or bare to call such charming scene
          'Argues a mind poss'd by care and spleen.'

          Onward he went, and fiercer grew the heat,
          Dust rose in clouds before the horse's feet;
          For now he pass'd through lanes of burning sand,
          Bounds to thin crops or yet uncultured land;
50   Where the dark poppy flourish'd on the dry
          And sterile soil, and mock'd the thin-set rye.

          'How lovely this!' the rapt Orlando said;
          'With what delight is labouring man repaid!
          'The very lane has sweets that all admire,
          'The rambling suckling, and the vigorous brier;
          'See! wholesome wormwood grows beside the way,
          'Where dew-press'd yet the dog-rose bends the spray;
          'Fresh herbs the fields, fair shrubs the banks adorn,
          'And snow-white bloom falls flaky from the thorn;

60   'No fostering hand they need, no sheltering wall,
     'They spring uncultured, and they bloom for all.'

     The Lover rode as hasty lovers ride,
     And reach'd a common pasture wild and wide;
     Small black-legg'd sheep devour with hunger keen
     The meagre herbage, fleshless, lank, and lean:
     Such o'er thy level turf, Newmarket! stray,
     And there, with other *black-legs*, find their prey:
     He saw some scatter'd hovels; turf was piled
     In square brown stacks; a prospect bleak and wild!
70   A mill, indeed, was in the centre found,
     With short sear herbage withering all around;
     A smith's black shed opposed a wright's long shop,
     And join'd an inn where humble travellers stop.

     'Ay, this is Nature,' said the gentle 'Squire;
     'This ease, peace, pleasure – who would not admire?
     'With what delight these sturdy children play,
     'And joyful rustics at the close of day;
     'Sport follows labour, on this even space
     'Will soon commence the wrestling and the race;
80   'Then will the village-maidens leave their home,
     'And to the dance with buoyant spirits come;
     'No affectation in their looks is seen,
     'Nor know they what disguise or flattery mean;
     'Nor aught to move an envious pang they see,
     'Easy their service, and their love is free;
     'Hence early springs that love, it long endures,
     'And life's first comfort, while they live, ensures:
     'They the low roof and rustic comforts prize,
     'Nor cast on prouder mansions envying eyes:
90   'Sometimes the news at yonder town they hear,
     'And learn what busier mortals feel and fear;
     'Secure themselves, although by tales amazed,
     'Of towns bombarded and of cities razed;
     'As if they doubted, in their still retreat,
     'The very news that makes their quiet sweet,

'And their days happy – happier only knows
'He on whom Laura her regard bestows.'

On rode Orlando, counting all the while
The miles he pass'd, and every coming mile;
100   Like all attracted things, he quicker flies,
The place approaching where th' attraction lies;
When next appear'd a *dam* – so call the place –
Where lies a road confined in narrow space;
A work of labour, for on either side
Is level fen, a prospect wild and wide,
With dikes on either hand by ocean's self supplied:
Far on the right the distant sea is seen,
And salt the springs that feed the marsh between;
Beneath an ancient bridge, the straiten'd flood
110   Rolls through its sloping banks of slimy mud;
Near it a sunken boat resists the tide,
That frets and hurries to th' opposing side;
The rushes sharp, that on the borders grow,
Bend their brown flow'rets to the stream below,
Impure in all its course, in all its progress slow:
Here a grave Flora scarcely deigns to bloom,
Nor wears a rosy blush, nor sheds perfume;
The few full flowers that o'er the place are spread
Partake the nature of their fenny bed;
120   Here on its wiry stem, in rigid bloom,
Grows the salt lavender that lacks perfume;
Here the dwarf sallows creep, the septfoil harsh,
And the soft slimy mallow of the marsh;
Low on the ear the distant billows sound,
And just in view appears their stony bound;
No hedge nor tree conceals the glowing sun,
Birds, save a wat'ry tribe, the district shun,
Nor chirp among the reeds where bitter waters run.

'Various as beauteous, Nature, is thy face,'
130   Exclaim'd Orlando: 'all that grows has grace;
'All are appropriate – bog, and marsh, and fen,
'Are only poor to undiscerning men;

'Here may the nice and curious eye explore
'How Nature's hand adorns the rushy moor;
'Here the rare moss in secret shade is found,
'Here the sweet myrtle of the shaking ground;
'Beauties are these that from the view retire,
'But well repay th' attention they require;
'For these, my Laura will her home forsake,
140   'And all the pleasures they afford partake.'

      Again, the country was enclosed, a wide
And sandy road has banks on either side;
Where, lo! a hollow on the left appear'd,
And there a Gipsy-tribe their tent had rear'd;
'Twas open spread, to catch the morning sun,
And they had now their early meal begun,
When two brown boys just left their grassy seat,
The early Trav'ller with their prayers to greet:
While yet Orlando held his pence in hand,
150   He saw their sister on her duty stand;
Some twelve years old, demure, affected, sly,
Prepared the force of early powers to try;
Sudden a look of languor he descries,
And well-feign'd apprehension in her eyes;
Train'd but yet savage, in her speaking face
He mark'd the features of her vagrant race;
When a light laugh and roguish leer express'd
The vice implanted in her youthful breast:
Forth from the tent her elder brother came,
160   Who seem'd offended, yet forbore to blame
The young designer, but could only trace
The looks of pity in the Trav'ller's face:
Within, the Father, who from fences nigh
Had brought the fuel for the fire's supply,
Watch'd now the feeble blaze, and stood dejected by:
On ragged rug, just borrow'd from the bed,
And by the hand of coarse indulgence fed,
In dirty patchwork negligently dress'd,

Reclined the Wife, an infant at her breast;
170   In her wild face some touch of grace remain'd,
Of vigour palsied and of beauty stain'd;
Her blood-shot eyes on her unheeding mate
Were wrathful turn'd, and seem'd her wants to state,
Cursing his tardy aid – her Mother there
With gipsy-state engross'd the only chair;
Solemn and dull her look; with such she stands,
And reads the milk-maid's fortune in her hands,
Tracing the lines of life; assumed through years,
Each feature now the steady falsehood wears:
180   With hard and savage eye she views the food,
And grudging pinches their intruding brood;
Last in the group, the worn-out Grandsire sits
Neglected, lost, and living but by fits;
Useless, despised, his worthless labours done,
And half protected by the vicious Son,
Who half supports him; he with heavy glance
Views the young ruffians who around him dance;
And, by the sadness in his face, appears
To trace the progress of their future years:
190   Through what strange course of misery, vice, deceit,
Must wildly wander each unpractised cheat!
What shame and grief, what punishment and pain,
Sport of fierce passions, must each child sustain –
Ere they like him approach their latter end,
Without a hope, a comfort, or a friend!
But this Orlando felt not; 'Rogues,' said he,
'Doubtless they are, but merry rogues they be;
'They wander round the land, and be it true,
'They break the laws – then let the laws pursue
200   'The wanton idlers; for the life they live,
'Acquit I cannot, but I can forgive.'
This said, a portion from his purse was thrown,
And every heart seem'd happy like his own.

    He hurried forth, for now the town was nigh –
'The happiest man of mortal men am I.'

Thou art! but change in every state is near,
(So while the wretched hope, the blest may fear);
'Say, where is Laura?' – 'That her words must show,'
A lass replied; 'read this, and thou shalt know!'

210   'What, gone!' – her friend insisted – forced to go: –
'Is vex'd, was teased, could not refuse her! – No?'
'But you can follow;' 'Yes:' 'The miles are few,
'The way is pleasant; will you come? – Adieu!
'Thy Laura!' 'No! I feel I must resign
'The pleasing hope, thou hadst been here, if mine:
'A lady was it? – Was no brother there?
'But why should I afflict me, if there were?'
'The way is pleasant:' 'What to me the way?
'I cannot reach her till the close of day.
220   'My dumb companion! is it thus we speed?
'Not I from grief nor thou from toil art freed;
'Still art thou doom'd to travel and to pine,
'For my vexation – What a fate is mine!

'Gone to a friend, she tells me; – I commend
'Her purpose: means she to a female friend?
'By Heaven, I wish she suffer'd half the pain
'Of hope protracted through the day in vain:
'Shall I persist to see th' ungrateful maid?
'Yes, I will see her, slight her, and upbraid:
230   'What! in the very hour? She knew the time,
'And doubtless chose it to increase her crime.'

Forth rode Orlando by a river's side,
Inland and winding, smooth, and full and wide,
That roll'd majestic on, in one soft-flowing tide;
The bottom gravel, flow'ry were the banks,
Tall willows, waving in their broken ranks;
The road, now near, now distant, winding led
By lovely meadows which the waters fed;
He pass'd the way-side inn, the village spire,
240   Nor stopp'd to gaze, to question, or admire;

On either side the rural mansions stood,
With hedge-row trees, and hills high-crown'd with wood.
And many a devious stream that reach'd the nobler flood.

'I hate these scenes,' Orlando angry cried,
'And these proud farmers! yes, I hate their pride:
'See! that sleek fellow, how he strides along,
'Strong as an ox, and ignorant as strong;
'Can yon close crops a single eye detain
'But he who counts the profits of the grain?
250 'And these vile beans with deleterious smell,
'Where is their beauty? can a mortal tell?
'These deep fat meadows I detest; it shocks
'One's feelings there to see the grazing ox; –
'For slaughter fatted, as a lady's smile
'Rejoices man, and means his death the while.
'Lo! now the sons of labour! every day
'Employ'd in toil, and vex'd in every way;
'Theirs is but mirth assumed, and they conceal,
'In their affected joys, the ills they feel:
260 'I hate these long green lanes; there's nothing seen
'In this vile country but eternal green;
'Woods! waters! meadows! Will they never end?
' 'Tis a vile prospect: – Gone to see a friend!' –

Still on he rode! a mansion fair and tall
Rose on his view – the pride of Loddon Hall:
Spread o'er the park he saw the grazing steer,
The full-fed steed, and herds of bounding deer:
On a clear stream the vivid sunbeams play'd,
Through noble elms, and on the surface made
270 That moving picture, checker'd light and shade;
Th' attended children, there indulged to stray,
Enjoy'd and gave new beauty to the day;
Whose happy parents from their room were seen
Pleased with the sportive idlers on the green.

'Well!' said Orlando, 'and for one so bless'd,
'A thousand reasoning wretches are distress'd;
'Nay, these so seeming glad, are grieving like the rest:
'Man is a cheat – and all but strive to hide
'Their inward misery by their outward pride.
280 'What do yon lofty gates and walls contain,
'But fruitless means to soothe unconquer'd pain?
'The parents read each infant daughter's smile,
'Formed to seduce, encouraged to beguile;
'They view the boys unconscious of their fate,
'Sure to be tempted, sure to take the bait;
'These will be Lauras, sad Orlandos these –
'There's guilt and grief in all one hears and sees.'

Our Trav'ller, lab'ring up a hill, look'd down
Upon a lively, busy, pleasant town;
290 All he beheld were there alert, alive,
The busiest bees that ever stock'd a hive:
A pair were married, and the bells aloud
Proclaim'd their joy, and joyful seem'd the crowd;
And now proceeding on his way, he spied,
Bound by strong ties, the bridegroom and the bride;
Each by some friends attended, near they drew,
And spleen beheld them with prophetic view.

'Married! nay, mad!' Orlando cried in scorn;
'Another wretch on this unlucky morn:
300 'What are this foolish mirth, these idle joys?
'Attempts to stifle doubt and fear by noise:
'To me these robes, expressive of delight,
'Foreshow distress, and only grief excite;
'And for these cheerful friends, will they behold
'Their wailing brood in sickness, want, and cold;
'And his proud look, and her soft languid air
'Will – but I spare you – go, unhappy pair!'

And now approaching to the Journey's end,
His anger fails, his thoughts to kindness tend,
310 He less offended feels, and rather fears t' offend:

Now gently rising, hope contends with doubt,
And casts a sunshine on the views without;
And still reviving joy and lingering gloom
Alternate empire o'er his soul assume;
Till, long perplex'd, he now began to find
The softer thoughts engross the settling mind:
He saw the mansion, and should quickly see
His Laura's self – and angry could he be?
No! the resentment melted all away –
320 'For this my grief a single smile will pay,'
Our trav'ller cried; – 'And why should it offend,
'That one so good should have a pressing friend?
'Grieve not, my heart! to find a favourite guest
'Thy pride and boast – ye selfish sorrows, rest;
'She will be kind, and I again be blest.'

While gentler passions thus his bosom sway'd,
He reach'd the mansion, and he saw the maid;
'My Laura!' – 'My Orlando! – this is kind;
'In truth I came persuaded, not inclined:
330 'Our friends' amusement let us now pursue,
'And I to-morrow will return with you.'

Like man entranced, the happy Lover stood –
'As Laura wills, for she is kind and good;
'Ever the truest, gentlest, fairest, blest –
'As Laura wills, I see her and am blest.'

Home went the Lovers through that busy place,
By Loddon Hall, the country's pride and grace;
By the rich meadows where the oxen fed,
Through the green vale that form'd the river's bed;
340 And by unnumber'd cottages and farms,
That have for musing minds unnumber'd charms;
And how affected by the view of these
Was then Orlando – did they pain or please?

Nor pain nor pleasure could they yield – and why?
The mind was fill'd, was happy, and the eye
Roved o'er the fleeting views, that but appear'd to die.

Alone Orlando on the morrow paced
The well-known road; the gipsy-tent he traced;
The dam high-raised, the reedy dykes between,
350 The scatter'd hovels on the barren green,
The burning sand, the fields of thin-set rye,
Mock'd by the useless Flora, blooming by;
And last the heath with all its various bloom,
And the close lanes that led the trav'ller home.

Then could these scenes the former joys renew?
Or was there now dejection in the view? –
Nor one or other would they yield – and why?
The mind was absent, and the vacant eye
Wander'd o'er viewless scenes, that but appear'd to die.

The Confidant

Anna was young and lovely – in her eye
The glance of beauty, in her cheek the dye;
Her shape was slender, and her features small,
But graceful, easy, unaffected all:
The liveliest tints her youthful face disclosed;
There beauty sparkled, and there health reposed;
For the pure blood that flush'd that rosy cheek
Spoke what the heart forbade the tongue to speak;
And told the feelings of that heart as well,
10 Nay, with more candour than the tongue could tell:
Though this fair lass had with the wealthy dwelt,
Yet like the damsel of the cot she felt;
And, at the distant hint or dark surmise,
The blood into the mantling cheek would rise.

Now Anna's station frequent terrors wrought
In one whose looks were with such meaning fraught:
For on a Lady, as an humble friend,
It was her painful office to attend.

Her duties here were of the usual kind –
20   And some the body harass'd, some the mind:
Billets she wrote, and tender stories read,
To make the Lady sleepy in her bed;
She play'd at whist, but with inferior skill,
And heard the summons as a call to drill;
Music was ever pleasant till she play'd
At a request that no request convey'd;
The Lady's tales with anxious looks she heard,
For she must witness what her Friend averr'd;
The Lady's taste she must in all approve,
30   Hate whom she hated, whom she loved must love;
These, with the various duties of her place,
With care she studied, and perform'd with grace;
She veil'd her troubles in a mask of ease,
And show'd her pleasure was a power to please.

Such were the Damsel's duties; she was poor –
Above a servant, but with service more:
Men on her face with careless freedom gazed,
Nor thought how painful was the glow they raised;
A wealthy few to gain her favour tried,
40   But not the favour of a grateful bride;
They spoke their purpose with an easy air,
That shamed and frighten'd the dependent fair;
Past time she view'd, the passing time to cheat,
But nothing found to make the present sweet;
With pensive soul she read life's future page,
And saw dependent, poor, repining age.

But who shall dare t' assert what *years* may bring,
When wonders from the passing *hour* may spring;
There dwelt a Yeoman in the place, whose mind

50 Was gentle, generous, cultivated, kind;
For thirty years he labour'd; fortune then
Placed the mild rustic with superior men:
A richer Stafford who had lived to save,
What he had treasured to the poorer gave;
Who with a sober mind that treasure view'd,
And the slight studies of his youth renew'd:
He not profoundly, but discreetly read,
And a fair mind with useful culture fed;
Then thought of marriage – 'But the great,' said he,
60 'I shall not suit, nor will the meaner me:'
Anna he saw, admired her modest air;
He thought her virtuous, and he knew her fair;
Love raised his pity for her humble state,
And prompted wishes for her happier fate;
No pride in money would his feelings wound,
Nor vulgar manners hurt him and confound:
He then the Lady at the Hall address'd,
Sought her consent, and his regard express'd;
Yet if some cause his earnest wish denied,
70 He begg'd to know it, and he bow'd and sigh'd.

The Lady own'd that she was loth to part,
But praised the damsel for her gentle heart,
Her pleasing person, and her blooming health;
But ended thus, 'Her virtue is her wealth.'

'Then is she rich!' he cried, with lively air;
'But whence, so please you, came a lass so fair?'

'A placeman's child was Anna, one who died
'And left a widow by afflictions tried;
'She to support her infant daughter strove,
80 'But early left the object of her love;
'Her youth, her beauty, and her orphan-state
'Gave a kind countess interest in her fate;
'With her she dwelt, and still might dwelling be,
'When the earl's folly caused the lass to flee;

177

'A second friend was she compell'd to shun,
'By the rude offers of an uncheck'd son;
'I found her then, and with a mother's love
'Regard the gentle girl whom you approve;
'Yet, e'en with me protection is not peace,
90   'Nor man's designs, nor beauty's trials cease:
'Like sordid boys by costly fruit they feel,
'They will not purchase, but they try to steal.'

Now this good Lady, like a witness true,
Told but the truth, and all the truth she knew;
And 'tis our duty and our pain to show
Truth this good lady had not means to know.
Yes, there was lock'd within the damsel's breast
A fact important to be now confess'd;
Gently, my muse, th' afflicting tale relate,
100   And have some feeling for a sister's fate.

Where Anna dwelt, a conquering hero came, –
An Irish captain, *Sedley* was his name;
And he too had that same prevailing art,
That gave soft wishes to the virgin's heart:
In years they differ'd; he had thirty seen
When this young beauty counted just fifteen;
But still they were a lovely lively pair,
And trod on earth as if they trod on air.

On love, delightful theme! the captain dwelt
110   With force still growing with the hopes he felt;
But with some caution and reluctance told,
He had a father crafty, harsh, and old;
Who, as possessing much, would much expect,
Or both, for ever, from his love reject:
Why then offence to one so powerful give,
Who (for their comfort) had not long to live?

With this poor prospect the deluded maid,
In words confiding, was indeed betray'd;

And, soon as terrors in her bosom rose,
120   The hero fled; they hinder'd his repose.
Deprived of him, she to a parent's breast
Her secret trusted, and her pains impress'd;
Let her to town (so prudence urged) repair,
To shun disgrace, at least to hide it there;
But ere she went, the luckless damsel pray'd
A chosen friend might lend her timely aid:
'Yes! my soul's sister, my Eliza, come,
'Hear her last sigh, and ease thy Anna's doom:'
' 'Tis a fool's wish,' the angry father cried,
130   But, lost in troubles of his own, complied;
And dear Eliza to her friend was sent,
T' indulge that wish, and be her punishment:
The time arrived, and brought a tenfold dread;
The time was past, and all the terror fled;
The infant died; the face resumed each charm,
And reason now brought trouble and alarm:

Should her Eliza – no! she was too just,
'Too good and kind – but ah! too young to trust.
Anna return'd, her former place resumed,
140   And faded beauty with new grace re-bloom'd;
And if some whispers of the past were heard,
They died innoxious, as no cause appear'd;
But other cares on Anna's bosom press'd,
She saw her father gloomy and distress'd;
He died o'erwhelm'd with debt, and soon was shed
The filial sorrow o'er a mother dead:
She sought Eliza's arms – that faithful friend was wed;
Then was compassion by the countess shown,
And all th' adventures of her life are known.

150   And now, beyond her hopes – no longer tried
By slavish awe – she lived a Yeoman's bride;
Then bless'd her lot, and with a grateful mind
Was careful, cheerful, vigilant, and kind:

179

The gentle husband felt supreme delight,
Bless'd by her joy, and happy in her sight;
He saw with pride in every friend and guest
High admiration and regard express'd:
With greater pride, and with superior joy,
He look'd exulting on his first-born boy;
160 To her fond breast the wife her infant strain'd,
Some feelings utter'd, some were not explain'd;
And she enraptured with her treasure grew,
The sight familiar, but the pleasure new.

Yet there appear'd within that tranquil state
Some threat'ning prospect of uncertain fate;
Between the married when a secret lies,
It wakes suspicion from enforced disguise:
Still thought the Wife upon her absent friend,
With all that must upon her truth depend;
170 'There is no being in the world beside,
'Who can discover what that friend will hide;
'Who knew the fact, knew not my name or state,
'Who these can tell cannot the fact relate;
'But thou, Eliza, canst the whole impart,
'And all my safety is thy generous heart.'

Mix'd with these fears – but light and transient these –
Fled years of peace, prosperity, and ease;
So tranquil all, that scarce a gloomy day
For days of gloom unmix'd prepared the way:
180 One eve, the Wife, still happy in her state,
Sang gaily, thoughtless of approaching fate;
Then came a letter, that (received in dread
Not unobserved) she in confusion read;
The substance this – 'Her friend rejoiced to find
'That she had riches with a grateful mind;
'While poor Eliza had, from place to place,
'Been lured by hope to labour for disgrace;
'That every scheme her wandering husband tried,
'Pain'd while he lived, and perish'd when he died.'

190 She then of want in angry style complain'd,
Her child a burthen to her life remain'd,
Her kindred shunn'd her prayers, no friend her soul
  sustain'd.

'Yet why neglected? Dearest Anna knew
'Her worth once tried, her friendship ever true;
'She hoped, she trusted, though by wants oppress'd,
'To lock the treasured secret in her breast;
'Yet, vex'd by trouble, must apply to one,
'For kindness due to her for kindness done.'

In Anna's mind was tumult, in her face
200 Flushings of dread had momentary place:
'I must,' she judged, 'these cruel lines expose,
'Or fears, or worse than fears, my crime disclose.'

The letter shown, he said, with sober smile, –
'Anna, your Friend has not a friendly style:
'Say, where could you with this fair lady dwell,
'Who boasts of secrets that she scorns to tell?'
'At school,' she answer'd: he 'at school!' replied;
'Nay, then I know the secrets you would hide;
'Some early longings these, without dispute.
210 'Some youthful gaspings for forbidden fruit:
'Why so disorder'd, love? are such the crimes
'That give us sorrow in our graver times?
'Come, take a present for your friend, and rest
'In perfect peace – you find you are confess'd.'

This cloud, though past, alarm'd the conscious wife,
Presaging gloom and sorrow for her life;
Who to her answer join'd a fervent prayer,
That her Eliza would a sister spare:
If she again – but was there cause? – should send,
220 Let her direct – and then she named a friend:
A sad expedient untried friends to trust,
And still to fear the tried may be unjust:

Such is his pain, who, by his debt oppress'd,
Seeks by new bonds a temporary rest.

Few were her peaceful days till Anna read
The words she dreaded, and had cause to dread: –

'Did she believe, did she, unkind, suppose
'That thus Eliza's friendship was to close?
'No! though she tried, and her desire was plain,
230   'To break the friendly bond, she strove in vain:
'Ask'd she for silence? why so loud the call,
'And yet the token of her love so small?
'By means like these will you attempt to bind
'And check the movements of an injured mind?
'Poor as I am, I shall be proud to show
'What dangerous secrets I may safely know:
'Secrets to men of jealous minds convey'd
'Have many a noble house in ruins laid:
'Anna, I trust, although with wrongs beset,
240   'And urged by want, I shall be faithful yet;
'But what temptation may from these arise,
'To take a slighted woman by surprise,
'Becomes a subject for your serious care –
'For who offends, must for offence prepare.'

Perplex'd, dismay'd, the Wife foresaw her doom;
A day deferr'd was yet a day to come;
But still, though painful her suspended state,
She dreaded more the crisis of her fate;
Better to die than Stafford's scorn to meet,
250   And her strange friend perhaps would be discreet:
Presents she sent, and made a strong appeal
To woman's feelings, begging her to feel;
With too much force she wrote of jealous men,
And her tears falling spoke beyond the pen;
Eliza's silence she again implored,
And promised all that prudence could afford.

For looks composed and careless, Anna tried;
She seem'd in trouble, and unconscious sigh'd:
The faithful Husband, who devoutly loved
His silent partner, with concern reproved:
'What secret sorrows on my Anna press,
'That love may not partake, nor care redress?'
'None, none,' she answer'd, with a look so kind,
That the fond man determined to be blind.

A few succeeding weeks of brief repose
In Anna's cheek revived the faded rose;
A hue like this the western sky displays,
That glows awhile, and withers as we gaze.

Again the Friend's tormenting letter came –
'The wants she suffer'd were affection's shame;
'She with her child a life of terrors led,
'Unhappy fruit! but of a lawful bed:
'Her friend was tasting every bliss in life,
'The joyful mother, and the wealthy wife;
'While she was placed in doubt, in fear, in want,
'To starve on trifles that the happy grant;
'Poorly for all her faithful silence paid,
'And tantalized by ineffectual aid:
'She could not thus a beggar's lot endure;
' She wanted something permanent and sure:
'If they were friends, then equal be their lot,
'And she was free to speak if they were not.'

Despair and terror seized the Wife, to find
The artful workings of a vulgar mind:
Money she had not, but the hint of dress
Taught her new bribes, new terrors to redress:
She with such feeling then described her woes,
That envy's self might on the view repose;
Then to a mother's pains she made appeal,
And painted grief like one compell'd to feel.

Yes! so she felt, that in her air, her face,
In every purpose, and in every place;
In her slow motion, in her languid mien,
The grief, the sickness of her soul, were seen.

Of some mysterious ill, the Husband sure,
Desired to trace it, for he hoped to cure;
Something he knew obscurely, and had seen
His wife attend a cottage on the green;
Love, loth to wound, endured conjecture long,
Till fear would speak, and spoke in language strong.

300

'All I must know, my Anna – truly know
'Whence these emotions, terrors, troubles flow;
'Give me thy grief, and I will fairly prove
'Mine is no selfish, no ungenerous love.'

Now Anna's soul the seat of strife became,
Fear with respect contended, love with shame;
But fear prevailing was the ruling guide,
Prescribing what to show and what to hide.

'It is my friend,' she said – 'but why disclose
'A woman's weakness struggling with her woes?
'Yes, she has grieved me by her fond complaints,
'The wrongs she suffers, the distress she paints:
'Something we do – but she afflicts me still,
'And says, with power to help, I want the will;
'This plaintive style I pity and excuse,
'Help when I can, and grieve when I refuse;
'But here my useless sorrows I resign,
'And will be happy in a love like thine.'

310

The Husband doubted; he was kind but cool: –
' 'Tis a strong friendship to arise at school;
'Once more then, love, once more the sufferer aid, –
'I too can pity, but I must upbraid:
'Of these vain feelings then thy bosom free,
'Nor be o'erwhelm'd by useless sympathy.'

320

The Wife again despatch'd the useless bribe,
Again essay'd her terror to describe;
Again with kindest words entreated peace,
And begg'd her offerings for a time might cease.

A calm succeeded, but too like the one
330 That causes terror ere the storm comes on:
A secret sorrow lived in Anna's heart,
In Stafford's mind a secret fear of art;
Not long they lasted – this determined foe
Knew all her claims, and nothing would forego;
Again her letter came, where Anna read,
'My child, one cause of my distress, is dead:
'Heav'n has my infant:' – 'Heartless wretch!' she cried,
'Is this thy joy?' – 'I am no longer tied:
'Now will I, hast'ning to my friend, partake
340 'Her cares and comforts, and no more forsake;
'Now shall we both in equal station move,
'Save that my friend enjoys a husband's love.'

Complaint and threats so strong, the Wife amazed,
Who wildly on her cottage-neighbour gazed;
Her tones, her trembling, first betray'd her grief
When floods of tears gave anguish its relief.

She fear'd that Stafford would refuse assent,
And knew her selfish Friend would not relent;
She must petition, yet delay'd the task,
350 Ashamed, afraid, and yet compell'd to ask;
Unknown to him some object fill'd her mind,
And, once suspicious, he became unkind:
They sate one evening, each absorb'd in gloom,
When, hark! a noise and rushing to the room,
The Friend tripp'd lightly in, and laughing said, 'I come.'

Anna received her with an anxious mind,
And meeting whisper'd, 'Is Eliza kind?'
Reserved and cool, the Husband sought to prove
The depth and force of this mysterious love.

To nought that pass'd between the Stranger-friend
And his meek partner seem'd he to attend;
But anxious, listen'd to the lightest word
That might some knowledge of his guest afford;
And learn the reason one to him so dear
Should feel such fondness, yet betray such fear.

Soon he perceived this uninvited guest,
Unwelcome too, a sovereign power possess'd;
Lofty she was and careless, while the meek
And humbled Anna was afraid to speak:
As mute she listen'd with a painful smile,
Her friend sate laughing and at ease the while,
Telling her idle tales with all the glee
Of careless and unfeeling levity.
With calm good sense he knew his Wife endued,
And now with wounded pride her conduct view'd;
Her speech was low, her every look convey'd –
'I am a slave, subservient and afraid.'
All trace of comfort vanish'd, if she spoke,
The noisy friend upon her purpose broke;
To her remarks with insolence replied,
And her assertions doubted or denied;
While the meek Anna like an infant shook,
Woe-struck and trembling at the serpent's look.

'There is,' said Stafford, 'yes, there is a cause –
'This creature frights her, overpowers and awes.'
Six weeks had pass'd – 'In truth, my love, this friend
'Has liberal notions; what does she intend?
'Without a hint she came, and will she stay
'Till she receives the hint to go away?'

Confused the Wife replied, in spite of truth,
'I love the dear companion of my youth.'
' 'Tis well,' said Stafford; 'then your loves renew;
'Trust me, your rivals, Anna, will be few.'

Though playful this, she felt too much distress'd
T' admit the consolation of a jest;
Ill she reposed, and in her dreams would sigh,
And murmuring forth her anguish, beg to die;
With sunken eye, slow pace, and pallid cheek,
She look'd confusion, and she fear'd to speak.

400   All this the Friend beheld, for, quick of sight,
She knew the husband eager for her flight;
And that by force alone she could retain
The lasting comforts she had hope to gain:
She now perceived, to win her post for life,
She must infuse fresh terrors in the wife;
Must bid to friendship's feebler ties adieu,
And boldly claim the object in her view:
She saw the husband's love, and knew the power
Her friend might use in some propitious hour.

410   Meantime the anxious Wife, from pure distress
Assuming courage, said, 'I will confess;'
But with her children felt a parent's pride,
And sought once more the hated truth to hide.

Offended, grieved, im patient, Stafford bore
The odious change, till he could bear no more;
A friend to truth, in speech and action plain,
He held all fraud and cunning in disdain;
But fraud to find, and falsehood to detect,
For once he fled to measures indirect.

420   One day the Friends were seated in that room
The Guest with care adorn'd, and named her home:
To please the eye, there curious prints were placed,
And some light volumes to amuse the taste;
Letters and music, on a table laid,
The favourite studies of the fair betray'd;
Beneath the window was the toilet spread,
And the fire gleam'd upon a crimson bed.

In Anna's looks and falling tears were seen
How interesting had their subjects been:
430 'Oh! then,' resumed the Friend, 'I plainly find
'That you and Stafford know each other's mind;
'I must depart, must on the world be thrown,
'Like one discarded, worthless and unknown;
'But, shall I carry, and to please a foe,
'A painful secret in my bosom? No!
'Think not your Friend a reptile you may tread
'Beneath your feet, and say, the worm is dead;
'I have some feeling, and will not be made
'The scorn of her whom love cannot persuade:
440 'Would not your word, your slightest wish, effect
'All that I hope, petition, or expect?
'The power you have, but you the use decline –
'Proof that you feel not, or you fear not mine.
'There was a time, when I, a tender maid,
'Flew at a call, and your desires obey'd;
'A very mother to the child became,
'Consoled your sorrow, and conceal'd your shame;
'But now, grown rich and happy, from the door
'You thrust a bosom-friend, despised and poor;
450 'That child alive, its mother might have known
'The hard, ungrateful spirit she had shown.'

Here paused the Guest, and Anna cried at length –
'You try me, cruel friend! beyond my strength:
'Would I had been beside my infant laid,
'Where none would vex me, threaten, or upbraid!'

In Anna's looks the Friend beheld despair;
Her speech she soften'd, and composed her air;
Yet, while professing love, she answer'd still –
'You can befriend me, but you want the will.'
460 They parted thus, and Anna went her way,
To shed her secret sorrows, and to pray.

Stafford, amused with books, and fond of home,
By reading oft dispell'd the evening gloom;
History or tale – all heard him with delight,
And thus was pass'd this memorable night.

The listening Friend bestow'd a flattering smile;
A sleeping boy the mother held the while;
And ere she fondly bore him to his bed,
On his fair face the tear of anguish shed.

470   And now his task resumed, 'My tale,' said he,
'Is short and sad, short may our sadness be!' –

'The Caliph Harun, as historians tell,
'Ruled, for a tyrant, admirably well;
'Where his own pleasures were not touch'd, to men
'He was humane, and sometimes even then;
'Harun was fond of fruits, and gardens fair,
'And woe to all whom he found poaching there:
'Among his pages was a lively Boy,
'Eager in search of every trifling joy;
480 'His feelings vivid, and his fancy strong,
'He sigh'd for pleasure while he shrank from wrong;
'When by the Caliph in the garden placed,
'He saw the treasures which he long'd to taste;
'And oft alone he ventured to behold
'Rich hanging fruits with rind of glowing gold;
'Too long he stay'd forbidden bliss to view,
'His virtue failing, as his longings grew;
'Athirst and wearied with the noontide heat,
'Fate to the garden led his luckless feet;
490 'With eager eyes and open mouth he stood,
'Smelt the sweet breath, and touch'd the fragrant food;
'The tempting beauty sparkling in the sun
'Charm'd his young sense – he ate, and was undone:
'When the fond glutton paused, his eyes around
'He turn'd, and eyes upon him turning found;
'Pleased he beheld the spy, a brother-page,

189

'A friend allied in office and in age;
'Who promised much that secret he would be,
'But high the price he fix'd on secrecy.

500   ' "Where you suspected, my unhappy friend,"
'Began the Boy, "where would your sorrows end?
' "In all the palace there is not a page
' "The Caliph would not torture in his rage:
' "I think I see thee now impaled alive,
' "Writhing in pangs – but come, my friend! revive;
' "Had some beheld you, all your purse contains
' "Could not have saved you from terrific pains;
' "I scorn such meanness; and, if not in debt,
' "Would not an asper on your folly set."

510   'The hint was strong; young Osmyn search'd his store
'For bribes, and found he soon could bribe no more;
'That time arrived, for Osmyn's stock was small,
'And the young tyrant now possess'd it all;
'The cruel youth, with his companions near,
'Gave the broad hint that raised the sudden fear;
'Th' ungenerous insult now was daily shown,
'And Osmyn's peace and honest pride were flown;
'Then came augmenting woes, and fancy strong
'Drew forms of suffering, a tormenting throng;
520   'He felt degraded, and the struggling mind
'Dared not be free, and could not be resign'd;
'And all his pains and fervent prayers obtain'd
'Was truce from insult, while the fears remain'd.

'One day it chanced that this degraded Boy
'And Tyrant-friend were fix'd at their employ;
'Who now had thrown restraint and form aside,
'And for his bribe in plainer speech applied:
' "Long have I waited, and the last supply
' "Was but a pittance, yet how patient I!
530   ' "But give me now what thy first terrors gave,
' "My speech shall praise thee, and my silence save."

'Osmyn had found, in many a dreadful day,
'The tyrant fiercer when he seem'd in play:
'He begg'd forbearance; "I have not to give;
' "Spare me awhile, although 't is pain to live:
' "Oh! had that stolen fruit the power possess'd
' "To war with life, I now had been at rest."

' "So fond of death," replied the Boy, ' 't is plain
' "Thou hast no certain notion of the pain;
540 ' "But to the Caliph were a secret shown,
' "Death has no pain that would be then unknown."

'Now,' says the story, 'in a closet near,
'The monarch seated, chanced the boys to hear;
'There oft he came, when wearied on his throne,
'To read, sleep, listen, pray, or be alone.

'The tale proceeds, when first the Caliph found
'That he was robb'd, although alone, he frown'd;
'And swore in wrath, that he would send the boy
'Far from his notice, favour, or employ;
550 'But gentler movements soothed his ruffled mind,
'And his own failings taught him to be kind.

'Relenting thoughts then painted Osmyn young,
'His passion urgent, and temptation strong;
'And that he suffer'd from that villain-Spy
'Pains worse than death, till he desired to die;
'Then if his morals had received a stain,
'His bitter sorrows made him pure again:
'To reason, pity lent her powerful aid,
'For one so tempted, troubled, and betray'd;
560 'And a free pardon the glad Boy restored
'To the kind presence of a gentle lord;
'Who from his office and his country drove
'That traitor-Friend, whom pains nor pray'rs could move;
'Who raised the fears no mortal could endure,
'And then with cruel av'rice sold the cure.

'My tale is ended; but, to be applied,
'I must describe the place where Caliphs hide.'

Here both the females look'd alarm'd, distress'd,
With hurried passions hard to be express'd.

570   'It was a closet by a chamber placed,
'Where slept a lady of no vulgar taste;
'Her friend attended in that chosen room
'That she had honour'd and proclaim'd her home;
'To please the eye were chosen pictures placed,
'And some light volumes to amuse the taste;
'Letters and music on a table laid,
'For much the lady wrote, and often played;
'Beneath the window was a toilet spread,
'And a fire gleam'd upon a crimson bed.'

580   He paused, he rose; with troubled joy the Wife
Felt the new era of her changeful life;
Frankness and love appear'd in Stafford's face
And all her trouble to delight gave place.

Twice made the Guest an effort to sustain
Her feelings, twice resumed her seat in vain,
Nor could suppress her shame, nor could support her
      pain:
Quick she retired, and all the dismal night
Thought of her guilt, her folly, and her flight;
Then sought unseen her miserable home,
590 To think of comforts lost, and brood on wants to come.

The Brothers

Than old *George Fletcher*, on the British coast,
Dwelt not a seaman who had more to boast:
Kind, simple, and sincere – he seldom spoke,
But sometimes sang and chorus'd – 'Hearts of oak!'
In dangers steady, with his lot content,
His days in labour and in love were spent.

He left a Son so like him, that the old
With joy exclaim'd, ' 'T is Fletcher we behold;'
But to his Brother when the kinsmen came,
10 And view'd his form, they grudged the father's name.

George was a bold, intrepid, careless lad,
With just the failings that his father had;
Isaac was weak, attentive, slow, exact,
With just the virtues that his father lack'd.

George lived at sea: upon the land a guest –
He sought for recreation, not for rest;
While, far unlike, his brother's feebler form
Shrank from the cold, and shudder'd at the storm;
Still with the Seaman's to connect his trade,
20 The boy was bound where blocks and ropes were made.

George, strong and sturdy, had a tender mind,
And was to Isaac pitiful and kind;
A very father, till his art was gain'd,
And then a friend unwearied he remain'd;
He saw his brother was of spirit low,
His temper peevish, and his motions slow;
Not fit to bustle in a world, or make
Friends to his fortune for his merit's sake;
But the kind sailor could not boast the art
30 Of looking deeply in the human heart;

Else had he seen that this weak brother knew
What men to court – what objects to pursue;
That he to distant gain the way discern'd,
And none so crooked but his genius learn'd.

Isaac was poor, and this the brother felt;
He hired a house, and there the Landman dwelt,
Wrought at his trade, and had an easy home,
For there would George with cash and comforts come:
And when they parted, Isaac look'd around,
40 Where other friends and helpers might be found.

He wish'd for some port-place, and one might fall,
He wisely thought, if he should try for all;
He had a vote – and were it well applied,
Might have its worth – and he had views beside;
Old Burgess Steel was able to promote
An humble man who served him with a vote;
For Isaac felt not what some tempers feel,
But bow'd and bent the neck to Burgess Steel;
And great attention to a Lady gave,
50 His ancient friend, a maiden spare and grave:
One whom the visage long and look demure
Of Isaac pleased – he seem'd sedate and pure;
And his soft heart conceived a gentle flame
For her who waited on this virtuous dame:
Not an outrageous love, a scorching fire,
But friendly liking and chastised desire;
And thus he waited, patient in delay,
In present favour and in fortune's way.

George then was coasting – war was yet delay'd,
60 And what he gain'd was to his brother paid;
Nor ask'd the Seaman what he saved or spent;
But took his grog, wrought hard, and was content;
Till war awaked the land, and George began
To think what part became a useful man:

'Press'd, I must go; why, then, 't is better far
'At once to enter like a British tar,
'Than a brave captain and the foe to shun,
'As if I fear'd the music of a gun.'
'Go not!' said Isaac – 'You shall wear disguise.'
70 'What!' said the Seaman, 'clothe myself with lies!' –
'Oh! but there's danger.' – 'Danger in the fleet?
'You cannot mean, good brother, of defeat;
'And other dangers I at land must share –
'So now adieu! and trust a brother's care.'

Isaac awhile demurr'd – but, in his heart,
So might he share, he was disposed to part:
The better mind will sometimes feel the pain
Of benefactions – favour is a chain;
But they the feeling scorn, and what they wish, disdain; –
80 While beings form'd in coarser mould will hate
The helping hand they ought to venerate;
No wonder George should in this cause prevail,
With one contending who was glad to fail:
'Isaac, farewell! do wipe that doleful eye;
'Crying we came, and groaning we may die;
'Let us do something 'twixt the groan and cry;
'And hear me, brother, whether pay or prize,
'One half to thee I give and I devise;
'For thou hast oft occasion for the aid
90 'Of learn'd physicians, and they will be paid;
'Their wives and children men support at sea,
'And thou, my lad, art wife and child to me:
'Farewell! – I go where hope and honour call,
'Nor does it follow that who fights must fall.'

Isaac here made a poor attempt to speak,
And a huge tear moved slowly down his cheek;
Like Pluto's iron drop, hard sign of grace,
It slowly roll'd upon the rueful face,
Forced by the striving will alone its way to trace.

Years fled – war lasted – George at sea remain'd,
While the slow Landman still his profits gain'd:
A humble place was vacant – he besought
His patron's interest, and the office caught;
For still the Virgin was his faithful friend,
And one so sober could with truth commend,
Who of his own defects most humbly thought,
And their advice with zeal and reverence sought:
Whom thus the Mistress praised, the Maid approved,
And her he wedded whom he wisely loved.

No more he needs assistance – but, alas!
He fears the money will for liquor pass;
Or that the Seaman might to flatterers lend,
Or give support to some pretended friend:
Still he must write – he wrote, and he confess'd
That, till absolved, he should be sore distress'd;
But one so friendly would, he thought, forgive
The hasty deed – Heav'n knew how he should live;
'But you,' he added, 'as a man of sense,
'Have well consider'd danger and expense:
'I ran, alas! into the fatal snare,
'And now for trouble must my mind prepare;
'And how, with children, I shall pick my way,
'Through a hard world, is more than I can say:
'Then change not, Brother, your more happy state,
'Or on the hazard long deliberate.'

George answer'd gravely, 'It is right and fit,
'In all our crosses, humbly to submit:
'Your apprehensions are unwise, unjust;
'Forbear repining, and expel distrust.' –
He added, 'Marriage was the joy of life,'
And gave his service to his brother's wife;
Then vow'd to bear in all expense a part,
And thus concluded, 'Have a cheerful heart.'

Had the glad Isaac been his brother's guide,
In the same terms the Seaman had replied;
At such reproofs the crafty Landman smiled,
And softly said – 'This creature is a child.'

Twice had the gallant ship a capture made –
And when in port the happy crew were paid,
140 Home went the Sailor, with his pockets stored,
Ease to enjoy, and pleasure to afford;
His time was short, joy shone in every face,
Isaac half fainted in the fond embrace:
The wife resolved her honour'd guest to please,
The children clung upon their uncle's knees;
The grog went round, the neighbours drank his health,
And George exclaim'd – 'Ah! what to this is wealth?
'Better,' said he, 'to bear a loving heart,
'Than roll in riches – but we now must part!'

150 All yet is still – but hark! the winds o'ersweep
The rising waves, and howl upon the deep;
Ships late becalm'd on mountain-billows ride –
So life is threaten'd, and so man is tried.

Ill were the tidings that arrived from sea,
The worthy George must now a cripple be;
His leg was lopp'd; and though his heart was sound,
Though his brave captain was with glory crown'd –
Yet much it vex'd him to repose on shore,
An idle log, and be of use no more:
160 True, he was sure that Isaac would receive
All of his Brother that the foe might leave;
To whom the Seaman his design had sent,
Ere from the port the wounded hero went:
His wealth and expectations told, he 'knew
'Wherein they fail'd, what Isaac's love would do;
'That he the grog and cabin would supply,
'Where George at anchor during life would lie.'

197

The Landman read – and, reading, grew distress'd: –
'Could he resolve t' admit so poor a guest?
170 'Better at Greenwich might the Sailor stay,
'Unless his purse could for his comforts pay;'
So Isaac judged, and to his wife appeal'd,
But yet acknowledged it was best to yield:
'Perhaps his pension, with what sums remain
'Due or unsquander'd, may the man maintain;
'Refuse we must not.' – With a heavy sigh
The lady heard, and made her kind reply: –
'Nor would I wish it, Isaac, were we sure
'How long this crazy building will endure;
180 'Like an old house, that every day appears
'About to fall – he may be propp'd for years;
'For a few months, indeed, we might comply,
'But these old batter'd fellows never die.'

The hand of Isaac, George on entering took,
With love and resignation in his look;
Declared his comfort in the fortune past,
And joy to find his anchor safely cast;
'Call then my nephews, let the grog be brought,
'And I will tell them how the ship was fought.'

190 Alas! our simple Seaman should have known,
That all the care, the kindness, he had shown,
Were from his Brother's heart, if not his memory, flown:
All swept away to be perceived no more,
Like idle structures on the sandy shore;
The chance amusement of the playful boy,
That the rude billows in their rage destroy.

Poor George confess'd, though loth the truth to find,
Slight was his knowledge of a Brother's mind:
The vulgar pipe was to the wife offence,
200 The frequent grog to Isaac an expense;
Would friends like hers, she question'd, 'choose to come,
'Where clouds of poison'd fume defiled a room?

'This could their Lady-friend, and Burgess Steel,
'(Teased with his worship's asthma) bear to feel?
'Could they associate or converse with him –
'A loud rough sailor with a timber limb?'

Cold as he grew, still Isaac strove to show,
By well-feign'd care, that cold he could not grow;
And when he saw his brother look distress'd,
210 He strove some petty comforts to suggest;
On his wife solely their neglect to lay,
And then t' excuse it, as a woman's way;
He too was chidden when her rules he broke,
And then she sicken'd at the scent of smoke.

George, though in doubt, was still consoled to find
His Brother wishing to be reckon'd kind:
That Isaac seem'd concern'd by his distress,
Gave to his injured feelings some redress;
But none he found disposed to lend an ear
220 To stories, all were once intent to hear:
Except his nephew, seated on his knee,
He found no creature cared about the sea;
But George indeed – for George they call'd the boy,
When his good uncle was their boast and joy –
Would listen long, and would contend with sleep,
To hear the woes and wonders of the deep;
Till the fond mother cried – 'That man will teach
'The foolish boy his loud and boisterous speech.'
So judged the father – and the boy was taught
230 To shun the uncle, whom his love had sought.

The mask of kindness now but seldom worn,
George felt each evil harder to be borne;
And cried (vexation growing day by day),
'Ah! brother Isaac! – What! I'm in the way!'
'No! on my credit, look ye, No! but I
'Am fond of peace, and my repose would buy
'On any terms – in short, we must comply:

'My spouse had money – she must have her will –
'Ah! Brother – marriage is a bitter pill.' –

240 George tried the lady – 'Sister, I offend.'
'Me?' she replied – 'Oh no! – you may depend
'On my regard – but watch your Brother's way,
'Whom, I, like you, must study and obey.'

  'Ah!' thought the Seaman, 'what a head was mine,
'That easy berth at Greenwich to resign!
'I'll to the parish' – but a little pride,
And some affection, put the thought aside.

  Now gross neglect and open scorn he bore
In silent sorrow – but he felt the more:
250 The odious pipe he to the kitchen took,
Or strove to profit by some pious book.

  When the mind stoops to this degraded state,
New griefs will darken the dependent's fate;
'Brother!' said Isaac, 'you will sure excuse
'The little freedom I'm compell'd to use:
'My wife's relations – (curse the haughty crew) –
.'Affect such niceness, and such dread of you:
'You speak so loud – and they have natures soft –
'Brother – I wish – do go upon the loft!'

260 Poor George obey'd, and to the garret fled,
Where not a being saw the tears he shed:
But more was yet required, for guests were come,
Who could not dine if he disgraced the room.
It shock'd his spirit to be esteem'd unfit
With an own brother and his wife to sit;
He grew rebellious – at the vestry spoke
For weekly aid – they heard it as a joke:
'So kind a brother, and so wealthy – you
'Apply to us? – No! this will never do:
270 'Good neighbour Fletcher,' said the Overseer,
'We are engaged – you can have nothing here!'

George muttered something in despairing tone,
Then sought his loft, to think and grieve alone;
Neglected, slighted, restless on his bed,
With heart half broken, and with scraps ill fed;
Yet was he pleased, that hours for play design'd
Were given to ease his ever-troubled mind;
The child still listen'd with increasing joy,
And he was sooth'd by the attentive boy.

280 At length he sicken'd, and this duteous child
Watch'd o'er his sickness, and his pains beguiled;
The mother bade him from the loft refrain,
But, though with caution, yet he went again;
And now his tales the Sailor feebly told,
His heart was heavy, and his limbs were cold:
The tender boy came often to entreat
His good kind friend would of his presents eat;
Purloin'd or purchased, for he saw, with shame,
The food untouch'd that to his uncle came;
290 Who, sick in body and in mind, received
The boy's indulgence, gratified and grieved.

'Uncle will die!' said George – the piteous wife
Exclaim'd, 'she saw no value in his life;
'But, sick or well, to my commands attend,
'And go no more to your complaining friend.'
The boy was vex'd, he felt his heart reprove
The stern decree. – What! punish'd for his love!
No! he would go, but softly, to the room,
Stealing in silence – for he knew his doom.

300 Once in a week the father came to say,
'George, are you ill?' – and hurried him away;
Yet to his wife would on their duties dwell,
And often cry, 'Do use my brother well:'
And something kind, no question, Isaac meant,
Who took vast credit for the vague intent.

But truly kind, the gentle boy essay'd
To cheer his uncle, firm, although afraid;
But now the father caught him at the door,
And, swearing – yes, the man in office swore,
And cried, 'Away! How ! Brother, I'm surprised,
'That one so old can be so ill advised:
'Let him not dare to visit you again,
'Your cursed stories will disturb his brain;
'Is it not vile to court a foolish boy,
'Your own absurd narrations to enjoy?
'What! sullen! – ha, George Fletcher! you shall see,
'Proud as you are, your bread depends on me!'

He spoke, and, frowning, to his dinner went,
Then cool'd and felt some qualms of discontent;
And thought on times when he compell'd his son
To hear these stories, nay, to beg for one:
But the wife's wrath o'ercame the brother's pain,
And shame was felt, and conscience rose in vain.

George yet stole up; he saw his Uncle lie
Sick on the bed, and heard his heavy sigh:
So he resolved, before he went to rest,
To comfort one so dear and so distress'd;
Then watch'd his time, but with a child-like art,
Betray'd a something treasured at his heart:
Th' observant wife remark'd, 'the boy is grown
'So like your brother, that he seems his own;
'So close and sullen! and I still suspect
'They often meet – do watch them and detect.'

George now remark'd that all was still as night,
And hasten'd up with terror and delight;
'Uncle!' he cried, and softly tapp'd the door;
'Do let me in' – but he could add no more;
The careful father caught him in the fact,
And cried, – 'You serpent! is it thus you act?
'Back to your mother!' – and, with hasty blow,
He sent th' indignant boy to grieve below;

Then at the door an angry speech began –
'Is this your conduct? – Is it thus you plan?
'Seduce my child, and make my house a scene
'Of vile dispute – What is it that you mean? –
'George, are you dumb? do learn to know your friends,
'And think awhile on whom your bread depends:
'What! not a word? be thankful I am cool –
'But, sir, beware, nor longer play the fool:
350 'Come! brother, come! what is it that you seek
'By this rebellion? – Speak, you villain, speak! –
'Weeping! I warrant – sorrow makes you dumb:
'I'll ope your mouth, impostor! if I come:
'Let me approach – I'll shake you from the bed,
'You stubborn dog – Oh God! my Brother's dead! –'

Timid was Isaac, and in all the past
He felt a purpose to be kind at least;
Nor did he mean his brother to depart,
Till he had shown this kindness of his heart:
360 But day by day he put the cause aside,
Induced by av'rice, peevishness, or pride.

But now awaken'd, from this fatal time
His conscience Isaac felt, and found his crime:
He raised to George a monumental stone,
And there retired to sigh and think alone;
An ague seized him, he grew pale, and shook –
'So,' said his son, 'would my poor Uncle look.'
'And so, my child, shall I like him expire.'
'No! you have physic and a cheerful fire.'
370 'Unhappy sinner! yes, I'm well supplied
'With every comfort my cold heart denied.'
He view'd his Brother now, but not as one
Who vex'd his wife, by fondness for her son;
Not as with wooden limb, and seaman's tale,
The odious pipe, vile grog, or humbler ale:
He now the worth and grief alone can view
Of one so mild, so generous, and so true;

203

'The frank, kind Brother, with such open heart,
'And I to break it – 'twas a daemon's part!'

380   So Isaac now, as led by conscience, feels,
Nor his unkindness palliates or conceals;
'This is your folly,' said his heartless wife:
'Alas! my folly cost my Brother's life;
'It suffer'd him to languish and decay,
'My gentle brother, whom I could not pay,
'And therefore left to pine, and fret his life away!'

He takes his Son, and bids the boy unfold
All the good Uncle of his feelings told,
All he lamented – and the ready tear
390 Falls as he listens, soothed, and grieved to hear.

'Did he not curse me, child?' – 'He never cursed,
'But could not breathe, and said his heart would burst:'
'And so will mine:' – 'Then, father, you must pray;
'My uncle said it took his pains away.'

Repeating thus his sorrows, Isaac shows
That he, repenting, feels the debt he owes,
And from this source alone his every comfort flows.
He takes no joy in office, honours, gain;
They make him humble, nay, they give him pain;
400 'These from my heart,' he cries, 'all feeling drove;
'They made me cold to nature, dead to love:'
He takes no joy in home, but sighing, sees
A son in sorrow, and a wife at ease;
He takes no joy in office – see him now,
And Burgess Steel has but a passing bow;
Of one sad train of gloomy thoughts possess'd,
He takes no joy in friends, in food, in rest –
Dark are the evil days, and void of peace the best.
And thus he lives, if living be to sigh,
410 And from all comforts of the world to fly,
Without a hope in life – without a wish to die.

Belinda Waters

Of all the beauties in our favour'd place,
BELINDA WATERS was the pride and grace.
Say ye who sagely can our fortunes read,
Shall this fair damsel in the world succeed?

    A rosy beauty she, and fresh and fair,
Who never felt a caution or a care;
Gentle by nature, ever fond of ease,
And more consenting than inclined to please.
A tame good nature in her spirit lives –
She hates refusal for the pain it gives:
From opposition arguments arise,
And to prevent the trouble, she complies.
She, if in Scotland, would be *fash'd* all day,
If call'd to any work or any play;
She lets no busy, idle wish intrude,
But is by nature negatively good.

    In marriage hers will be a dubious fate:
She is not fitted for a high estate; –
There wants the grace, the polish, and the pride;
Less is she fitted for a humble bride:
Whom fair Belinda weds – let chance decide!

    She sees her father oft engross'd by cares,
And therefore hates to hear of men's affairs.
An active mother in the household reigns,
And spares Belinda all domestic pains.
Of food she knows but this, that we are fed: –
Though, duly taught, she prays for daily bread,
Yet whence it comes, of hers is no concern –
It comes! and more she never wants to learn.

She on the table sees the common fare,
But how provided is beneath her care.
Lovely and useless, she has no concern
About the things that aunts and mothers learn;
But thinks, when married, – if she thinks at all, –
That what she needs will answer to her call.

To write is business, and, though taught to write,
She keeps the pen and paper out of sight:
What once was painful she cannot allow
To be enjoyment or amusement now.
She wonders why the ladies are so fond
Of such long letters, when they correspond.
Crowded and cross'd by ink of different stain,
She thinks to read them would confuse her brain;
Nor much mistakes; but still has no pretence
To praise for this, her critic's indolence.

Behold her now! she on her sofa looks
O'er half a shelf of circulating books.
This she admired, but she forgets the name,
And reads again another, or the same.
She likes to read of strange and bold escapes,
Of plans and plottings, murders and mishaps,
Love in all hearts, and lovers in all shapes.
She sighs for pity, and her sorrows flow
From the dark eyelash on the page below;
And is so glad when, all the misery past,
The dear adventurous lovers meet at last –
Meet and are happy; and she thinks it hard,
When thus an author might a pair reward –
When they, the troubles all dispersed, might wed –
He makes them part, and die of grief instead!

Yet tales of terror are her dear delight,
All in the wintry storm to read at night;
And to her maid she turns in all her doubt, –
'This shall I like? and what is that about?'

She had 'Clarissa' for her heart's dear friend –
Was pleased each well-tried virtue to commend,
And praised the scenes that one might fairly doubt,
If one so young could know so much about:
Pious and pure, th' heroic beauty strove
70 Against the lover and against the love;
But strange that maid so young should know the strife,
In all its views, was painted to the life!
Belinda knew not – nor a tale would read,
That could so slowly on its way proceed;
And ere Clarissa reach'd the wicked town,
The weary damsel threw the volume down.
'Give me,' she said, 'for I would laugh or cry,
' "Scenes from the Life," and "Sensibility;"
' "Winters at Bath," – I would that I had one!
80 ' "The Constant Lover," the "Discarded Son,"
' "The Rose of Raby," "Delmore," or "The Nun."
'These promise something, and may please, perhaps,
'Like "Ethelinda," and the dear "Relapse." '
To these her heart the gentle maid resign'd,
And such the food that fed the gentle mind.

II

P. – Knew you the fair BELINDA, once the boast
Of a vain mother, and a favourite toast
Of clerks and young lieutenants, a gay set
Of light admirers? – Is she married yet?

90   F. – Yes! she is married; though she waited long,
Not from a prudent fear of choosing wrong,
But want of choice. – She took a surgeon's mate,
With his half pay, that was his whole estate.

Fled is the charming bloom that nature spread
Upon her cheek, the pure, the rosy red –
This, and the look serene, the calm, kind look, are fled.
Sorrow and sadness now the place possess,
And the pale cast of anxious fretfulness.

She *wonders* much – as, why they live so ill, –
100 Why the rude butcher brings his weekly bill, –
She wonders why that baker will not trust, –
And says, most truly says, – 'Indeed, he must.'
She wonders where her former friends are gone, –
And thus, from day to day, she wonders on.

Howe'r she can – she dresses gaily yet,
And then she wonders how they came in debt.
Her husband loves her, and in accent mild,
Answers, and treats her like a fretted child;
But when he, ruffled, makes severe replies,
110 And seems unhappy – then she pouts, and cries
'She wonders when she'll die!' – She faints, but never dies.

'How well my father lived!' she says. – 'How well,
'My dear, your father's creditors could tell!'
And then she weeps, till comfort is applied,
That soothes her spleen or gratifies her pride:
Her dress and novels, visits and success
In a chance-game, are soft'ners of distress.

So life goes on! – But who that loved his life,
Would take a fair Belinda for his wife?
120 Who thinks that all are for their stations born,
Some to indulge themselves, and to adorn;
And some, a useful people, to prepare,
Not being rich, good things for those who are,
And who are born; it cannot be denied,
To have their wants and their demands supplied.

She knows that money is a needful thing,
That fathers first, and then that husbands bring;
Or if those persons should the aid deny,
Daughters and wives have but to faint and die,
130 Till flesh and blood can not endure the pain,
And then the lady lives and laughs again.

To wed an ague, and to feel, for life,
Hot fits and cold succeeding in a wife;
To take the pestilence with poison'd breath,
And wed some potent minister of death,
Is cruel fate – yet death is then relief;
But thus to wed is ever-during grief.

Oft have I heard, how blest the youth who weds
Belinda Waters! – rather he who dreads
140 That fate – a truth her husband well approves,
Who blames and fondles, humours, chides, and loves.

The Cousins

I

P. – I left a frugal Merchant, who began
Early to thrive, and grew a wealthy man;
Retired from business with a favourite Niece,
He lived in plenty, or if not – in peace.
Their small affairs, conforming to his will,
The maiden managed with superior skill.
He had a Nephew too, a brother's child, –
But James offended, for the lad was wild:
And Patty's tender soul was vex'd to hear,
10 'Your Cousin James will rot in gaol, my dear;
'And now, I charge you, by no kind of gift
'Show him that folly may be help'd by thrift.'
This Patty heard, but in her generous mind
Precept so harsh could no admission find.

Her Cousin James, too sure in prison laid,
With strong petitions plied the gentle maid,
That she would humbly on their Uncle press
His deep repentance, and his sore distress;

How that he mourn'd in durance, night and day,
And which removed, he would for ever pray.

'Nought will I give, his worthless life to save,'
The Uncle said; and nought in fact he gave:
But the kind maiden from her pittance took
All that she could, and gave with pitying look;
For soft compassion in her bosom reign'd,
And her heart melted when the Youth complain'd.
Of his complaints the Uncle loved to hear,
As Patty told them, shedding many a tear;
While he would wonder how the girl could pray
For a young rake, to place him in her way,
Or once admit him in his Uncle's view;
'But these,' said he, 'are things that women do.'

Thus were the Cousins, young, unguarded, fond,
Bound in true friendship – so they named the bond –
Nor call'd it love – and James resolved, when free,
A most correct and frugal man to be.
He sought her prayers, but not for heavenly aid:
'Pray to my Uncle,' and she kindly pray'd –
'James will be careful,' said the Niece; 'and I
'Will be as careful,' was the stern reply.

Thus he resisted, and I know not how
He could be soften'd – Is he kinder now?
Hard was his heart; but yet a heart of steel
May melt in dying, and dissolving feel.

II

F. – What were his feelings I cannot explain,
His actions only on my mind remain.
He never married, that indeed we know,
But childless was not, as his foes could show. –
Perhaps his friends – for friends, as well as foes,
Will the infirmities of man disclose.

When young, our Merchant, though of sober fame,
Had a rude passion that he could not tame;
And, not to dwell upon the passion's strife,
He had a Son, who never had a wife;
The father paid just what the law required,
Nor saw the infant, nor to see desired.
That infant, thriving on the parish fare,
Without a parent's love, consent, or care,
Became a sailor, and sustain'd his part
60   So like a man, it touch'd his father's heart: –
He for protection gave the ready pay,
And placed the seaman in preferment's way;
Who doubted not, with sanguine heart, to rise,
And bring home riches, gain'd from many a prize.
But Jack – for so we call'd him – Jack once more,
And never after, touch'd his native shore:
Nor was it known if he in battle fell,
Or sickening died – we sought, but none could tell.
The father sigh'd – as some report, he wept;
70   And then his sorrow with the Sailor slept;
Then age came on; he found his spirits droop,
And his kind Niece remain'd the only hope.

Premising this, our story then proceeds –
Our gentle Patty for her Cousin pleads;
And now her Uncle, to his room confined,
And kindly nursed, was soften'd and was kind.
James, whom the law had from his prison sent,
With much contrition to his Uncle went,
And, humbly kneeling, said, 'Forgive me, I repent.'
80   Reproach, of course, his humbled spirit bore;
He knew for pardon anger opes the door;
The man whom we with too much warmth reprove,
Has the best chance our softening hearts to move;
And this he had – 'Why, Patty, love! it seems,'
Said the old man, 'there's something good in James.
'I must forgive; but you my child, are yet,
'My stay and prop; I cannot this forget.

'Still, my dear Niece, as a reforming man,
'I mean to aid your Cousin, if I can.'
90   Then Patty smiled, for James and she had now
Time for their loves, and pledged the constant vow.

    James the fair way to favouring thoughts discern'd –
He learn'd the news, and told of all he learn'd;
Read all the papers in an easy style,
And knew the bits would raise his Uncle's smile;
Then would refrain, to hear the good man say,
'You did not come as usual yesterday:
'I must not take you from your duties, lad,
'But of your daily visits should be glad!'

100   Patty was certain that their Uncle now
Would their affection all it ask'd allow;
She was convinced her lover now would find
The past forgotten and old Uncle kind.
'It matters not,' she added, 'who receives
'The larger portion; what to one he leaves
'We both inherit! let us nothing hide,
'Dear James, from him in whom we both confide.'
'Not for your life!' quoth James. 'Let Uncle choose
'Our ways for us – or we the way shall lose.
110   'For know you, Cousin, all these miser men –
'Nay, my dear James!' –
                    'Our worthy Uncle, then,
'And all like Uncle like to be obey'd
'By their dependants, who must seem afraid
'Of their own will: – If we to wed incline,
'You'll quickly hear him peevishly repine,
'Object, dispute, and sundry reasons give,
'To prove we ne'er could find the means to live;
'And then, due credit for his speech to gain,
'He'll leave us poor – lest wealth should prove it vain.
120   'Let him propose the measure, and then we
'May for his pleasure to his plan agree.

'I, when at last assenting, shall be still
'But giving way to a kind Uncle's will;
'Then will he deem it just, amends to make
'To one who ventures all things for his sake;
'So, should you deign to take this worthless hand,
'Be sure, dear Patty, 't is at his command.'

But Patty questioned – 'Is it, let me ask,
'The will of God that we should wear a mask?'
This startled James: he lifted up his eyes,
And said with some contempt, besides surprise,
'Patty, my love! the will of God, 't is plain,
'Is that we live by what we can obtain;
'Shall we a weak and foolish man offend,
'And when our trial is so near our end?'

This hurt the maiden, and she said, ' 'T is well!
Unask'd I will not of your purpose tell,
'But will not lie.' –
                    'Lie! Patty, no, indeed,
'Your downright lying never will succeed!
'A better way our prudence may devise,
'Than such unprofitable things as lies.
'Yet, a dependant, if he would not starve,
'The way through life must with discretion carve,
'And, though a lie he may with pride disdain,
'He must not every useless truth maintain.
'If one respect to these fond men would show,
'Conceal the facts that give them pain to know;
'While all that pleases may be placed in view,
'And if it be not, they will think it true.'

The humble Patty dropp'd a silent tear,
And said, 'Indeed, 't is best to be sincere.'
James answer'd not – there could be no reply
To what he would not grant nor could deny:

But from that time he in the maiden saw
What he condemn'd; yet James was kept in awe;
He felt her virtue, but was sore afraid
For the frank blunders of the virtuous maid.

Meantime he daily to his Uncle read
The news, and to his favourite subjects led:
160   If closely press'd, he sometimes staid to dine,
Ate of one dish, and drank one glass of wine;
For James was crafty grown, and felt his way
To favour, step by step, and day by day;
He talk'd of business, till the Uncle prized
The lad's opinion, whom he once despised,
And, glad to see him thus his faults survive,
'This Boy,' quoth he, 'will keep our name alive.
'Women are weak, and Patty, though the best
'Of her weak sex, is woman like the rest:
170   'An idle husband will her money spend,
'And bring my hard-earn'd savings to an end.'

Far as he dared, his Nephew this way led,
And told his tales of lasses rashly wed,
Told them as matters that he heard, – 'He knew
'Not where,' he said: 'they might be false or true;
'One must confess that girls are apt to dote
'On the bright scarlet of a coxcomb's coat;
'And that with ease a woman they beguile
'With a fool's flattery, or a rascal's smile;
180   'But then,' he added, fearing to displease,
'Our Patty never saw such men as these.'

'True! but she may – some scoundrel may command
'The girl's whole store, if he can gain her hand:
'Her very goodness will itself deceive,
'And her weak virtue help her to believe;
'Yet she is kind; and, Nephew! go, and say,
'I need her now – You'll come another day.'

In such discourses, while the maiden went
About her household, many an hour was spent,
Till James was sure that when his Uncle died,
He should at least the property divide:
Nor long had he to wait – the fact was quickly tried.

The Uncle now to his last bed confined,
To James and Patty his affairs resign'd;
The doctor took his final fee in hand,
The man of law received his last command;
The silent priest sat watching in his chair,
If he might wake the dying man to prayer, –
When the last groan was heard; then all was still,
And James indulged his musings – on the Will.

This in due time was read, and Patty saw
Her own dear Cousin made the heir-by-law.
Something indeed was hers, but yet she felt
As if her Uncle had not kindly dealt;
And but that James was one whom she could trust,
She would have thought it cruel and unjust.
Ev'n as it was, it gave her some surprise,
And tears unbidden started in her eyes;
Yet she confess'd it was the same to her,
And it was likely men would men prefer.
Loth was the Niece to think her Uncle wrong;
And other thoughts engaged her – 'Is it long
'That custom bids us tarry ere we wed,
'When a kind Uncle is so lately dead?
'At any rate,' the maiden judged, ' 't is he
'That first will speak – it does not rest with me.'

James to the Will his every thought confined,
And found some parts that vex'd his sober mind.
He, getting much, to angry thoughts gave way,
For the poor pittance that he had to pay,
With Patty's larger claim. Save these alone,
The weeping heir beheld the whole his own;

Yet something painful in his mind would dwell, –
'It was not likely, but was possible:' –
No – Fortune lately was to James so kind,
He was determined not to think her blind:
'She saw his merit, and would never throw
'His prospects down by such malicious blow.'

Patty, meanwhile, had quite enough betray'd
230 Of her own mind to make her James afraid
Of one so simply pure: his hardening heart
Inclined to anger – he resolved to part:
Why marry Patty? – if he look'd around
More advantageous matches might be found;
But though he might a richer wife command,
He first must break her hold upon his hand.

She with a spinster-friend retired awhile,
'Not long,' she said, and said it with a smile.
Not so had James determined: – He essay'd
240 To move suspicion in the gentle maid.
Words not succeeding, he design'd to pass
The spinster's window with some forward lass.
If in her heart so pure no pang was known,
At least he might affect it in his own.
There was a brother of her friend, and he,
Though poor and rude, might serve for jealousy.
If all should fail, he, though of schemes bereft,
Might leave her yet! – They fail'd, and she was left.

Poor Patty bore it with a woman's mind,
250 And with an angel's, sorrowing and resign'd.
Ere this in secret long she wept and pray'd,
Long tried to think her lover but delay'd
The union, once his hope, his prayer, his pride; –
She could in James as in herself confide:
Was he not bound by all that man can bind,
In love, in honour, to be just and kind?

Large was his debt, and when their debts are large,
The ungrateful cancel what the just discharge;
Nor payment only in their pride refuse,
But first they wrong their friend, and then accuse.
Thus Patty finds her bosom's claims denied,
Her love insulted, and her right defied.
She urged it not; her claim the maid withdrew,
For maiden pride would not the wretch pursue:
She sigh'd to find him false, herself so good and true.

Now all his fears, at least the present, still, –
He talk'd, good man! about his uncle's will, –
'All unexpected,' he declared, – 'surprised
'Was he – and his good uncle ill-advised:
'He no such luck had look'd for, he was sure,
'Nor such deserved,' he said, with look demure;
'He did not merit such exceeding love,
'But his, he meant, so help him God, to prove.'
And he has proved it! all his cares and schemes
Have proved the exceeding love James bears to James.

But to proceed, – for we have yet the facts
That show how Justice looks on wicked acts;
For, though not always, she at times appears –
To wake in man her salutary fears.

James, restless grown – for no such mind can rest –
Would build a house, that should his wealth attest;
In fact, he saw, in many a clouded face,
A certain token of his own disgrace;
And wish'd to overawe the murmurs of the place.

The finish'd building show'd the master's wealth,
And noisy workmen drank his Honour's health –
'His and his heirs' – and at the thoughtless word
A strange commotion in his bosom stirr'd.
'Heirs! said the idiots?' – and again that clause
In the strange Will corrected their applause.

Prophetic fears! for now reports arose
That spoil'd 'his Honour's' comforts and repose.
A stout young Sailor, though in battle maim'd,
Arrived in port, and his possessions claim'd.
The Will he read: he stated his demand,
And his attorney grasp'd at house and land.
The Will provided – 'If my son survive,
He shall inherit;' and lo! Jack's alive!
Yes! he was that lost lad, preserved by fate,
300 And now was bent on finding his estate.
But claim like this the angry James denied,
And to the law the sturdy heir applied.
James did what men when placed like him would do –
Avow'd his right, and fee'd his lawyer too:
The Will, indeed, provided for a son;
But was this Sailor youth the very one?

Ere Jack's strong proofs in all their strength were
    shown,
To gain a part James used a milder tone;
But the instructed tar would reign alone.

310   At last he reign'd: to James a large bequest
Was frankly dealt; the Seaman had the rest –
Save a like portion to the gentle Niere,
Who lived in comfort, and regain'd her peace.
In her neat room her talent she employ'd,
With more true peace than ever James enjoy'd.
The young, the aged, in her praise agreed –
Meek in her manner, bounteous in her deed;
The very children their respect avow'd:
' 'T was the good lady,' they were told, and bow'd.

320   The merry Seaman much the maid approv'd, –
Nor that alone – he like a seaman loved;
Loved as a man who did not much complain,
Loved like a sailor, not a sighing swain;

Had heard of wooing maids, but knew not how –
'Lass, if you love me, prithee tell me now,'
Was his address – but this was nothing cold –
'Tell if you love me;' and she smiled and told.

He brought her presents, such as sailors buy,
Glittering like gold, to please a maiden's eye,
330   All silk, and silver, fringe and finery;
These she accepted in respect to him,
And thought but little of the missing limb.
Of this he told her, for he loved to tell
A warlike tale, and judged he told it well: –
'You mark me, love! the French were two to one,
'And so, you see, they were ashamed to run;
'We fought an hour; and then there came the spot
'That struck me here – a man must take his lot; –
'A minute after, and the Frenchman struck:
340   'One minute sooner had been better luck;
'But if you can a cripple cousin like,
'You ne'er shall see him for a trifle strike.'

Patty, whose gentle heart was not so nice
As to reject the thought of loving twice,
Judged her new Cousin was by nature kind,
With no suspicions in his honest mind,
Such as our virtuous ladies now and then
Find strongly floating in the minds of men.
So they were married, and the lasses vow'd
350   That Patty's luck would make an angel proud:
'Not but that time would come when she must prove
'That men are men, no matter how they love:' –
And she has prov'd it; for she finds her man
As kind and true as when their loves began.

James is unhappy; not that he is poor,
But, having much, because he has no more;
Because a rival's pleasure gives him pain;
Because his vices work'd their way in vain;

219

And, more than these, because he sees the smile
360 Of a wrong'd woman pitying man so vile.

He sought an office, serves in the excise,
And every wish, but that for wealth, denies;
Wealth is the world to him, and he is worldly wise.
But disappointment in his face appears;
Care and vexation, sad regret and fears
Have fix'd on him their fangs, and done the work of years.

Yet grows he wealthy in a strange degree,
And neighbours wonder how the fact can be:
He lives alone, contracts a sordid air,
370 And sees with sullen grief the cheerful pair;
Feels a keen pang, as he beholds the door
Where peace abides, and mutters, – 'I am poor!'

Notes

Line references are shown in sloping numerals

INEBRIETY; A POEM. First published in 1775, 'Inebriety' is one of Crabbe's earliest poems. The choice of drunkenness as a subject need not surprise us once we note the fondness of eighteenth-century poets for ranging widely in search of matter for verse and recall their interest in didactic poetry. 'Inebriety' is not an entirely satisfactory poem because the severe moralizing is at odds with the comic descriptions of the rural scene; but it contains impressive passages, and shows that Crabbe is already at ease in handling the couplet form. It is recognizably Augustan in its concern to persuade us of the justness of its argument by appeal to history. The version here used is the cut one of 1834.

In the poetry of Pope we find frequent allusions to the great past – especially that of Augustan Rome – which provide an implied comment on the comparative worth of the present. Commonly, comparison is employed to make an ironic contrast: the present in no way measures up to the past. It will be noticed that Crabbe uses this tactic in 'Inebriety'. For example, he gives the names of heroic and virtuous Ancients to his own characters in order to underline how far they are from possessing such qualities. And in addition he alludes to the great literature of the past to show how that, too, serves values nowhere to be met with in the scenes he describes. In a sense it is this that makes the poem unsatisfactory; the drunkenness with which Crabbe is concerned can hardly be erected into a central indictment of the viciousness of his age. But intermittently at least, Crabbe seems to want to make such an indictment. And this, I think, is the reason he begins his poem by drawing on the opening lines of Pope's great poem *The Dunciad*, which had been very precisely and exhaustively concerned with the degeneracy of contemporary society. lines *1–8* of 'Inebriety' in fact, are closely modelled on lines 1–8 of *The Dunciad* (1742).

9 ff. The pattern for this sort of descriptive verse had been set by James Thomson in *The Seasons*. 'Sable' means black, 'verdure' greenery.

25. Crabbe shows off medical knowledge here, of circulation of the blood. 'Venal road' means vein. The idea is that a cold person needs liquor to restore him to warmth.

37. ''rrac' is Arrack, a name given in eastern countries to any spirituous liquor. It thus stands for any drink which is exotic and expensive. 'Turtle' means the flesh of turtle, again an expensive delicacy.

39. 'Colin' is a name traditionally given to peasants in pastoral poetry. e.g. Spenser's *Colin Clout's Come Home Again.*

55. 'Lucina' is the moon.

57. 'silent ether' – ether is a word for air frequently to be found in eighteenth-century poetry, and reflects the age's intense interest in Newtonian science. It is often called 'silent' because though it fills all space it is subtle and imperceptible.

60. 'Bacchanalian' – a follower of Bacchus, god of wine.

73–8. A mock-epic simile of the kind used by Pope and Fielding, for example. The epic simile in English literature originates in Milton's *Paradise Lost*; the mock-epic simile is a device similar to the ironic appeal to history: it demonstrates the gap between the subject's pretensions and actuality.

86. 'ambient' means surrounding.

88. 'rooky pinions' – the image of the heavy black bird which the words summon up, suggests to us the heaviness of head that goes with a hangover from drinking, and as well perhaps the blackness of bile that, according to the still prevalent theory of the 'humours', caused melancholy, an after effect of inebriety.

109. Here we meet the first of the occasions in the poem when Crabbe implicitly comments on his characters by giving them names which point to their lack of qualities that go with the historical personage intended. Flaminius was a great democratic leader who lived *c.* 230–200 B.C. and who frequently and bravely challenged the senatorial government.

121–40. These lines are closely modelled on a famous passage in Pope's *Essay on Man*, Epistle I, lines 99 ff, in which Pope makes an ironic contrast between the ignorant simplicity of the 'poor Indian' and the 'wiser thou' whose conceit in his knowledge threatens to make him 'The GOD of GOD!'

124. 'the muddy ecstasies of beer' – in the eighteenth century, beer was clarified only by the large breweries. Small breweries, who brewed for quick consumption, inevitably produced 'clouded' beer.

178. 'rubric' – Crabbe plays on the word here, which not only means red, and thus indicates that the vicar has spilt wine over his white neckbands, but also means the rule for divine service.

196. Levites were priests in Palestine.

201. Curio is a name common to several low-born, democratic and incorruptible Romans.

209–16. In their attack on dullness, these lines recall Dryden's famous attack on Shadwell in *MacFlecknoe*. Dryden was one of Crabbe's favourite poets, and dullness is a cardinal sin for the Augustans, representing for them the negation of true human worth: it is opposed to wit and reason and reduces man to the level of the animals.

217–20. A reference to the fourteenth of John Gay's *Fables*.

221. 'Fabricio' – Luscinus Fabricus *c.* 282 B.C. was poor, austere, incorruptible and a military hero, who became a moral example to Roman youth.

230. 'Titan' – the sun.

232. 'Timon' – not the famous misanthrope but the literary sceptic, born *c.* 320 B.C., died in Athens 250 B.C. Timon wrote parodies of all dogmatic philosophies.

249. Horace was an important poet to the eighteenth century, especially Pope. He was seen as always on the side of good sense and standing for the most cherishable values. In his poetry he warned against all forms of excess, and in *Odes*, Book I, no. 27, attacked drunkenness. He thus does the opposite of vindicating the bowl, and the Timon who becomes 'Horace in English' to his companions merely demonstrates how little he is entitled to the name of a great poet.

258–9. The reference to garret and frantic poet points to Grub Street, where so many literary hacks lived in eighteenth-century London, and which quickly came to be associated with drudging poverty; and very probably Crabbe is referring to Hogarth's famous engraving, *The Distressed Poet*, often called *The Poet in the Garret*.

266. 'Milo' – T. Annius Milo was a great friend of Cicero, the most famous of all orators who, when Milo was banished from Rome, prepared an oration in his defence. Crabbe ironically compares the dignity of the relationship between Cicero and Milo with the fawning plagiarism of his Milo, who is so far from being the military figure that the original Milo had been, that he is more like the Milonius mentioned in Horace's *Satires* Book I, no. 5, a drunken buffoon living in Rome, accustomed to dance whenever intoxicated.

280–91. Notice the Augustan attitudes made explicit in these closing lines, and the balancing judgments enacted in the couplet form.

THE VILLAGE, *Book I.* In the opening passage of the poem, Crabbe emphasizes the absurdity of assuming that the end of the eighteenth century can lay claim to possessing the ideal world of pastoral retreat which Virgil had celebrated in his *Eclogues.* Goldsmith in *The Deserted Village* and Langhorne in *The Country Justice* spoke of such a world as though it was a present reality; Crabbe insists that the reality of rural life makes it impossible to write of it in the terms Virgil used. Corydon and Tityrus are the names of shepherds in the *Eclogues,* Mincio is the river Mincius, and Mantua is the town of which he was a native.

27. 'DUCK' – Stephen Duck (1705–56) the so-called 'thresher-poet' was a farmhand now remembered for his *Poems on Several Occasions* (1736). He was something of a celebrity in the eighteenth century because his triumph as a poet was against the odds.

29–30. Here Crabbe says that it is absurd to pretend that the drab meanness and harshness of contemporary agricultural labour can be identified with the free and noble labour celebrated by Virgil.

53–4. Crabbe's declaration of intent. Notice that in the couplet itself Crabbe manages to stress his own attitudes. Truth is contrasted to Bards, who make up pleasing lies about rural life. The rhyme-word 'not' finalizes, as it were, Crabbe's point. And we note, indeed, how the decisiveness of statement owes everything to the way in which the rhyme seals it off. The couplet as employed here is a perfect way to end a discussion.

63–78. Perhaps the best-known lines of the poem, these specify some of the ills of rural life. Our attention is drawn to the way in which nature is far from friendly to man's efforts to cultivate her. Weeds lord it over the harvest with an authority that belies the 'idealizing' view of nature as adapting herself to man's needs. Every art and care of human accomplishment are denied by the rank weeds that 'reign o'er the land'; they, not men, are the masters. And the hostile dominance of nature is pointed up by the precision with which Crabbe identifies the weeds with an insolent and tyrannous rule: such words as 'nodding', 'paints', 'high', 'waves', sufficiently render the sense of nature's effortless and insulting control over human effort. And the dominant tyranny is sounded by such words as 'hardy', 'clasping', 'cling'. The descriptions are, moreover, realistic in that they properly show how the weeds prevent the rye from finding the sun it needs for healthy growth, and how they choke it to death. Taken together, the realism and its accompanying rendering of nature's tyrannous power expose the falseness of Langhorne's and Goldsmith's belief that nature exists to serve man.

93–100. Crabbe has in mind a passage from *The Deserted Village*, lines 16–24, in which Goldsmith speaks of the village games and sports which he sees as an essential part of rural life. Crabbe's point is that such a vision has nothing to do with the actual truth.

109–12. Crabbe is here attacking Langhorne's belief that it is cities, not rural life, that are the Haunts of Rapine, Harbours of Disease. And he may also have in mind no. 71 of Johnson's paper, the *Idler*, in which we read of one Dick Shifter, who after reading Virgil mistakes literary praise of rural retirement for the real thing and goes to live in the country. But having bought himself an estate, Shifter soon discovers that pastoral, life is not all he had imagined it to be, and after five days of discomfort and disillusionment he returns to London.

113. 'finny tribe' – it is common to eighteenth-century poetry to turn a noun into an adjective by adding a final 'y' and attach it to a generalized, collective noun in order to avoid the particularization which was felt irrelevant to the poet's concerns. As Imlac puts it in Johnson's *Rasselas*, 'The business of a poet . . . is to examine, not the individual, but the species; to remark general properties and large appearances: he does not number the streaks of the tulip, or describe the different shades in the verdure of the forest' (chapter x).

144. 'dog-star' – Sirius, the chief star of a constellation which rises during July and August, that is, the hottest part of the year.

229. The typical eighteenth-century village poorhouse was a disgracefully ill-kept jerrybuilt place. Because of land enclosure the number of poor increased vastly throughout the century, so that existing institutions became even less able to cope with them. The normal attitude to the village poor was that they were designing rogues who tried to steal from the parish rather than do an honest day's work, and that they must therefore be given no encouragement in their trickery. Thus the squalor and misery of those forced 'on the parish'.

232. 'wheel' – spinning-wheel.

283. As an apothecary who had trained as a doctor, Crabbe knew well enough the extent to which quacks lived off the poor, through the cynical agency of parish appointments.

304. In *The Deserted Village* Goldsmith described with approval the vicar who was passing rich on forty pounds a year. For Goldsmith such a man was 'to all the country dear'. Crabbe's point is that the average vicar is not to be recognized in Goldsmith's words.

305–17. During the eighteenth century the Anglican Church came in for a good deal of contemptuous regard because of the number of its ordained priests who were the younger sons of wealthy families, and who found the priesthood a vocation that interfered very little with their private pleasures. Jane Austen's novel *Mansfield Park* is very much alive to the offensiveness of this.

342–3. The language here is close to the poetry of graveyard melancholy which is found in quantity in the eighteenth century and includes among its better-known examples, Gray's *Elegy in a Country Churchyard* and Edward Young's *Night Thoughts*. This poetry meditated in a relaxed, commonly too indulgent way, on death, the mutability of life, the frailty of human hopes. The setting is normally a churchyard, the time evening. It may be noted, however, that Crabbe's lines are not mere indulgence.

Book II. 399–401. The peer's disease is syphilis. It is interesting to note that Crabbe here anticipates the last stanza of Blake's poem 'London'. Both poets suggest that a breakdown of community sense and responsibility in favour of selfishness will harm all. The idea is far more powerfully developed in Blake's poem, but Crabbe certainly shows here a strong awareness of the need for social responsibility, for each man to admit that he is not an island entire unto himself. Such awareness is a strong motivating force in the work of the major Augustan writers.

414. Meaning that the hostess wrote what was owing to her on the wall.

418. 'Hall' – each town had its Hall, a place for the holding of any public business, and at which Courts of Justice met periodically.

442. For Crabbe the word 'luxurious' retained its meaning of lustful, lecherous.

448. At this point the poem changes for the worse. We enter upon a eulogy to the Rutland family, for a while Crabbe's employers, though never really his patrons. This sort of flattering address is not, of course, unfamiliar in seventeenth- and eighteenth-century poetry, since writers might depend for their livelihood on the favours of the rich; but it began to die out during the latter half of the eighteenth century as writers became increasingly professional and self-supporting and there- fore independent of patronage. The crucial moment in this process of emancipation was Dr Johnson's tremendous letter to Lord Chesterfield. It will be remembered from the introduc- tion that Crabbe had recently been rescued from his desperate poverty by the efforts of Burke; and he probably had every reason to be grateful to the Rutlands. Still, the last 100 lines of *The Village* have nothing to do with what has gone before and form a curious and unsatisfactory conclusion to the poem. In fact we know it was written some while after the rest of the poem, for *The Village* in its original form had been submitted to Dr Johnson before Crabbe became chaplain to the Duke of Rutland, son of the famous Marquis of Granby. The particular occasion of the conclusion was the death in action of the Duke's brother, Lord Robert Manners, 12 April 1782.

SIR EUSTACE GREY. This poem is one of Crabbe's major triumphs. Technically, it shows amazing adroitness in the handling of a difficult stanza-form that could easily take control of the sense, yet never does. Psychologically, it is the first example of Crabbe's subtle exploration of a diseased and tortured mind. Morally, it shows his Augustan concern with restraint, the avoidance of any excess – moral, physical or spiritual. Socially, it is intelligently alert to the emotional effects of religious revivalism, especially Methodism, which was so important at the end of the eighteenth century and which had affected to the point of madness the lives of the poets Christopher Smart, William Cowper and possibly William Collins.

'*Scene – A Mad-House*'. Conditions in either private or public asylums during the eighteenth century varied so widely that generalization is impossible. At one end there was unbelievable squalor and brutality, with the unfortunate inmates the comic spectacle for visitors; at the other humanitarian effort and decent care. Sir Eustace Grey's asylum obviously belongs to the better type; the presence of the sympathetic professional physician is itself enough to demonstrate this.

6. A projector is defined in Dr Johnson's *Dictionary* as 'one who forms wild, impracticable schemes'. As we might expect, the examples of men rising to sudden wealth through manufacturing and industrial enterprise during the seventeenth and eighteenth centuries created almost a class of projectors. Compare line *66*.

87. 'Varnish higher' – a phrase taken from painting. Varnish was applied to a finished canvas to preserve it from Time's injurious hand.

112. We are given here what may be a confused admission that Sir Eustace Grey knew of his wife's sin or that he had driven her to it. It amounts to a near confession of his being a moral hypocrite. His sense of guilt over this and his subsequent revenge is what drives him mad. And I think that his mad visions are intimately related to his past history and the guilt which attends it.

200. Out of the available fashion for the picturesque – that is, such images might readily occur to Sir Eustace Grey's mind – Crabbe fashions a 'mad' picture of ruined splendour. For the picturesque was a fashion towards the end of the eighteenth century which found especially compelling whatever was irregular and rough in art and nature: melancholy ruins were seen as essentially picturesque. But there is a deep relevance to Sir Eustace's apparently random vision; for clearly his own life is one of ruined splendour: his wealth, name, contentment have been destroyed.

220–8. Ostensibly a description of a visit to the polar regions – 'stream' is a column of light shooting up at dawn at the poles –

this again goes deeper, I think. The terrifying cold light is the light of conscience directed by an omniscient power – God. And God is always imaged as Light in the eighteenth century. The following stanzas suggest that because of this penetrating light Sir Eustace knows himself to be beyond the world of ordinary men, and no longer fully human. Thus he travels to 'Cities of whom no travellers tell', and is irresistibly led to tombs – again the imagery of graveyard melancholy would be available to the mind of a cultivated man – because he thinks himself beyond redemption and therefore as good as dead.

There then follow stanzas which deal implicitly with the destruction of personality, in which Sir Eustace as social outcast all but loses his claim to being human. We may note how nearly he is here compared to the mad Lear and Mad Tom.

316. This marks a change of direction. What we have now is the beginning of religious mania such as affected the eighteenth-century poet Christopher Smart who, after years of debauchery, began suddenly to fall on his knees and pray in public places. A similar terrifying and mentally disabling feeling of irreparable sin is here admitted. The gloomy sense of man's inevitably corrupt nature runs through revivalist thought: and one is saved, not by works, but by Grace, the sudden decision of God which man cannot affect. Revivalist religion is emotional in the extreme; thus Augustan distrust of it. So when, line *331*, Sir Eustace says that 'reason on her throne would shake', we are to understand that in fact she has already fallen and that what he pretends is reasonable is far otherwise. We are therefore prepared for the discovery of salvation in the next stanza.

'Seal'd among the few'. This refers directly to the revivalist belief that once you are aware of being filled with Grace you have joined the ranks of the 'Elect', the word Sir Eustace himself uses later, line *380*. (It was Cowper's sense that he was unalterably excluded from Grace and hence condemned to eternal damnation that occasioned his madness.)

The stanzas that follow are full of Revivalist terminology and fairly closely modelled on the diction of Methodist hymnals, and the shift of stanza pattern is to echo Methodist hymnology. *404 ff.* In the last four stanzas of the poem, the Physician speaks as the ideal Augustan representative in pointing to the folly of excess in this case of Pride and its ability to bring the highest tumbling down from Reason to 'a frenzied child of grace'. As

I have noted in my Introduction, the last words of the poem are almost a paraphrase of Dr Johnson.

PHOEBE DAWSON. This and the following extract are taken from Part II of *The Parish Register*, called 'Marriages'. Although I do not like cutting, these episodes are reasonably detachable; indeed *The Parish Register* as a whole is concerned with separate tales which build up a fairly complete picture both of a Parish and attitudes to and ways of 'Births', 'Marriages' and 'Burials'.
1. 'Lammas fair' – harvest festival, held on the 1st of August. *19–26*. Note here the intelligence of Crabbe's psychological insights; these will stand a good deal of careful investigation. *41–5*. The imagery taken from painting is properly functional. Though 'painted' would, if left to itself, be mere cliché, it is given real point by the following 'highly colour'd' and 'strongly drew'. We can see now that 'blissful view' is merely a work of artifice, and that its deceitfulness is inseparable from its allure. 'Prospect' is a wide landscape – the word hints at a large country estate planned by a wealthy owner to include a prospect. Thus Phoebe's lover suggests to her a future of wealth and ease. This, she knows, is 'false' because too 'highly colour'd'. Yet its allure remains, and the insidious promise for the future would be strong to a servant girl. This is another fine example of the way Crabbe uses his language to reach for the psychological subtleties of the occasion.

SIR EDWARD ARCHER. *5*. 'taste' – Note the careful positioning of this word made to rhyme with 'chaste.' Fanny Price is reduced to the level of a casual possession of the 'amorous knight', a phrase whose apparent courtesy is undermined by Crabbe's implicit moral attitude to his 'taste'. He has a taste for her as he might have for some kinds of painting, or clothes or food. In other words, the man of taste treats a person not of his class merely as an object to gratify his whim. And what follows is very insistent on the fact of class separateness and the human indifference this occasions. Archer's warnings of Fanny's future are, of course, real and terrible; but Fanny can resist allure as Phoebe Dawson could not. And we may note the extreme sensuality of Archer's concluding words – especially lines *56–7* – and the excess they indicate, which from her point of view makes resistance that much more necessary, and possible.

74. This fine line clearly enough shows up Archer's flaw; he cannot comprehend a strength of personal relationship that survives the wreck of physical beauty. The cast of mind that could produce a line such as this has its sombre element; but it has, too, a realistic strength in its knowledge of human affairs that makes so purely a negative attitude as cynicism impossible.

LADY OF THE HALL. This is from 'Burials', the third part of *The Parish Register*.

14–27. Crabbe here condemns the Lady's irresponsibility and shows the disorder that proceeds from it. We remember the Augustan insistence on social responsibility, the strong awareness that each man must honour society's claim on him. The results of the Lady's refusal to do this are inevitable: she is cheated by her servant, her wealth and estate are destroyed; and her dependants – the poor – are made to suffer.

28–41. These lines show the fake pomp that attends her funeral. Crabbe images the affair in stage-terms, which makes clear his attitude to it. There is no true involvement, only 'acting', dissembling. And we may note that the whole thing is so badly done as to become meaningless. For the Augustans, art instructed through pleasing, but 'this poor farce' can neither please the fancy nor touch the heart. In other words the Lady's whole life is seen in retrospect as meaningless and therefore valueless; it is a sort of non-existence (we may further note that everything of hers has perished). The non-existence is brought home with grim impressiveness in lines *60–1*. The worms find no body at all. Even in death she denies her human function!

THE BOROUGH. This is Letter I of the long poem, *The Borough*. Although in his preface to the poem Crabbe denies he has any place in mind, his Borough clearly owes a good deal to Aldeburgh. We should note, however, that the poem's narrator is not Crabbe. Indeed, as he says, 'When the reader enters into the poem he will find the author retired from view, and an imaginary personage brought forward to describe his Borough for him'. And we must also note that the random nature of the personage's description cleverly solves the problem of suggesting the Borough's variety without requiring him to detail it.

20. 'squalid' – of appearance: thin and miserable-looking, dull and undernourished.

32. 'Lily' – 'The white water-lily, Nymphæa alba' (Crabbe's own note). As we shall see, he is very keen on botanical accuracy in this and other poems.

41. 'Samphire Banks' – 'The jointed glasswort, Salicornia, is here meant, not the true samphire, the Crithmum maritimum:' 'Salt-wort', 'The Salsola of Botanists' (Crabbe's notes).

52. *Hoys* are small passenger and goods vessels; a *pink* has a very narrow stern; a *snow* has two masts resembling the main and foremasts of a ship, and a third small mast just abaft the main-mast.

84. 'The curvature of planks for the sides of a ship, etc., is, I am informed, now generally made by the power of steam. Fire is, nevertheless, still used for boats and vessels of the smaller kind' (Crabbe's note).

121 'prime' – to prune. In this and the next line we have a hint that the newer fashion in landscape gardening has reached the Borough. Crabbe's speaker is traditionally Augustan in his preference for the gardens that imitated nature, 'untutored and at ease'. But by the end of the century this ideal had been replaced for a more 'artificial' style, whose most famous exponents were Sir Uvedale Price, Richard Payne Knight and Humphry Repton.

127. The fields were guarded from the poor, who thieved and poached as necessity drove them. You might compare Wordsworth's lyrical ballad, 'Goody Blake and Harry Gill', for a comparable awareness of this indication of social malaise.

130. 'tenters' – hooks; 'repulsive' means able to repulse.

134. A quotation from Pope's description of the monument in London.

147. 'crag' a shelly sand found only on the East Coast of England.

150. 'gale' – bog-myrtle.

151. 'radiant beauty' – not poetic diction, but botanical precision. 'radiant' means extending radially, as do the petals of sun-dew flowers.

169. 'Embrown'd and horrid' – this is poetic diction; the two terms are traditionally associated – they can be found together in Dryden and Pope.

171. 'Of the effect of these mists, known by the name of fogbanks, wonderful and, indeed, incredible relations are given; but their property of appearing to elevate ships at sea, and to bring them in view, is, I believe, generally acknowledged' (Crabbe's note).

196–7. The appearance of porpoises off-shore presages bad weather. It is characteristic that Crabbe should move towards this sombrely realistic account of storm and death at sea at the end of the opening letter. It combines the Augustan sense of the hovering presence of death with his own recognition of the harsh actualities of life for most people of the Borough.

ELLEN ORFORD. This is Letter XX of *The Borough*. It opens with a biting attack on the unreality of much popular literature of the period. The Augustanism that motivates the attack is very strong here; bad literature is positively dangerous because it instructs us falsely. It encourages interests and beliefs that can meet only with constant thwarting. Thus Crabbe directs his attention particularly to the vogue for 'sentimental' and 'Gothic-horror' novels, produced in vast quantities at the end of the eighteenth century, and attacked by Jane Austen in *Northanger Abbey* and *Sense and Sensibility*.

5. 'The lad's or boy's love, of some counties, is the plant southern-wood, the Artemisia Abrotanum of botanists' (Crabbe's note).

34. Darnley-Cottages and *Maple-Vales*. *Darnley-Vale* (1789) was a sentimental novel, written by a Mrs Bonhote. By mixing up names, Crabbe implies how difficult it is to remember individual works from this glut of popular fiction. In every sense of the word, the novels are undistinguished performances.

49–50. Crabbe here refers to Gothic horror novels, especially one by M. G. Lewis, called *The Monk* (1795), which was so popular it earned the author his nickname 'Monk Lewis'.

51. Banditti are also a feature of Gothic novels, perhaps most famously in Mrs Radcliffe's *The Italian* (1797). Mrs Radcliffe is a favourite author of Catherine Morland, the heroine of *Northanger Abbey*.

58. The flagging imagination of Gothic novelists made for frequent use of the word 'inexpressible'.

93. I do not know to which novel Crabbe is here referring; if indeed it existed. But Wales increasingly figures in the popular fiction of the period; wild, desolate and rugged, it suited the atmosphere of these works.

101. 'Clementina' – possibly Crabbe is hinting at Mrs Charlotte Smith's *Celestina* (1791) which deals with incest.

142–5. Note how Crabbe draws attention to the representative course of Ellen's life. She is no uniquely suffering individual, of the sort to be found in the novels he has earlier castigated. And what follows stresses the ordinariness of Ellen's experience. Yet in doing so it remarkably and beautifully celebrates her resilience and ability to endure; the real and cherishable modest virtue of her courage makes tawdry and unimportant the improbable sufferings of the put-upon heroines of popular fiction. Notice in this connection the important passage, lines *181–99*, and the way the novelistic moment (lines *187–9*) is validly present, (Ellen's grief is very great) but outlived. Life, that is, goes on, as lines *198–9* make clear.

234–53. We have here another example of Crabbe's dealing with the more severe kind of Methodism. Sir Eustace Grey had felt himself one of the Elect; Ellen's husband feels himself one of the damned, and Crabbe's recognition of the dire effects of this on a kindly human being constitute his strong objection to such an unreasonable religion.

274–7. Crabbe does not really let Ellen tell us why her son was hanged, but it may well have been for sedition or being a member of a revolutionary faction. The arguments of the 'Worst of the bad', allowances having been made for Ellen's unsympathetic rendering of them, sound as though they may have their source in Tom Paine's *Rights of Man* (1791). Certainly during the 1790s the government became scared of possible attempts to imitate the French Revolution; and to an extent the fear was justified. Thus government spies were constantly infiltrating into working-men's meetings and causing the arrest of many.

Notice how finely Crabbe attends to Ellen's deep feelings for her son and the manner of his death. Though she repeatedly says she can speak no more, in fact she wrenches the whole story out; we sense how alive her agony still is, how strong the compulsion that forces her into speech.

291. 'cart' – in which condemned criminals were dragged through the streets on their way to the gallows.

328–37. Though at first glance the lines may seem pathetic, or a mistaken attempt to urge the consolations of piety, attentively considered they properly illuminate Ellen's character, her resilient strength and courage. Crabbe presents us with a very simple woman; yet in the way he presents her there is no shade of condescension.

PETER GRIMES. Letter XXII of *The Borough*. Without doubt this is a masterpiece, and one of the few of Crabbe's poems that are reasonably well known, especially since the success of Benjamin Britten's operatic version. In a note to the poem, Crabbe wrote: 'The character of Grimes, his obduracy and apparent want of feeling, his gloomy kind of misanthropy, the progress of his madness, and the horrors of his imagination, I must leave to the judgment and observation of my readers. The mind here exhibited is one untouched by pity, unstung by remorse, and uncorrected by shame; yet is this hardihood of temper and spirit broken by want, disease, solitude, and disappointment: and he becomes the victim of a distempered and horror-stricken fancy. It is evident, therefore, that no feeble vision, no half-visible ghost, not the momentary glance of an unbodied being, nor the half-audible voice of an invisible one, would be created by the continual workings of distress on a mind so depraved and flinty.' We note Crabbe's psychological concern in these words.

21. 'hot spirit' – probably rum, or it could be gin. They were cheap enough.

23. 'prove his freedom and assert the man' – I think we have here another reference to the revolutionary democratic cant, as Crabbe would see it, of the end of the eighteenth century; the spirit of Tom Paine lurks behind Grimes's assertion.

59–65. These lines refer to the practice of parish apprenticeship, by means of which workhouse pauper children would for a trifling sum be given to masters looking for apprentices. Commonly, the workhouse overseers hoped the masters would come from another parish, since it then became that parish's turn to provide for the pauper if he was cast off by his master. But since the labour gained was cheap and easily exploitable, the chances of this happening were extremely slight. Naturally, the system led to the indifferent brutality recorded in Crabbe's poem and Dickens's *Oliver Twist*.

171–204. In this description the extraordinary attention to detail makes the desolate environment so vividly realized that we sense how powerfully it will impress itself on Grimes's mind. There is a total absence of the human; the feeling of isolation is terrific. And, too, the discordance of Grimes's mind is manifested in what he notes of the non-human life around him – in, for example, his awareness of the 'clanging golden-eye'.

208. 'reach' – 'The reaches in a river are those parts which extend from point to point. Johnson has not the word precisely in this sense; but it is very common, and, I believe, used wheresoever a navigable river can be found in this country' (Crabbe's note).

240 'resigned' – abandoned.

251. 'furious' – violently agitated, verging on madness.

252. 'distempered' – insane.

254. 'parish-bed' – a bed in the workhouse.

PRISONS. Letter XXIII of *The Borough*. In a prefatory Note Crabbe said: 'It has always been held as a salutary exercise of the mind, to contemplate the evils and miseries of our nature: I am not therefore without hope, that even this gloomy subject of Imprisonment, and more especially the Dream of the Condemned Highwaymen, will excite, in some minds, that mingled pity and abhorrence which, while it is not unpleasant to the feelings, is useful in its operations. It ties and binds us to all mankind by sensations common to us all, and in some degree connects us, without degradation, even to the most miserable and guilty of our fellow-men.'

33. 'debtor'. Debtors' prisons existed into the nineteenth century. Dickens's great novel, *Little Dorrit*, is much concerned with one.

59. 'vends' – sells.

70. 'anchorite' – literally, a religious recluse. Crabbe's is a grim joke.

97. 'bound' – the man had offered himself as financial guarantor for a friend wanting to borrow money, which meant he must supply any money his friend could not repay. Wordsworth's *Michael* is a poem which records the disasters that overtake a bondsman.

109–12. Note here how the repeated rhyme suggests the woman's endless prevarications.

158. The reference here is to Pope's translation of the *Odyssey*, Book XI.

289–332. Note how the gathering details of the dream, the concreteness of the remembered life, manifest an absorption that makes the breaking-in of the watchman's call extremely painful. Crabbe's prefatory note is justified by the poem's ending. We are strongly aware of the human vitality implicit in the condemned man's dream, how fully it identifies him with all that is living.

Tales in Verse

PROCRASTINATION. For an analysis of this poem, see my Introduction, p. 28.

41. 'fond' – useless.

43. 'still' – always.

77. 'tabby vest' – tabby was a name for watered silk-taffeta with a wavy line running through it. It was very fashionable at the time.

85. 'Allusion is here made, not to the well-known species of *sumach*, called the poison-oak, *toxicodendron*, but to the *upas*, or poison-tree of Java: whether it be real or imaginary, this is no proper place for enquiry' (Crabbe's note).

90. 'stocks' – investments.

103. 'she changed her book' – that is, she changed from 'tender tales' to 'books devout'.

169–71. Remember she has virtually given up reading. These are now mere objects of possession, not properly used – 'level' and 'polished' suggest what irrelevant art has gone into perverting the books' purpose.

184. 'tilted boats' – rowing-boats with awnings, suggesting both expense and improper secrecy.

266. A 'trim spark' is a nautical expression for a ship in good fighting order. Rupert is made to speak in character.

275. 'trepann'd' – tricked financially.

306. 'parish-gift' – financial assistance. He is now 'on the Parish'.

310. 'badge-man's blue' – as a badge-man, Rupert is licensed to beg by the Parish, who supply his coat of blue serge cloth.

THE FRANK COURTSHIP. From his attacks on Methodism, we would expect Crabbe to have a keen dislike of nonconformist religions. The attitude is typically Augustan, distrusting whatever is extreme and poses a threat to the Anglican Church. Crabbe's distrust stems from this reasoning: that nonconformists in their personal form of religion take too much on themselves; they do not sufficiently recognize the frailty of human kind which, because of its inevitable flaws, need a tradition on which to rely. Nonconformism is thus a kind of pride, a foolish assumption that man is better than he is, and can accomplish more than is in fact possible.

16. 'spleen' – melancholy.

34. Cromwellians who put Charles I to death.

40. 'Saints' – 'This appellation is here used not ironically, nor with malignity; but it is taken merely to designate a morosely devout people, with peculiar austerity of manners' (Crabbe's note).

46. 'merchant born' – it is a fact that the nonconformist sects were almost entirely drawn from the ranks of the merchant and manufacturing middle-class.

58. Cromwell is of course the Protector. The Augustans had little time for him; he had, after all, dared personal intervention against the weight of tradition.

60. On more than one occasion Cromwell refused to let unacceptable members into the House, and dismissed the session prematurely.

72. 'fail'd' – gone bankrupt. Note the suggestion in the word used, that this is immoral.

75. Gretna Green, the scene of many sudden, elopers' marriages.

93. As 'failure' is immoral, so 'frugal and rich' are virtues to nonconformists.

117. 'meeting' – a nonconformist congregation.

130. 'vestal' – pure and virginal.

136. 'simulation' – pretence.

141. 'franks' – a superscribed signature by a person (e.g. an M.P.) allowing letter to be sent free of charge. Human contact, we note, may not take precedence over thrift.

155. 'drab' – a woollen cloth, of a dull light brown colour. Josiah's wearing drab would mark him out, since men's dress at the end of the century was fashionably gay in colour.

200. 'tricks and honours' – terms used in card-games.

234. 'ductile' – easily led.

236. 'gaping' – yawning.

242. 'soft' – a stock poetic word in the eighteenth century. As normally used it means agreeable or pleasant; as linked here with 'soft'ning' it implies morally enervating.

260. 'doubtful' – fearful.

363. The line means 'To take the heart captive, and once it is caught to reject it'.

375. 'Am I well' – a fine play on words, which tells us much about the girl's pert poise. She flirts with the 'Doctor' by asking him if in fact she pleases him, is good-looking. The phrase is one of 'polite' raillery, at which we would expect the girl to be expert.

375. 'light' – her dress, that is, is daringly and fashionably low-cut. But 'light' has its moral connotation also, of frivolous and near-wanton.

392. 'naughty' – the word is near to the meaning of 'wicked'.

414. 'Speakst thou then at meeting' – meaning: do you testify at prayer meetings? It was the habit in certain sects for individuals to testify to their sense of grace when the spirit so moved them.

430. 'long-skirted' – the sense is of dress no longer fashionable, indeed so ostentatiously unfashionable that it is almost a fashion in itself. Certainly it implies considerable self-consciousness on the part of the wearer.

491. 'grace' – means both seemly and becoming, and, of course, hints at the more religious meaning which the girl picks up in her answer. How beautifully managed this dialogue is, witty, keenly retentive of the sense of the personalities, yet able to imply a quality of generosity to which they win through. These lines alone can leave us in no doubt as to why Jane Austen prized Crabbe so highly.

THE WIDOW'S TALE. See my Introduction (p. 22) for comment on the opening of this poem.

2. 'school' – the meaning is of a finishing-school.

7. 'disposed' – brought into a state of – by her expensive education.

20. 'farinaceous food' – dumplings.

21. 'saline' – salt.

26. 'hinds' – literally farm-workers, but also means rustic, unkempt. In the same line 'cut and come again' is a phrase implying abundance.

40. 'business' – house affairs, to be taken as a serious fulltime occupation.

55. 'nymph' – notice how the word by its very poetical conventionality, suggests the way the girl sees herself as a tragic heroine out of literature; we are back with the sentimental novels that Crabbe had attacked in 'Ellen Orford'. That Nancy sees herself as a tragic heroine becomes clear in her conversation with the Widow. Equally clear, is the Widow's realistic good sense in condemning the girl's romantic and literary visions, so at odds with the actual. We have here a case of sense versus sensibility.

146. 'prison' – the word limits by its own excess; we are aware of how much the word points at Nancy's unrealistic attitude.

179–93. The Widow's speech is strikingly familiar to the view upheld in *Sense and Sensibility* that reason must control the passions. When in that novel Marianne Dashwood finally breaks away from her indulgence of feeling, her sister recognizes 'in the whole of her subsequent manner . . . the direction of mind awakened to reasonable exertion' (ch. 46). And earlier, Elinor herself has concealed her own anguish, and as she eventually tells Marianne, she has been supported in her own unhappiness 'by feeling that I was doing my duty' (ch. 37). Man, that is, is a social animal, owing no more to himself than what he owes to society.

245. 'resign' – abandon it, give it up.

288. 'contemn' – despise.

307. 'retired' – sent away.

359. 'competence' – good financial circumstances.

391. See note on lines *17–21* of 'Belinda Waters', p. 250.

417. 'storm' – assault.

ARABELLA. Each of the *Tales in Verse* is preceded by quotations from Shakespeare. I have not felt it necessary to include them, but the ones prefixed to 'Arabella' are so felicitous that in their case I make an exception.

> Thrice blessed they that master so their blood –
> But earthly happier is the rose distill'd,

> Than that which, withering on the virgin thorn,
> Grows, lives and dies in single blessedness
> > *Midsummer Night's Dream.*

> I something do excuse the thing I hate,
> for his advantage whom I dearly love.
> > *Measure for Measure.*

> Contempt, farewell! and maiden pride adieu!
> > *Much Ado About Nothing.*

These quotations fairly indicate the mellow tolerance and human good sense that inform Crabbe's handling of his poem and its heroine.

1. 'guide' – Dr Rack is the town's vicar.

23. 'her sex's dread' – this testifies to the fact that Arabella is an 'advanced' woman in the sense that she is intellectually emancipated. She is a 'blue-stocking' as women became called who, at about the middle of the eighteenth century, organized themselves into groups for cultivating the mind with serious subjects. How serious can be gauged from line *28*. Berkeley, Bacon, Hobbes and Locke are English philosophers, the last three of whom were much in favour during the eighteenth-century. Indeed Bishop Berkeley (1688–1756) Thomas Hobbes (1588–1679) and John Locke (1632–1704) are in many ways the century's law-givers in moral, social, political and psychological matters.

32. Hannah More (1745–1833) and Mrs Elizabeth Montagu (1720–1800) were both blue-stockings. As learned ladies their conversational standards would be high, so for Arabella to be able to converse with them fixes the advanced degree of her own intellectual accomplishments. My feeling is that Crabbe's attitude to Arabella does not exclude a certain amusement: the alliterations of Berkeley and Bacon, More and Montagu do obtrude rather (and why, after all, Bacon if not for alliteration? The names of other philosophers would do equally well, if not better.)

50. 'some savage foe' – this shows Arabella's contempt for the excessively feminine and willingly subordinate attitude of other women. Men are to be treated as equals only.

68. 'No spurious offspring drain his private purse.' – he had no illegitimate children for whose upbringing he had secretly to pay.

81. 'a man of parts' – a term of praise, meaning that Doctor Campbell was a man of various accomplishments. We may note that although 'a man of parts' was often taken as synonymous with 'ideal' or enviably complete, this is by no means Arabella's idea.

155. 'fondly' – has here almost the meaning of mistakenly though excessive feeling.

189. 'maiden vot'ress' – dedicated to virginity.

193. 'over-nice' – too scrupulous in his judgment of behaviour.

194. 'false sublime' – sublime is a word that looms large in eighteenth-century discussion of feelings. It refers to the highest or deepest of emotions. We can be sure that Crabbe as a man who distrusted extremes, was uneasy with the sublime.

201. 'venal turn-coat' – a man who changes his political views for reward.

207. Belinda, that is, has managed to get rid of an illegitimate child.

231. 'zeal', – a word to be linked with 'enthusiasm' and 'sublime'. It indicates an excess, a tendency to the extreme which sacrifices the adjustment of balances necessary for truly civilized human beings. In the eighteenth-century the word almost always had a religious connotation; it indicated the emotional fervour of nonconformism. It is used again of the 'maiden vot'ress' in line *262* and also line *310*.

273. 'engage' – bind, secure. The sense is of the callbirds attracting others into their cages.

275. 'naughty' – evil, wicked.

314–15. After 1772 any slave brought to England was free as soon as he set foot on English soil.

337. At the end of his poem, Crabbe added the following note: 'As the author's purpose in this tale may be mistaken, he wishes to observe that conduct like that of the lady's here described must be meritorious or censurable just as the motives to it are pure or selfish; that these motives may in a great measure be concealed from the mind of the agent; and that we often take credit to our virtue for actions which spring originally from our tempers, inclinations, or our indifference. It cannot therefore be improper, much less immoral, to give an instance of such self-deception.'

THE LOVER'S JOURNEY. This poem may be said to provide Crabbe's contribution to the great Romantic debate about the functioning of the imagination. The debate is extremely complex, and it would be wrong to pursue it far here. But we may say that essentially it turns on the question of whether the imagination projects or discovers reality. Does the poet discover more in the world by means of the imagination than is open to the ordinary eye; or is what he sees merely the product of his private mind? This problem exercised all the major Romantic poets, and in particular it bulks large in the work of Blake, Coleridge and Wordsworth, the last of whom introduced the word 'joy' into his discussions of the imagination's way of knowing the universe, in order to suggest that the poet sees the truth, because he has been filled with an inspiration that derives from God. Not that Wordsworth put it quite in Christian terms; but 'joy' in the eighteenth century is a technical term that defines the accession of spiritual grace. Since literary theory during the century came to place more and more emphasis on the poet's need for inspiration, 'joy' became a convenient term to harmonize the concepts of inspiration and grace, and so guard against the charge that the imagination's powers were the fruit of private or fanatical delusions. As might be expected, Crabbe's view of the mind's discovering powers is sceptical in the extreme. For him, indeed, imagination is projective, as the opening lines of the poem make clear, and in this he directly challenges the sort of experience Wordsworth had claimed in 'Tintern Abbey', where he wrote of his belief that with

> an eye made quiet by the power
> Of harmony, and the deep power of joy,
> We see into the life of things.

Yet having said this, I must hasten to add that 'The Lover's Journey' is not a solemn or reflective poem. On the contrary, it is a delightful comedy, 'a pretty fancy, and well executed', as Jeffrey said.

8. 'peculiar' – here means belonging exclusively to.

21. 'Laura' – perhaps the most famous name in all love-poetry, it was bestowed on the lady to whom Petrarch addressed his many love-poems. Orlando, it will be remembered, is the valiant lover of *As You Like It*. There is nothing very severe in Crabbe's indicating the 'fancy' of his youthful lovers.

40. 'cup-moss' – a lichen.

45. 'Care and spleen' – it was an assumption of the Romantics that the imagination's power failed when the poet's mind turned spontaneously towards the state of mind they variously termed melancholy, despair, dejection. Wordsworth's 'Resolution and Independence' and Coleridge's 'Dejection Ode' treat of the subject, and Crabbe touches on it here in speaking of care and spleen (defined in Dr Johnson's *Dictionary* as 'melancholy; hypochondriacal vapours').

49. 'Bounds' – boundary.

50–61. Notice how these lines echo Crabbe's concern with the grim reality of the peasant's life that he had made the subject of *The Village.* The herbs that 'spring uncultured' – including the wormwood whose bitterness only a lover could distinguish by the epithet 'wholesome' – are in fact the weeds that lord it over the labourer's efforts to cultivate his crop.

55. 'suckling' is an obsolete (Suffolk) dialect word meaning honey-suckle: 'rambl*ing* suckl*ing*' is an unfortunate locution.

63. 'common pasture' – prior to enclosure of it, the 'common' was where all villagers had the right to pasture their livestock.

67. '*blacklegs*' – the term refers to race-course gamblers or sharpers, whose name probably derives from their appearing generally in boots.

68–9. The scattered hovels would belong to those wanderers who built themselves huts some little distance from the village. Until enclosure all villagers had the right to cut peat from the common for fuel (the 'square brown stacks').

74–81. Notice that this part of Orlando's speech picks up the theme that Goldsmith had elaborated in the *Deserted Village* and which Crabbe had satirized in *The Village.*

116. 'Flora' – 'The ditches of a fen so near the ocean are lined with irregular patches of a coarse and stained lava; a muddy sediment rests on the horse-tail and other perennial herbs, which in part conceal the shallowness of the stream; a fat-leaved pale-flowering scurvy-grass appears early in the year, and the razor-edged bull-rush in the summer and autumn. The fen itself has a dark and saline herbage; there are rushes and *arrow-head*, and in a few patches the flakes of the cotton-grass are seen, but more commonly the *sea-aster*, the dullest of that numerous and hardy genus; the *thrift*, blue in flower, but withering and remaining withered till the winter scatters it;

the *saltwort*, both simple and shrubby; a few kinds of grass changed by their soil and atmosphere, and low plants of two or three denominations undistinguished in a general view of the scenery; – such is the vegetation of the fen when it is at a small distance from the ocean; and in this case there arise from it effluvia strong and peculiar, half saline, half putrid, which would be considered by most people as offensive, and by some as dangerous; but there are others to whom singularity of taste or association of ideas has rendered it agreeable and pleasant' (Crabbe's note). The comedy of this detailed description gets its kick from the closing words.

122. 'sallows' – a low-growing type of willow.

123. A mallow is a common wild plant with a very sticky sap. Notice how our feeling about this description is manipulated by Crabbe's getting two strong stresses together, which taken with the alliteration makes for a very forceful rendering of his description. 'And the soft, slimy mallow'.

131. 'All are appropriate' – Orlando's argument is not original. Crabbe is poking fun at an eighteenth-century belief that the perfect design of the universe proved the existence of a benevolent God (the belief included among its assumptions the existence of the desert as necessary for camels. If no desert then no camels, which would make for a gap in creation).

133. 'nice' – attentive to details.

136. 'shaking ground' – a bog or marsh.

163. 'fences' – hedges. The gipsies should not, of course, steal from the boundaries of enclosed land; but again we might look to 'Goody Blake and Harry Gill' for a sense of the evils of enclosure in creating vice.

175. 'engross'd' means both monopolized and absorbed. The word is not subtle, but it does release a very funny image.

196. 'But this Orlando felt not' – the implicit censure of Orlando's moral insensibility may serve to remind us that at the time the gipsy was a frequent symbol of disorder and threat to social peace. It is in these terms that a gipsy encampment is seen in Cowper's *The Task*, where we are told (Book 1),

> Strange! that a creature rational, and cast
> In human mould, should brutalize by choice
> His nature.

And this image of the gipsies' deliberate denial of humanity (the Augustan note is very strong) is also present in *Emma*, where the gipsies intrude on the world of Highbury as something malevolently non-human.

250. In fact, of course, the bean-flower has a particularly fragrant smell.

283. 'Seduce' – in the sense of win over by attractiveness and also lead astray.

316. 'the settling mind' – the phrase indicates that Orlando is passing from the extremes of joy and melancholy to the 'settled' calm and balanced state of mind which was for Crabbe the most desirable.

346. 'that but appear'd to die' – the words are rather too compressed. Crabbe means that no sooner did the views appear than that they died away from Orlando's gaze, his mind being full of other matters.

THE CONFIDANT. Though in many ways less brilliant than other of the *Tales*, 'The Confidant' is a fine poem. Our enjoyment of it derives partly from the sheer dexterity with which Crabbe handles the narrative, and partly from his presentation of married happiness which is at once believable and unemphatic. And we take pleasure, too, in the decent tact with which Crabbe brings out the husband's goodness. In the end, indeed, it is the very discretion of the poem that assures its success.

21. 'Billets' – billet-doux, love-letters.

23. 'inferior skill' – the sense is that she had to be careful not to win; as an inferior that would be intolerable to the Lady.

37. 'careless' – note how the word defines their human indifference to her because of her social inequality. The same is true of the word 'easy' in line *41.*

52. 'Mild' is a word that hints that he is as good as his social superiors.

57. 'discreetly' – the sense is, judiciously.

66. 'confound' – shame him.

77. 'placeman' – a term given to any holder of public office, though it usually signified contempt since the office would be held out of motives of self-interest rather than fitness.

86. 'rude' – violent and offensive. In the eighteenth century a 'double-standard' morality existed, whereby although daughters were expected to remain chaste, it was thought blameless and even worthy of sons to have some sexual experience. The position of a servant-girl was thus unfortunate since she could expect no protection from her employers; sons were encouraged, not 'checked'. Yet were she to become pregnant she would find herself on the streets quick enough. Defoe's *Moll Flanders* and Richardson's *Pamela* are two eighteenth-century novels which deal with the plight of servant girls because of the 'double-standard' morality.

142. 'innoxious' – free from mischievous effects.

264. 'fond' – here suggesting the strength of his feelings determined him to go against his reasons.

288. The sense is that even the incarnation of selfish envy wouldn't wish to make her suffer more.

311. 'fond' – here nearer to foolish.

317. 'resign' – abandon.

367. 'sovereign' – supreme or overriding. That is, she usurps the husband's own power.

472 'The Caliph Harun'. 'The sovereign here meant is the Haroun or Harun al Raschid, who died early in the ninth century: he is often the hearer and sometimes the hero, of a tale in the Arabian Nights' entertainment' (Crabbe's note).

509. 'asper' – a small silver Turkish coin.

THE BROTHERS. The opposition of characters in this poem is similar to that between Tom Jones and Blifil in Fielding's *Tom Jones*, but with one crucial difference. For Crabbe does not deal in black and white: Isaac is not absolute evil; in E. M. Forster's phrase, he is a 'moral consumptive'. Forster, however, was not speaking of Isaac when he made the remark (in 'Notes on the English Character,' an essay in *Abinger Harvest*) but of John Dashwood, who appears in *Sense and Sensibility*, and whom Forster characterizes as 'an unconscious hypocrite'. He means to do well, does ill and still thinks he has done well. Again we see the links between Crabbe and Jane Austen and we may refer back to Crabbe's concluding note to 'Arabella' and his remark that 'motives may in a great measure be concealed from the mind of the agent'. Isaac is a harsher study of moral hypocrisy than Arabella; but though harsh it does not push to the cruder extremes of Fielding's moral attitudes. In this instance, Crabbe's is a subtler art.

4. 'Hearts of Oak' was a song written in and very popular during the eighteenth-century.

22. 'pitiful' – full of pity for.

34. 'genius' – individual talent.

41. 'post-place' – in other words, Isaac wanted to be a place-man. See note on 'The Confidant', line *77*.

45. A Burgess was an M.P. for a borough.

59. 'coasting' – carrying cargo from port to port round the island.

63. Crabbe probably has in mind the declaration of war against France 1795.

65. 'Press'd' – press-ganged, a method whereby men were literally captured by sailors and forced into serving on board ship.

97. 'Pluto's iron-drop' – as god of the underworld, Pluto was traditionally represented as implacably hard of heart. Iron-ore was fancifully said to be Pluto's tears solidified.

107. 'zeal' – meeting this word again, reminds us of Crabbe's distrust of the zealous. It alerts us to Isaac's nonconformist-like devotional attitude, his capacity for moral humbug.

159. See note on lines *17–21* of 'Belinda Waters'.

170. 'Greenwich' – the name for disabled sailors.

177. 'kind' – a play on words: kind of course means generous; it also means 'in kind', i.e. typically.

202. 'defiled' – polluted.

204. 'Teas'd' – has a stronger meaning than now – vexed.

246. George plans to go 'on the Parish', as we remember Rupert had done in 'Procrastination'.

257. 'niceness' – fastidiousness, suggesting an excess of this.

266–7. Applied for poor relief.

270 'Overseer' – an officer who has care of the Parochial provision for the poor.

271. 'engaged' – fully committed, meaning all the money is used.

304–5. Notice how Isaac is here the moral consumptive, how he fits Crabbe's note to 'Arabella'.

401. 'nature' – natural feelings and responsibilities. Literally, Isaac is saying he denied his humanity.

POSTHUMOUS TALES. It is difficult to date the actual composition of the *Posthumous Tales* with any great accuracy. Crabbe's sons added a rather apologetic preface to the volume in which they acknowledged that had their father 'lived to edit these compositions, he would have considered it necessary to bestow on them a good deal more of revision and correction, before finally submitting them to the eye of the world. [We] perceived that his language had not always effected the complete development of his ideas; that images were here and there left imperfect – nay, trains of reflection rather hinted than expressed; and that, in many places, thoughts in themselves valuable could not have failed to derive much additional weight and point, from the last touches of his own pen.' Such remarks suggest that Crabbe was working on at least some of these poems at the time of his death. And of course this may well have been the case. Yet others were certainly planned and written a good deal earlier. In a letter of 1823 Crabbe told a Mrs Leadbetter, 'In my "Farewell and Return" I suppose a young man to take leave of his native place, and to exchange *Farewells* with his friends and acquaintance there – in short, with as many characters as I have fancied I could manage. These, and their several situations and prospects, being briefly sketched, an interval is supposed to elapse; and our youth, a youth no more, *returns* to the scene of his early days. Twenty years have passed; and the interest, if there be any, consists in the completion, more or less unexpected, of the history of each person to whom he had originally bidden farewell.' We have his sons' assurance that Crabbe intended *The Farewell and Return* to be published as a separate volume, and indeed it makes up the bulk of *Posthumous Tales*. Moreover, the letter to Mrs Leadbetter suggests that the volume was well in hand in 1823. Why, then, was it not published? Can we include it with the sons' remarks on the posthumous volume as a whole and assume that Crabbe did not live to complete it? Or do we assume that though it was finished, Crabbe decided not to publish? And if so, why did he come to such a decision? Was it because of the comparative failure of *Tales of the Hall*? or, as I think more likely, his recognition that the idea outlined in the letter to Mrs Leadbetter was too slight to sustain a volume, and that much of the writing lacked the terseness and power of his major phase. We note Crabbe's own cautious remark in the letter – 'the interest, if there be any'. Perhaps that is no more than his customary modesty; but my feeling is that Crabbe came to recognize that the interest was not perhaps sufficient to justify his own efforts at tidying-up the manuscript for publication. A letter to his son George, written in October 1831, makes it clear that Crabbe thought a posthumous volume might be financially worth while, though he himself was prepared to make no great claims for its intrinsic merit. With characteristic wit he writes: 'There are, in my recess at home, where they have been long undisturbed, another series of Stories, – in number and quantity sufficient for a volume; and as I suppose they are much like the former in execution, and sufficiently different in events and characters, they may hereafter, in peaceable times, be worth something to you; and the more, because I shall, whatever is mortal of me, be at rest in the chancel of Trowbridge Church; for the works of authors departed are generally received with some favour, partly as they are old acquaintances, and in part because there can be no more of them.'

The above remarks make it plain that I do not have so high a regard for *Posthumous Tales* as for the great volumes of 1810 and 1812. Yet it would be unfair and insensitive to suggest there is not a great deal of good and even excellent writing in them. 'The Cousins' and 'Belinda Waters' do, I hope, fairly represent the best of *Posthumous Tales* and show that even when not at the height of his powers, Crabbe attained a level that should be the envy of other, more highly praised poets. Both tales come from the planned volume, *The Farewell and Return*.

BELINDA WATERS. The opening description of Belinda is very characteristic. We note the extraordinary wit and poise of the lines, and the subtlety of discriminations – in, for example, 'And more consenting than inclined to please'. We note, too, the controlled reversal of expectation: 'She hates refusal for the pain it gives', seems unambiguous praise until we recognize two lines later that the person who suffers may well be herself. 'fash'd' (line *13*) means bothered, vexed, put to perpetual inconvenience.

17–21. Marriage is a social responsibility; Belinda's nature is such that she seems incapable of acting responsibly. The idea is picked up in the crucial word of line *32*, where she is spoken of as 'lovely and useless'. 'Usefulness' and its opposite are very important concepts to Crabbe; to be useful is to be fulfilling yourself as a human being, and it necessarily implies that you are also fulfilling your duty to others, discharging your social responsibility. The word is employed importantly for example in the 'Widow's Tale' (line *391*) and 'The Brothers' (line *159*).

47. 'circulating books' – books from circulating libraries. Such libraries became increasingly popular during the nineteenth century. In the following lines Crabbe works over familiar territory, the attack on silly novels that had engaged him in 'Ellen Orford'. It is clear that he sees such novels as not merely silly but positively harmful to a person of Belinda's nature; they encourage a further retreat from life's actualities. It is clear, too, that Belinda's reading-matter dates from the end of the eighteenth-century, rather than the beginning of the nineteenth.

65. '*Clarissa*' – Richardson's famous novel, about a seduced but essentially innocent girl who refuses to marry her seducer and dies. The novel was extremely popular in the eighteenth century. Dr Johnson professed a high regard for it because it was true to life and essentially moral and instructive. Belinda's throwing it away thus tells us a good deal about her (though allowance might be made for its extreme length).

78. As in 'Ellen Orford', Crabbe rings the changes on novel titles. 'Scenes from the life' is perhaps meant for *Features From Life* (1788) by Elizabeth Blower, while 'Sensibility' hardly needs an original. The titles that follow indicate themes and conventions popular to the novel of the period. 'Winters at Bath' refers to the popularity of that town as a setting for the novel of romance; 'The Constant Lover', looks towards the recurrent theme of love surviving all disasters; 'Discarded Son' indicates the theme of the hard-hearted father; 'The Rose of Raby' is almost certainly meant for an historical romance, a mode increasingly popular towards the end of the century and destined to help Sir Walter Scott, as well as Southey, Tom Moore and Byron, who all wrote historical romances in verse; 'Delmore', may just be *Melmoth the Wanderer*, by Leslie Maturin, though that famous horror novel wasn't written until 1820; 'The Nun' echoes Lewis's *The Monk* (1795); 'Ethelinda' is a variant of Fanny Burney's sentimental *Evelina* (1778); and the 'Relapse' very probably hints at the theme of adultery or the failed wife.

84. As elsewhere in Crabbe, 'resign'd' means abandoned.

86. 'P' – this signifies the man who has left his native place in youth and is now returned to enquire about his former acquaintances and friends. Note how in these four lines the enjambments lead us to a qualification of praise for Belinda: *boast, toast, gay set*: the last words of the lines have much of their gloss removed by the opening words of the following lines.

90. 'F' – the friend who informs 'P' of the subsequent fate of acquaintances.

98. Note here the withheld word. 'Pale cast of thought' is a famous phrase in *Hamlet*; but Belinda can't be dignified by the word: instead we get 'anxious fretfulness'. The absence of the expected word leads us to sense how the absence of thought itself caused Belinda a life of 'anxious fretfulness'.

137. 'during' – enduring.

141. Note the typical Crabbe reversal of expectation in this line: it ends with the word we hardly expect to find after what has gone immediately before. It is perfectly in character for Crabbe not to overstate his moral theme, or to attempt to flatten out the surprises of human nature. 'chide' has a stronger meaning than now. The sense is, reprove or scold. We notice how the catalogue of the husband's attitudes itself suggests the inevitable variety of feelings Belinda occasions. The poem as a whole bears striking evidence of Crabbe's full and sympathetic judgment of human beings. His attitude to Belinda is severe, yet not dismissive.

THE COUSINS. *14*. 'Precept' – as it turns out, of course, the precept is 'right'. But nobody could think Patty wrong. As always, Crabbe, while aware of the complexities of moral judgment, shows that precept must be judged not only in action, but by a consideration of the actors. The test of moral theory is human experience.

19 and *20*. James's words hint at untruthfulness because they are too absolute. 'durance' – hard in prison chains.

54. 'He who had no wife yet had a child'.

57. 'parish fare' – that is, was brought up as a pauper child, by the Parish.

73. 'premising' – infending this as the beginning of an action.

108–10. Note how the element of coarseness, even brutality in James's speech, suggests a good deal about him.

140–1. 'prudence' – in action the moral precept is open to suspicion as it had been in 'Procrastination'. And we note the play on the word 'unprofitable'; the word to be taken financially as well as in its meaning of beneficial.

153–7. These brilliant lines direct us to the make-up of James's mind. Their psychological insights are shrewd and subtle.

We notice how the couplet form contains the balancing, the weighing of attitudes on James's part.

232. 'Inclined' – again, a word that directs us to the process of James's mind. In one sense his heart mechanically leans to anger; in another, James favours a tactic of anger (inclined also means favourably disposed) because it will get rid of Patty. Crabbe shows that James is responsible for his behaviour, even if it might seem like a 'natural' progression.

247–8. Note the terseness of this, the sense of solution easily contained in the couplet. Here the containing couplet can very clearly show James's heartlessness – it is all so neat and tidy.

281. Ostentatious wealth in the building of great houses, is a vice attacked by the 'line' of poets whose values in this respect. Crabbe inherits: by Ben Jonson, ('To Penshurst') Carew ('To Saxham') Marvell ('Upon Appleton House') and Pope ('Fourth Moral Essay–On the Use of Riches'). In all these poems a careful distinction is made between the great houses that gather to them the necessary social virtues and responsibilities which constitute their greatness, and those which are built for 'envious show' and which can hope only to rival the other houses in size and pomp, since they are destitute of the moral values which makes a house truly great.

In telling us of the house that James built we see an example of how by careful scaling-down, Crabbe can adapt this tradition to his own concerns.

304. 'fee'd' – hired, though the word can also mean bribed, a meaning that perhaps isn't absent here.

339. 'struck' – surrendered. Notice the degree of realism in Jack's speech, similar to Rupert's in 'Procrastination'.

343. 'nice' – scrupulous.

Appendix

The following lines, taken from the episode of the Lady of the Hall, in the *Parish Register*, show all formal resources of the couplet.

> No fire the kitchen's cheerless grate display'd;
> No cheerful light the long-closed sash convey'd;
> The crawling worm, that turns a summer fly,
> Here spun his shroud and laid him up to die
> The winter-death: – upon the bed of state,
> The bat shrill shrieking woo'd his flickering mate;
> To empty rooms the curious came no more,
> From empty cellars turned the hungry poor,
> And surly beggars cursed the ever-bolted door.

The first couplet is a *closed* couplet: that is to say, its meaning is enclosed within the two lines, grammatically it is complete. The next couplet is *open*: because of the *enjambment* after 'die' we have to read on into the next couplet to complete the sense. Enjambment may of course be used in a closed couplet; indeed a little below the passage quoted we have:

> Unlike the darkness of the sky, that pours
> On the dry ground its fertilising showers;

but this is not so frequent. The last three lines of the passage form a *triplet*: three lines rather than the usual two take the one rhyme. And the last line is an *alexandrine*, a line frequently employed to close a triplet. This line has twelve syllables instead of the normal ten that make for the *decasyllabic* line that is the staple of Crabbe's couplet writing. And it may be noted that for all his use of enjambment, Crabbe's lines are mostly *end-stopped*.

We may notice in this passage how Crabbe animates his lines by syntactical variation, avoiding the possible monotony that he also guards against by exploiting the formal resources I have pointed out. In the first couplet, for example, we recognize the way 'cheerless' is played off against 'cheerful', 'fire' against 'light'. In what follows we become aware of whole years as the measure of the decay of the Hall; the crawling worm turns a summer fly and then dies the winter-death. A seasonal cycle is enacted with an improper leisure (improper in that nature has invaded what man should govern), and the verbs 'turns' 'spun' and 'laid him up' fully express this. Moreover, the open couplet testifies to this leisured possession of the Hall, since it fills more space, takes more time to read, than the closed couplet. In the following couplet we are forced to attend to the juxtaposition of 'bed of state' and 'the bat'. The one stands for social position and proper human fruitfulness, the other for what, absurdly and wrongly, has usurped these things; and we note how the word 'shrieking' sustains our awareness of what is wrong. In the triplet we note the alternation of 'To' and 'From', 'came' and 'turned'; and we note also that in the first line noun precedes verb, and that in the second line this syntactical arrangement is reversed with the effect of making it possible that the poor were turned away, or themselves abandoned the Hall.

This gives an indication of what Crabbe can do with the couplet. But there are many other effects to be won. First, antithesis. In the Introduction I noted how a couplet on the footman Daniel reduced his pretensions to absurdity and did it by implied antithesis of the rhyme words.

> And thus, with clouded cane, a fop complete,
> He stalk'd, the jest and glory of the street.

Crabbe frequently uses his couplet so that a statement contained in the first line is undercut in the second. Related to this is the way he uses the couplet to reverse expectations. Again, in the Introduction I pointed out how the first couplet of 'Procrastination' does this.

> Love will expire – the gay, the happy dream
> Will turn to scorn, indiff'rence, or esteem:

Esteem is not the word we expect to find, but because it is a rhyme word it has the necessary authority to pull us up short and make us aware of the complexity of judgment in human affairs. It avoids the cynical. In short, the couplet can accommodate a complexity of judgment that shows itself either as antithesis – the two sides of the coin, or reversal of expectation – the indication that there is another side, or balance – the acceptance of opposed sides as necessary for final assessment. This balancing we see at play in some lines from 'Arabella'.

> On Captain *Bligh* her mind in balance hung –
> Though valiant, modest; and reserved, though young:
> Against these merits must defects be set –
> Though poor, imprudent; and though proud, in debt:
> In vain the captain close attention paid;
> She found him wanting, whom she fairly weighed.

I think it is unnecessary to show how Crabbe exemplifies the process of Arabella's balancing judgments in these lines.

But though each couplet requires compression as a unit, this is not to deny that Crabbe needs a strong forward thrust to his verse; his art, after all, is a narrative art. How does he manage this? Some more lines from 'Arabella' help to show.

> Men she avoided; not in childish fear,
> As if she thought some savage foe was near;
> Not as a prude, who hides that man should seek,
> Or who by silence hints that they should speak;
> But with discretion all the sex she view'd,
> Ere yet engaged pursuing or pursued;
> Ere love had made her to his vices blind,
> Or hid the favourite's failings from her mind.

First, we notice this is all one sentence. That in itself is some reason to read forward. But the sentence is broken down into fairly separate parts. We notice, however, that the use of negatives 'not in childish fear', 'Not as a prude' prepare us for a future positive answer. How did she avoid men? In addition, we have negative statements that occupy four lines; for a full answer we expect another four to balance them. And that is in fact what we get. Moreover, we read on not just to find out the reason for Arabella's avoidance of men, but because we cannot linger over the lines. Statements are firmly made and as firmly dismissed. The closed couplets of this passage brook no argument, and there is nothing for it but to read ahead.

This handling of the couplet is, indeed, supremely important in Crabbe and I would think that he learned much from Dryden in this respect. Like Dryden, Crabbe has a sense of the pace necessary for sustained narrative; it isn't so much that he hurries you along as that he gives you no encouragement to linger. The rhyme powerfully finishes off what has been said, it resolves statement or argument with a justness we feel to be proper not only because antithesis, reversal or balance are themselves a complete movement, but because the proximity of rhyme words – and rhyme words cannot come closer than in the couplet – convey a powerful sense of completion. And where there is no completion you have anyway to read on.

As a last point we may consider the use Crabbe makes of dialogue in his couplet. The most dazzling example is, without doubt, the end of 'The Frank Courtship', which seems to me to mark a high point in the history of the couplet. But just because its virtues are so extreme it will perhaps be helpful to take an example that reveals a customary competence. The encounter between Dinah and the returned Rupert provides what we need.

> 'See! my good friend,' and then she raised her head,
> 'The bloom of life, the strength of youth is fled;
> 'Living we die; to us the world is dead;
> 'We parted bless'd with health, and I am now
> 'Age-struck and feeble – so I find art thou;
> 'Thine eye is sunken, furrow'd is thy face,
> 'And downward looks't thou – so we run our race;
> 'And happier they whose race is nearly run,
> 'Their troubles over, and their duties done.'
>
> 'True, lady, true – we are not girl and boy,
> 'But time has left us something to enjoy.'
> 'What! thou has learn'd my fortune? – yes, I live
> 'To feel how poor the comforts wealth can give:
> 'Thou too perhaps art wealthy; but our fate
> 'Still mocks our wishes, wealth is come too late.'
>
> 'To me nor late nor early; I am come
> 'Poor as I left thee to my native home:
> 'Nor yet,' said Rupert, 'will I grieve; 'tis mine
> 'To share thy comforts, and the glory thine;
> 'For thou wilt gladly take that generous part
> 'That both exalts and gratifies the heart . . .'

There is, of course, a great deal more of this dialogue, but from the snatch I have quoted certain points can be made. First we note the way Dinah converts the loss of youth's strength into the caricature picture of old age, which she pins onto Rupert as well as herself; and the remark 'so I find art thou' owes most of its force, even sense of sudden inspiration (she is looking for an argument not to honour her earlier vow) to the fact of the couplet. Think how diminished the charge would seem if 'thou' was not a rhyme word. Rupert sweeps the charge away with a good-humoured impatience that puts it in proper perspective: 'we are not girl and boy'. Immediately we notice that his straightforward energy of statement counteracts her careful assessments of their demerits for marriage. Such care has she taken indeed, that she tries to slip away from the awkwardness of her present situation by a generalizing statement that falls pat into the couplet form.

> And happier they whose race is nearly run,
> Their troubles over, and their duties done.

It is this Rupert sweeps aside, and in general it is noticeable that Crabbe has his words flow over the ends of lines; Rupert's speech not only breaks through the politeness of the couplet form, its energy belies Dinah's implied judgment that he is a feeble old man. We may notice, too, the way Crabbe has Dinah pick up Rupert's word 'enjoy'. 'What! thou hast learn'd my fortune?' It is of course that she has been really worried about, and Crabbe very cleverly makes her reveal her true anxiety.

DICTION AND IMAGERY

In a note it is impossible to do more than outline the way Crabbe handles diction and imagery, but I can at least suggest what is characteristic to him in these matters. First, there is his handling of technical terms, mostly botanical, though they also include nautical, legal and political. Closely linked with this is his accuracy in naming places and occupations: borough, village, placeman, burgess and so on. These elements of Crabbe's dictional resources make for a keen validity in his work; the precise realization of locality makes his people very much creatures of their environment; and we should note that this is a very different one from that of the Augustans. Thus

Crabbe has to deny himself much of their diction, because it would be out of place in his world. But we recognize his use of buried quotation and allusion and of 'sublime' or 'poetical' diction in order to 'place' his own concerns and characters (examples are given in the Introduction and Notes). It can therefore be said that he employs some of the resources of Augustan diction, but for particular effects.

Where he is more like the Augustans is in his use of words that define moral and social interests that are derived from theirs: and of these words we may cite the frequent appearance and crucial positioning of, for example, zeal, fond, feeling, kind (meaning both generous, and of the race, typical), heart, duty, useful, man, reason, judge, just, care, prudence, hope (like the Augustans, Crabbe saw the course of human life as one in which we are all 'condemn'd to hope's delusive mine', in Dr Johnson's words; what matters is the resolution with which we meet the unexpected disasters that lie in wait for us).

Lastly, Crabbe's handling of speech should be noted, and especially the way he uses it either to give a measure of realism to his characters – see, for example, Rupert in 'Procrastination', and George in 'The Brothers' – or, more subtly to tell us something about the character of the speaker. And here mention may be made of Sir Edward Archer, James (in 'The Cousins') and Nancy ('The Widow's Tale') though the practice abounds in the poetry of the major phase.

Of Crabbe's use of imagery the Notes have something to say and to try and amplify on them here would involve me in a long essay. All that need be said at this point is that Crabbe customarily handles his images to bring out the psychological state of mind he so brilliantly explores – most astonishingly in Sir Eustace Grey, perhaps, though not most subtly – and also to give point to his moral concerns. In this connection it will be enough to suggest that he uses terms drawn from painting and acting not merely to make a description more lively, but to indicate possible gaps between illusion (the work of feelings, fondness, self-deception, etc.) and sad reality. In addition, we should never lose sight of the care with which Crabbe employs descriptive language, so that the vivid relationship between character and environment is made plausible – in the description of the solitary scene in 'Peter Grimes' or Dinah's possessions in 'Procrastination', to name two examples at random. Descriptive poetry is of course an eighteenth-century obsession, but whereas in much of the verse of Thomson, Dyer and Green, 'description held the place of sense', in Crabbe it is always functional. If we glance at a famous passage in 'Peter Grimes' we shall see how this is so.

Thus by himself compell'd to live each day,
To wait for certain hours the tide's delay;
At the same time the same dull views to see,
The bounding marsh-bank and the blighted tree;
The water only, when the tides were high,
When low, the mud half-cover'd and half-dry;
The sun-burnt tar that blisters on the planks,
And bank-side stakes in their uneven ranks;
Heaps of entangled weeds that slowly float,
As the tide rolls by the impeded boat.

When tides were neap, and, in the sultry day,
Through the tall bounding mud-banks made their way,
Which on each side rose swelling, and below
The dark warm flood ran silently and slow;
There anchoring, Peter chose from man to hide,
There hang his head, and view the lazy tide
In its hot slimy channel slowly glide;
Where the small eels that left the deeper way
For the warm shore, within the shallows play;
Where gaping muscles, left upon the mud,
Slope their slow passage to the fallen flood; –
Here dull and hopeless he'd lie down and trace
How sidelong crabs had scrawled their crooked race;
Or sadly listen to the tuneless cry
Of fishing gull or clanging golden-eye;
What time the sea-birds to the marsh would come,
And the loud bittern, from the bull-rush home,
Gave from the salt-ditch side the bellowing boom:
He nursed the feelings these dull scenes produce,
And loved to stop beside the opening sluice;
Where the small stream, confined in narrow bound,
Ran with a dull, unvaried, saddening sound;
Where all, presented to the eye or ear,
Oppress'd the soul with misery, grief, and fear.

Dull scenes they may be, but where else in English literature can we find so exact a rendering of their dullness? Yet it is not mere objective description, not just matter of fact. We notice, for example, the repetition of the word 'slow'. And we recognize that Peter's mind is attuned through enforced leisure to the sluggish movements in these dull scenes. And how brilliantly the sluggishness is demonstrated. 'There hang his head, and view the lazy tide | In its hot slimy channel slowly glide.' In the second of these lines the adjectives and adverb hold up the sentence's movement towards its verb. It is not merely that the words accurately describe the tide's lazy movement and therefore show how much leisure Peter himself has to devote to watching it; by weighing the sentence down they enact the slowness. It is so with the line about the mussels who 'Slope their slow passage to the fallen flood'. The long vowels and alliterative devices demand a slow reading. And also we notice the accuracy with which Peter sees the activity: the verb 'slope' is a triumph of observation that may be set beside that of the crabs who 'scrawl'd their crooked race'. But it is not only Peter's eye that is perforce attuned to minute study of these dull scenes. His ear also registers them. The accuracy with which he identifies the 'clanging golden-eye' and the bittern's 'bellowing boom' is more evidence of how much time he has for these things and how they impress themselves on his senses. That these dull scenes are not random objective description but selected by the state of Peter's mind may finally be suggested by the couplet 'Where the small stream, confin'd in narrow bound, | Ran with a dull, unvaried, sadd'ning sound'. If Crabbe was a Romantic poet he would have written 'saddened sound'. But being Crabbe he refuses to speak of nature in human terms; what he does is suggest how the natural scene can be related to human perception. The description of the stream is objective, yet to Peter, no matter how unconscious he is of the process, it can be identified with his own position. For he, too, is confined in a narrow bound, forced to go to this spot day after day, and his life is therefore dull and unvaried. 'Dull' indeed is the crucial word because it is both objective description of the sound the stream makes and subjectively can be seen as indicating Peter's present life. And that is why the sound of the stream finally is 'sadd'ning': it makes him aware of his plight.

Even where Crabbe is not writing as well as he clearly is in this passage, it is difficult to accuse him of emptiness or irrelevance in his handling of imagistic language. Let us take an admittedly not very good line. 'Where rosy pleasures smile, whence real blessings flow' can hardly be accounted a distinguished performance (it comes from 'Prisons'). Yet admitting as much we can still say that it has the virtue of being clear in meaning and relevant to Crabbe's concern in the poem. 'Rosy' sufficiently defines health and good looks which the criminal life dissipates; and through its connections with virginity it hints at an innocence which is the opposite of the criminal's guilt and viciousness. 'Flow' is pretty much of a cliché, and yet even so validly implies both abundance and unrestrained movement, blessings the criminal cannot know. We may also note here how Crabbe gives the line some animation by creating an internal balance: both halves of the line have four words, they follow the same grammatical pattern, and there is a balancing of alliteration: wr | wr |.

Further Reading

There is still not a good modern edition of Crabbe's Collected Poems. We must still make do with the eight-volume one edited by his sons which also contains the *Life* by his son George, or the three-volume edition edited by Sir A. M. Ward (Cambridge University Press, 1903–5). There is, too, a volume of *New Poems*, edited by Arthur Pollard (Liverpool Univ. Press, 1960).

The Life of George Crabbe by his son has been separately published in the World's Classics series with an introduction by E. M. Forster (Oxford University Press, 1932), and with an introduction – better than Forster's – by Edmund Blunden (Cresset Press, 1947).

The fullest biography is by René Huchon, *George Crabbe and his Times* (Murray, 1907), which also attempts criticism, though not very well. A better, though modest critical study, is Lilian Haddakin's *The Poetry of Crabbe* (Chatto and Windus, 1955). Other critical studies include Oliver Sigworth's *Nature's Sternest Painter* (Univ. of Arizona, 1965) and Peter New's *Crabbe* (Cambridge University Press, 1975).

The following works also contain essays on Crabbe: George Saintsbury, *Essays in English Literature* vol. 1 (1889), and *A History of Nineteenth Century Literature, 1780–1895* (1896) both published by Macmillan; Ezra Pound, *Literary Essays* (ed. T. S. Eliot) and *A.B.C. of Reading*, (published by Faber and now available as paperbacks); F. R. Leavis, *Revaluation* (Chatto and Windus, 1936); E. M. Forster, *Two Cheers for Democracy* (Edward Arnold, 1951); Frank Whitehead in *The Pelican Guide to English Literature No. 5: From Blake to Byron*; and A. E. Rodway, *The Romantic Conflict* (Chatto and Windus, 1963). There is also a useful anthology of his contemporaries' reviews and views of Crabbe in *Romantic Perspectives*, eds. P. Hodgart and T. Redpath (Harrap, 1964).